BASIC ETHICS IN ACTION

BASIC ETHICS

SECOND EDITION

MICHAEL BOYLAN

PEARSON

Prentice
Hall

Upper Saddle River, NJ 07458

Library of Congress Cataloging-in-Publication Data

Boylan, Michael.
  Basic ethics / Michael Boylan.— 2nd ed.
    p. cm. — (Basic ethics in action)
  Includes bibliographical references and index.
  ISBN-13: 978-0-13-600655-8 (alk. paper)
  ISBN-10: 0-13-600655-8 (alk. paper)
  1. Ethics. I. Title.
  BJ1012.B615 2009
  170—dc22

                                    2008002556

Senior Editor: Dave Repetto
Editor-in-Chief: Sarah Touberg
Marketing Manager: Sasha Anderson-Smith
Senior Managing Editor: Mary Rottino
Production Liaison: Fran Russello
Senior Operations Specialist: Brain Mackey
Operations Specialist: Cathleen Petersen
Cover Design: Margaret Kenselaar

Cover Illustration/Photo: Lindsey
  Prudhomme
**Composition/Full-Service Project
  Management:** Katie Boilard/
  Pine Tree Composition, Inc.
Printer/Binder: R.R. Donnelley
  & Sons Company

Credits and acknowledgments borrowed from other sources and reproduced, with permission, in this textbook appear on appropriate page within text.

Pearson Prentice Hall™ is a trademark of Pearson Education, Inc.
Pearson® is a registered trademark of Pearson plc
Prentice Hall® is a registered trademark of Pearson Education, Inc.

Pearson Education LTD. London
Pearson Education Singapore, Pte. Ltd
Pearson Education, Canada, Inc.
Pearson Education—Japan
Pearson Education Australia PTY, Limited

Pearson Education North Asia, Ltd., Hong Kong
Pearson Educación de Mexico, S.A. de C.V.
Pearson Education Malaysia, Pte. Ltd
Pearson Education, Upper Saddle River,
  New Jersey

10 9 8 7 6 5 4 3 2 1
ISBN-(10):   0-13-600655-8
ISBN-(13): 978-0-13-600655-8

For Rebecca

CONTENTS

The second edition of *Basic Ethics* has undergone many changes. The overarching strategy has been to create a book that will work in at least three sorts of classes: (a) a class that will use *Basic Ethics* as the sole textbook to be supplemented as the instructor sees fit with current events or other contemporary materials that will help the students personally to come to grips with ethical theory and its underlying principles; (b) a class that will use *Basic Ethics* as the principal text to help explain primary readings in ethics; (c) a class that will use *Basic Ethics* along with one or more of the other books in the series *Basic Ethics in Action* to balance theory with applied ethics. All three approaches have pedagogical merit. I believe the new structuring and format of the book will better support these three course designs.

There have been a number of people who have also used the first edition for the purpose of ethics seminars for nonuniversity audiences. I also believe that this second edition is set out to allow more flexibility in dipping in and out of the book.

I have also expanded the normative theories examined to include the anti-realist ethical approaches of noncognitivism and contractarianism.

The contents is structured with three foci: The Basic Questions, The Basic Answers, and Putting it All Together. The questions in the first section are answered by the various ethical theories and normative approaches outlined in the second section. Finally, the last chapter forms the basis for the reader to integrate her own values and embrace an ethical approach to life.

For many, the fourteen chapters could be covered in the traditional fourteen-week semester. Those on different calendars (such as the quarter system) or those using the book as a resource for an ethics seminar can fashion their own best combination.

Each chapter begins with a quick preview. The material is presented in the context of examples and thought experiments. Each chapter ends with an integrative exercise that ties the chapter together. Some professors will have these done formally and turned in for a grade. Others will use these integrative exercises to focus class discussion. The last chapter of the book is meant to act as a capstone for the term. Many will structure their term paper around this final exercise.

Finally, each chapter highlights a few key terms that are conceptually important in order to grapple with material presented. These are collected in a glossary at the end of the book.

In summary, the new features of the book include:

- Expanded coverage of normative theories to include noncognitivism and contractarianism
- An overall structure that sets up foundational problems in ethical theory in the first section of the book that are variously addressed by the different ethical theories in the second section of the book
- A fourteen-chapter format to fit into most semester calendars
- A preview of each chapter
- Thought experiments and examples that help the student better engage with the text
- Key terms that are highlighted to assist the reader in grappling with issues raised (and reviewed in a glossary)
- An integrative exercise at the end of each chapter to test proficiency in comprehension and application of the material in that chapter
- A final chapter that is designed to help the student pull together much of the book and which can help structure a term paper that is grounded in pedagogy established for this purpose

Of course all of this is presented within the context of this author's worldview theory of ethics that allows students to begin with the values and understanding of the world that they already possess, and from there to transition to new levels of awareness.

In addition to those I acknowledged in the first edition I would like to add: Paul Churchill, David Cummiskey, Lisa Newton, Rosemarie Tong, Gabriel Palmer-Fernandez, Wanda Teays, and many others who have assisted me in developing my thinking for this second edition. My thanks to Julie Kirsch for her comments on the chapter on virtue ethics, to Adam Kovach on his organizational suggestions, and to Sarah Holle for her expertise in helping me reformat the presentation to make the book more useful. As always, I thank my family for their continued support of all that I do.

Michael Boylan
Marymount University
Arlington, VA

PART

I

THE BASIC QUESTIONS

LIVING IN A WORLD OF VALUES

WHO WE ARE AND WHAT WE VALUE

We begin our examination "in the middle of things." We are of various ages. We are female or male, theistic or agnostic or atheistic, lovers of opera or the latest pop music. We all vary greatly in who we are: who we think we are and what others judge us to be. All of us come to these pages with our own personal stories. When one considers all this diversity, it seems amazing that we are able to talk meaningfully with each other about anything.

It is my contention that rational discourse implies a common body of knowledge to which each party refers when examining some subject.[1] One of those common areas of knowledge might be various agreed-upon scientific facts about the world. Another may be various common values we hold. In some ways, the former connects us to almost *all* other people (because it implies universality) while the latter connects us only to those who share our values (i.e., the defined community is necessarily smaller).

2

The community of those who agree about the truths of science is large. As a result of this, many value the conclusions of science. We trust our lives to surgeons and physicians who prescribe treatments based upon this common body of knowledge.

Communities of people who hold other sorts of values are generally smaller than the community of those who agree about the truths of science. Be that as it may, it is probably the case that these smaller communities of particular values may say more about who we are and how we relate to others, than anything else about us. What are these values and how do we come to possess them? This is obviously a question that is best dealt with by developmental psychology. However, generally we can say that some of these values are given to us and some we choose for ourselves.

There are many values which each of us holds. We value goods having to do with our work and how it is carried out. We value goods that are tied up in our recreation. We are also particular about our family values and those of other communities in which we reside (such as the city, county, state, and nation—as well as the Boy and Girl Scouts, churches, mosques, and synagogues, etc.). This book is interested primarily in those values called ethics. We will try not to forget those other values (because they are always important), but before we make an effort at integration (see Chapter 14: "Formulating Your Own Answer"), it will be necessary to get through some basic concepts and then to explore some ways people have expressed ethical value.

WHAT IS ETHICS?

There is some disagreement about this. The various answers are given in Part 2 of this book. Some view **ethics** as all about intuiting what is true from some other realm. Others think that it is a conventional linguistic/cultural exercise at descriptivism. Still others (including this author) believe that it is about realistic assessments about the world that inform upon the grounding of normativity. Thus, for this author, ethics is the science concerning the "right and wrong" of **human action**. My definition, from the standpoint of moral realism, means that ethics is first a "science." By "science" I mean an activity which is studied rationally and systematically and whose conclusions seek to be exact.

Second, ethics concerns "right" and "wrong." These terms refer to judgments that assign praise or blame. In the case of ethics, these judgments are usually assigned to people or to actions according to some standard. Just what this standard *is* and how it is justified is a source of some controversy.

Third, the subject matter in question is human action. This does not mean that other types of actions may not come into the examination, for example animals, trees, and the oceans, but these other entities only come into question inasmuch as they are objects of human action. Thus, how a human treats a dog, a forest, or a waterway may be questions of ethics, but how dogs treat each other, or how trees interact, or how the molecules of water collide are *not* questions of ethics. This is because it is assumed[2] that humans are the only rational creatures (meaning, roughly, that they exhibit characteristics of deductive and inductive logic which are expressed in an operationally observable set of behaviors which can be classified as a language— namely, that such behaviors exhibit [at least] syntax and grammar),[3] and that this rationality is empowered with some modicum of free choice about what we do.

Because of this ability to rationally choose, we acquire ownership of and responsibility for the reasonably foreseen consequences of our actions. It is due to this ownership and responsibility that "good" or "bad" are assigned as value judgments according to some recognized "norm" which applies to all (or at least to some) people. In short, human action refers to humans interacting with humans or with anything else in such a way that we assume it originated from free rational choice.

Such a definition eliminates many types of things. First, it eliminates speculations that are not primarily systematic or rational. These systematic and rational justifications can be termed "good reasons for acting." What would be eliminated by such a restriction would be justifications based *solely* upon emotion, desire, or mere whimsy (though reason and emotion working together would fit).[4]

Second, this definition does not pertain to anything to which a neutral or merely descriptive depiction might apply. This might include actions such as "combing one's hair" or "whether to place the new picture on the right or the left wall." These activities are distinguished because they do not affect others in their sphere of action nor would they affect the self through violation of essential duties to the self. I do not diminish another nor myself (generally speaking) if I should choose the spaghetti or the linguini for my dinner entrée.[5]

Third, it does not apply to non-human entities (animals, vegetables, and minerals) except as they come into contact with humans.[6]

Fourth, it does not apply to actions that are not the result of free, rational deliberation. Thus, if one is coerced into certain actions by physical or severe psychological means, one is absolved from moral responsibility along some kind of sliding scale representing diminished capacity.[7] For example, if I strap you down and overpower you and then take your hand and make you push "the button" for a nuclear attack, you are not responsible for the results—for you could not have done otherwise. On the other hand, if you were somewhat—or even greatly influenced by someone but nevertheless you could have done something to prevent some action that you would have then committed, then I think that *some* responsibility rests upon you. This is because moral responsibility rests upon the free choice *to do otherwise.* This is not an "all or nothing" proposition. Therefore, according to a sliding scale one is proportionally responsible according to how free he really was.

Ethics really requires at least two agreements about freedom: (a) the metaphysical understanding that we are *positively* free to commit certain actions and (b) the ethical consideration about how we are to understand limitations on this freedom respecting our *blame* for committing this or that action.

These aspects of definition need to be supplanted by the rationale for thinking about ethics at all. *Why should we study ethics?* The answer to this question is somehow embedded in the purpose of our humanity: we are rational, purposive beings living together. Sometimes these purposes conflict. When this happens we can respond in one of two ways: (a) we can "muscle out" the other party so that our will can reign supreme; or (b) we can introspectively consider the ground of human action and act according to our best understanding of the proper mode of conduct.

But why should we introspect? This is certainly one of the most essential questions humans must consider. I have always been influenced by the dictum of Socrates: "The unexamined life is not worth living." It is the contention of philosophical ethics that each of us has a duty to examine himself or herself. It is not enough to exist like a piece of driftwood floating on the sea of life. This is because free, rational deliberation is an essential part of our ability to be autonomous individuals. And unless we are autonomous agents, there is no real participation in ethics. When there is no real participation in ethics, we give up a fundamental aspect of what it means to be a human being.

It is a fundamental feature of who we are as people that we participate in ethics such that we are diminished without such participation. None would choose to be diminished, thus none would choose to deny this duty to himself or herself.[8] Nonetheless, we know that many fail in this. What are we to say about such people? How can we justify our judgments?

These are just two questions for which we will seek answers as we develop our exploration into ethics and values.

THE INDIVIDUAL: METAETHICS, NORMATIVE ETHICS, AND APPLIED ETHICS

The above discussion has raised a number of questions that need answers. These answers require a reasoned and systematic response. Each of these basic inquiries begins with our own experience and can be phrased in the form of questions of increasing generality:

a. A particular moral problem arises such as, "What should I do when my prenatal testing shows that I am carrying a Down's syndrome baby?"

b. To answer (a) implies recourse to a norm by which I can assess my options via-à-vis the "rightness" and "wrongness" of said actions. What is the standard by which we will judge human action as good or bad? How do we know that the standard we have set out is the correct standard?

c. To answer this last query, we need to establish a group of principles by which the process of (b) itself can be critically evaluated, in order to ascertain whether the standards in (b) are ones we should adopt for ourselves.

These principles should address the further questions of:

i. How do we arrive at the standard?

ii. What is the range and scope of the standard?

iii. What formal characteristics should a good standard possess?

Questions (a), (b), and (c) all deal with the right and wrong in human action—but they address different issues. They begin from our personal experience with a moral problem. The struggle to solve the problem suggests a series of approaches that are increasingly abstract.

This experientially learned order (also called the *genetic order*) begins with the phenomenon of someone faced with a difficult situation. (One begins with the empirical fact and proceeds to an account that is more abstract.) If this process is followed over time, we see that someone has begun with a situation that confronted him or her and ends up addressing abstract, general principles that would apply to a large range of cases.

This is, in many ways, similar to the activities of the scientist who begins with observations of nature and proceeds to general rules of biology/chemistry/physics that account not only for *this* event, but also for all similarly structured events.

Once the more abstract, general principles have been established, then one can move in the opposite direction to solve the difficulty, that is, moving from the more abstract to the empirical case at hand. This process is called the *logical order*. The logical order is occasioned by the former process (the genetic order). In the logical order one begins with the abstract and moves to the empirical.

Imagine that you were writing a science textbook. You would begin with certain abstract assumptions about science. These would be set out as the laws of science. These laws or general principles would generally apply to situations of that sort. Thus, if you wrote in your textbook the Newtonian formula $F = ma$ (force equals mass times acceleration), then any particular problem that was an instance of this would be "tagged" to this formula and subsumed under it. Students reading the book would learn the general rule and how to recognize instances of this rule and then when the appropriate instance of that rule occurred, they would treat that instance as a case falling under the law '$F = ma$.'

Such a process is about recognizing the territory of the appropriate or covering law. Thus the logical order works from the abstract to the particular while the genetic order works from the particular to the abstract.

In ethics the most concrete area is **applied ethics** that deals with applying normative theories to actual moral situations. **Normative ethics** is next since it creates a system by which a large number of similar cases can be dealt with under the constraints of acting under some well-defined prescription. Last is **metaethics**.[9] Metaethics is a series of investigations that intend to offer critical support to the process of creating a moral theory and the operation of its implementation. Since this is an *essay* on ethics, I will begin with the logical order in my presentation.

Metaethics refers to the most general investigation about how to go about creating and applying a theory that prescribes how we should act. There are many issues and discussions which have developed in this area of ethical study—more than can be set out in such a brief treatment as this, however; in the depiction of the ethical theories themselves (see part 2) some further elaboration of many key distinctions are set forth.

One central issue concerns the *origins* of the theories. This, in turn, engenders several related questions: "How do we know these theories are correct?" "How are these theories justified?" "What do these theories tell us about the world?"

These (and other) questions are important because they set the stage for our being able to construct a normative theory of ethics. In this way metaethics serves normative ethics just as philosophy of science serves those who create theories of science. There is a sense of creating the boundaries of acceptable discourse.

One of the principal questions in metaethics in the twentieth century has been whether one could derive an "ought" statement from an "is" statement. If you cannot, then "oughts" occur from nonfactual (i.e., nonrational) sources. Why do people hold such a position? Let's examine this through an example.

> Premise: John says to Mary, "There is a poisonous cobra under your chair."
> Conclusion: John then says, "You ought to get out of your chair and run" or more simply "Get out of your chair and run!"

What is the relationship between the premise and the conclusion? On first glance it might seem as if the factual premise implies the conclusion. In this case we would have an "is" (or factual statement) implying an "ought" (or prescriptive statement).

However, others might demur. They would say that there are suppressed premises in this paradigm. These might include:

> 1'. A poisonous cobra will kill you.
> 1". You do not wish to be killed.
> 1'''. The only way to avoid being killed is to get out of your chair and run.

Premise 1' and 1''' are both factual statements, but 1' is a suppressed premise that is also normative. The whole argument would go differently if one were to assert that *he were indifferent to being killed*. This means that 1' is really equivalent to "You *ought* not wish to be killed." In this way the detractor would contend that a hidden "ought" has been smuggled into the premises. If this is true, then one has not derived an "ought" from an "is" but rather an "ought" from an "ought."

Thus, the detractor of there being a derivation of an "ought" from an "is" would assert that in every supposed example of such a purported derivation, there is a suppressed premise which contains a "hidden 'ought.'"

There are other important questions in metaethics. For example, perhaps the basis of ethical value cannot be determined rationally. Those who would make such an assertion fall into two camps: (a) the cognitivists who emphasize the role of rationally informed emotion such as "sympathy" and "care" (as in ethical feminism) and (b) the noncognitivists.

I will defer my discussion of ethical feminism until Chapter 7. The noncognitivists believe that the basis of ethical theory is not legitimately in knowledge. In a deep sense it is a matter of "taste." For example, few of us would contend that there is an intellectual basis for liking Fortnum and Mason's Irish Breakfast Tea over Bewley's variety of the same. The softer taste of the latter is preferred by some, while the sharper, tannic aspect of the former is the choice of others.

The noncognitivists will contend that no matter how hard one tries, that matters of value cannot be traced back to matters of fact. For example, on the above example concerning tea, one could say that good tea has a sharper, tannic taste, therefore; Bewley's is better. "However," the critic would contend, "how do we know that sharper and tannic are better and how do we measure them?" This can be a problem, the noncognitivists contend. There is *no* pure standard for good tea that all would agree to: this is why we have so many types of tea!

There are various other noncognitivist strategies that I will not elaborate here—such as linguistic analysis and emotivism. These are interesting and are treated in Chapter 9.

For now, let us focus our considerations on how we are able to talk about ethical theories. Metaethics creates a structure by which such discourse is possible by elucidating the architecture by which normative ethics is possible. Throughout this book many of you will say to yourselves, "But that claim depends upon some more abstract, unacknowledged concept. I want to explore that logically prior concept!" This sort of exhortation is the origin of metaethical speculation. Do not shy away from bringing up these thoughts in class!

THE SOCIETY: SOCIAL AND POLITICAL ETHICS

A second way of thinking about ethics is in the social/political sphere. The difference between these two perspectives is that in the personal realm it is rather easier to parse the issues involved: Jamal is talking to Juanita about why he is canceling his invitation to the senior prom. To analyze the case one need only consider the practical situations of Jamal and Juanita and then to ascertain what moral principles/maxims/virtues might apply. Once these have been ascertained, the process is comparatively straightforward.

However, things become much more complicated in the social world. Here, we must situate ourselves into a world involving others. One of the best ways to do this is via a thought experiment about what we all desire most (see page 10).

I feel confident that all of us would choose the food and water. This is because it is essential to our ability to act (without it we would die). Fancy clothes are nice, but they are not as embedded as food and water. All of our primary goods of agency—on the *first level* the food, clothing, and shelter that allow us to live and actually *be agents* and on the *second level* those goods necessary to *be effective agents* (such as education and the recognition of fundamental human dignity)—are far ahead of fancy dress clothing.

WARM-UP THOUGHT EXPERIMENT 1–1: EMBEDDEDNESS— AN INTRODUCTION

If you were cast away on a desert island what would you desire most? A year's supply of food and water that might see you through until a ship might rescue you, or an Italian designer's latest formal wear that is sure to make you look your best? How do you base your response? ■

In the survivalist mode there may or may not be enough to eat. The twentieth century is certainly full of examples of cities in the midst of war that have had to resort to extreme measures in order to survive.[10] Other circumstances such as great poverty, environmentally induced famine and political oppression often put large numbers of human beings at risk of losing that which is most primary.

Beyond the basic goods of agency there are other goods that we either possess or seek to possess. I call these goods secondary goods. These include property (both real and portable), and intangible goods such as social status and self-esteem. The secondary goods are divided according to their relationship to the basic conditions of action.

The secondary goods have three groups. In the first group are the life enhancing goods (medium to high-medium embeddedness). These goods seek to enable the agent to compete at an equal starting line. These goods are not as important as basic goods because basic goods enable: a) the biological conditions of action and b) the basic societal skills as well as the basic human rights that allow any effective action. However, that is not to say that life enhancing secondary goods are in any way trivial. They are not. They promote equality of action and equal opportunity.

The middle level of secondary goods are those that are useful to us (medium to low-medium embeddedness). These goods are the prudential goods that most of us can reasonably strive for as a primary material precondition to living the sort of life that will make us happy. Again, there is some relativity here because what might please one person in one country/historical era might not satisfy another.

The lowest level of secondary goods are the luxury goods (low embeddedness). These goods are aimed at providing pleasurable accessories to action. Luxury goods come in all sorts of packages. Some are small (such as gourmet coffee beans) while others are very large (such as a membership in an exclusive country club). The point here is that this class is the farthest removed from the fundamental conditions for action.[11]

I contend that the moral claim for goods decreases as one moves away from the basic conditions of action. Thus, for example, being a member of a social class that faces discrimination within a society is far closer to effective action (life enhancing) than possessing a portable compact disc music player (luxurious). This means that the good involved (respecting the member of the discriminated class) has greater moral value than possessing the portable compact disc music player.[12] This is because being discriminated against (like African Americans in the United States) can negatively affect one's self-esteem and ability to be an effective agent. Since it is assumed that (in order to be good) before anything else, each of us wants to commit voluntary, purposive action—anything that is an unfair[13] hindrance to action strikes against our fundamental human nature. Each person alive on the earth—now or at any time anywhere—can legitimately claim to fulfill what is his natural potential (at least respecting fundamental human agency). If there is a reciprocal relation between legitimate claims to goods by individuals (and groups of individuals) and the duty of the society to provide those goods to said individuals, then this distinction about proximity to action is very important. This is because the society has a *duty* to provide individuals with those goods that are proximate to action— either as basic goods or level-one secondary goods that are very fundamental/life enhancing (such as not being discriminated against). However, society *does not* have a duty to provide agents with goods that might be useful for action, but are not fundamental (level-two and level-three secondary goods). For example, it might be useful to own a cell phone. One might be a more effective agent with a cell phone, but it still does not pass the test for being a fundamental secondary good since one can still fulfill a large range of effective action without one. A cell phone is nice, but it is not necessary.[14] A cell phone is not fundamentally life enhancing and is several levels removed from basic goods.

Thus, targeting society's resources toward alleviating the negative consequences of discrimination would be (on this account) more morally defensible than using society's resources to provide people cell phones. And in our desert island example, since the basic goods of agency are of far greater importance (to human agency) than secondary goods, it is clear that one would choose a year's supply of food and water over an equally costly (in money) designer outfit.

THE MORAL STATUS OF BASIC GOODS

The general point is that (concerning moral issues), there is a hierarchy of claims to goods that may be ranked according to their proximity to action. In the first class there are basic goods. These are ranked on two levels. These levels correspond to their proximity to one's ability to act. We all wish to act before anything else because without action we cannot become good. On the first level (most deeply embedded) are those goods that are biologically related to acting at all: food (a minimum number of calories given a certain body mass), clothing (protection of the core body temperature so that it might be above 94 degrees Fahrenheit), shelter (providing core body temperature protection and reasonable opportunity to sleep), and protection from unwarranted bodily harm (without some modicum of safety we will perish).

The second level of basic goods (deeply embedded) concentrates upon providing the agent with the goods necessary to be an effective actor within a particular society. These goods are what any agent could claim in order to act at a basic level of proficiency within that society. These goods are of two types. The first sort of second-level basic good refers to education and skills that are necessary within some society. Because these requirements are societally/historically specific, there is some relativism regarding the actual goods involved. However, the more theoretical requirement is universal, namely that there are goods affecting education and skills that all members of that society need in order to be effective agents at a basic level.

The second sort of level-two basic goods are those having to do with human liberties such as those set out in the U.S. Bill of Rights and the United Nations Universal Declaration of Human Rights. These goods are also necessary in order to be effective actors in any given society.

Since basic goods are more essential for action than secondary goods, moral rights claims for basic goods will trump secondary goods rights claims. Within each category, the more primary a level is to action the more it will take precedence over the less primary.

All of these rights claims are grounded in the definition of what it means to be an agent and an objective evaluation of what every agent deems primary to him or her above all else (i.e., the ability to execute purposive action in order to become good).

Thus, on the moral level the term "embeddedness" refers to the proximity to the conditions of action (as discussed above). This means that the strength of an agent's claim to any particular good is relative to its embeddedness in the table. Underlying this is the notion that what is natural for all agents to desire most (the ability to commit free, purposive action) is also justified. This can be set out more precisely in the following argument.[15]

Argument 1–1: The Moral Status of Basic Goods[16]

1. All people, by nature, desire to be good—Fundamental Assumption
2. In order to become good, one must be able to act—Fact
3. All people, by nature, desire to act—1, 2
4. People value what is natural to them—Assertion
5. What people value they wish to protect—Assertion
6. All people wish to protect their ability to act—3–5
7. Fundamental interpersonal "oughts" are expressed via our highest value systems: morality, aesthetics, and religion—Assertion
8. All people must agree, upon pain of logical contradiction, that what is natural and desirable to them individually is natural and desirable to everyone collectively and individually—Assertion
9. Everyone must seek personal protection for her own ability to act via morality, aesthetics, and religion—6, 7
10. Everyone, upon pain of logical contradiction, must admit that all other humans will seek personal protection of his or her ability to act via morality, aesthetics, and religion—8, 9
11. All people must agree, upon pain of logical contradiction, that since the attribution of the basic goods of agency are predicated generally, that it is inconsistent to assert idiosyncratic preference—Fact
12. Goods that are claimed through generic predication apply equally to each agent and everyone has a stake in their protection—10, 11
13. Rights and duties are correlative—Assertion
14. Everyone has at least a moral right to the basic goods of agency and others in the society have a duty to provide those goods to all—12, 13

What is the essence of Argument 1–1? It is that the basis of our social/political understanding of others lies in our acceptance that there is a generic attribution of claim rights to those goods necessary for action. This recognition causes us to connect to those people and try to deliver these goods to those without these goods.

A further specification of these goods would also be useful. There might be numerous categorizations of what hierarchical order is most empirically grounded, but my best guess is something like this:

The Table of Embeddedness

Basic Goods

Level One: Most Deeply Embedded[17] (That which is absolutely necessary for human action): food, clothing, shelter, protection from unwarranted bodily harm

Level Two: Deeply Embedded (That which is necessary for effective basic action within any given society)

- Literacy in the language of the country
- Basic mathematical skills
- Other fundamental skills necessary to be an effective agent in that country, e.g., in the United States some computer literacy is becoming increasingly important
- Some familiarity with the culture and history of the country in which one lives
- The assurance that those you interact with are not lying to promote their own interests
- The assurance that those you interact with will recognize your human dignity (as per above) and not exploit you as a means only
- Basic human rights such as those listed in the U.S. Bill of Rights and the United Nations Universal Declaration of Human Rights

Secondary Goods

Level One: Life Enhancing (Medium to high-medium on embeddedness)

- Basic societal respect
- Equal opportunity to compete for the prudential goods of society
- Ability to pursue a life plan according to the personal worldview imperative
- Ability to participate equally as an agent in the shared community worldview imperative

Level Two: Useful (Medium to low-medium embeddedness)

- Ability to utilize one's real and portable property in the manner she chooses
- Ability to gain from and exploit the consequences of one's labor regardless of starting point
- Ability to pursue goods that are generally owned by most citizens, e.g., in the United States today a telephone, television, and automobile would fit into this class

Level Three: Luxurious (Low embeddedness)

- Ability to pursue goods that are pleasant even though they are far removed from action and from the expectations of most citizens within a given country, e.g., in the United States today a European vacation would fit into this class
- Ability to exert one's will so that she might extract a disproportionate share of society's resources for her own use

Some may quarrel with some of the ranking, but the general point is that there is such a ranking. If this is agreed to, and if these goods are proportionally linked to the possibility of action (what we all want most), then the acceptance of the argument on the moral status of basic goods along with the **table of embeddedness** constitute a moral basis upon which we should all confront others. At the very minimum, according to the wealth of the society, claims for lower-level goods should always be trumped by claims for more basic goods. This has nothing to do with charity. It is a valid human right that entails a correlative duty. All people deserve these goods. This is one way to understand the foundation of social/political ethics. The manner in which each reader responds to this standpoint constitutes an answer to one of the basic questions in ethics.

KEY TERMS

- ethics
- human action
- applied ethics
- normative ethics
- metaethics
- table of embeddedness

A THOUGHT EXPERIMENT: INDIVIDUAL AND SOCIAL ETHICS

Directions: Write a two and a half page essay (750 words) on the thought experiment below. Try to fashion your response using your own opinions with some of the distinctions made in this chapter (see Key Terms).

The President of the United States and the Congress have just passed a new tax law that seeks to deliver health insurance to all people in the United States regardless of their ability to pay. This may sound like a good thing—after all, protection from unwarranted bodily harm has been interpreted as supporting health care rights (a level-one basic good). The down side is that there is a special surtax that is being levied on those with incomes in the top 5 percent of taxpayers. This will affect *you*. You have gone to school to become a tax accountant. Your family has had to sacrifice mightily for this. Your mother had to take out a second mortgage on her house. Now, at graduation, is the time that you were to gain the fruits of your and your family's sacrifice. However, because of your field and your grades, you have a chance—right out of college—to get into that top 5 percent! Why should you have to pay for the health care of others who did not overcome the same obstacles that you did? You also want to get married. Your fiance is in primary education—not much money there. If this new hefty tax goes into effect it may affect your ability to marry right out of college and buy a house. Since you've studied tax law you see that you could easily break the law on an ambiguous provision and never be caught. This would ensure that your new marriage would start out with a financial bang. What do you do? Do you pay your fair tax share? Do you cheat (knowing that you will probably never be caught/convicted because the rule is ambiguous)? What do you owe your fiance? What do you owe the disadvantaged in your country?

NOTES

1. See Michael Boylan, *The Process of Argument* (Englewood Cliffs, NJ: Prentice Hall, 1988, rpt Lanham, MD: University Press of America, 1995), Chapter 1.
2. Though with some primates, this assumption may be controversial. If, for example, it were proven that dolphins were rational, then it would follow that "human action" is too narrow. In this case, "the action of rational creatures" would be more apt.
3. Some may claim that the standards for syntax, grammar, deductive, and inductive logic are all derived from humans interacting with humans. This is probably true. There may be a bias here.
4. In fact I try to integrate the two in Michael Boylan, *A Just Society* (Lanham, MD and Oxford: Rowman and Littlefield, 2004), Chapter 2.
5. This example illustrates that I believe that morality is not only about action, but also about the proper distribution of one's personal activities within the context of others. It seems to me that there are many activities that are not proximately related to the rational interests of others (nor falling under the scope of the personal worldview imperative that it be "good") and therefore such actions are not to be judged in the purview of ethical analysis. I will term this other type of analysis "prudential" (in one's personal interest).
6. The status of the interaction with animals and nature is controversial. See my article, "Worldview and the Value-Duty Link" in *Environmental Ethics*, ed. Michael Boylan (Upper Saddle River, NJ: Prentice Hall, 2001).
7. It should be clear that I am *not* talking about cases in which people have not even thought about what they are doing. Rather, these examples are about coercion.
8. It should be acknowledged here that "duty" is very important to my own personal conception of ethics. Those who would hold a consequentialist view would assign different values here. For a further discussion, compare the arguments as presented in Chapter 13.
9. Please note that the ethical noncognitivists think of metaethics rather differently. For them it begins with second-order linguistic discourse: talking about a proposition. For a discussion of this see Chapter 9.
10. One need not go far to prove this point. In the Second World War the siege of Leningrad and Stalingrad are poignant examples of people deprived of level-one basic goods [see: Anthony Beevor, *Stalingrad: The Fateful Siege, 1942–43* (NY: Penguin, 1999) and Harrison Evans Salisbury, *The 900 Days: The Siege of Leningrad* (NY: Da Capo Press, 1985)]. Of course there is also the horrific conditions in the Nazi concentration camps [see: Zygmunt Bauman, *Modernity and the Holocaust* (Ithaca, NY: Cornell University Press, 1989)] and, unfortunately many more. Even at the writing of this book millions around the world suffer the loss of level-one basic goods daily.
11. It seems to me that luxury goods, themselves, can be broken into several classes rated according to the amount of societal resources/money required to convey this good. Thus, a compact disc music player is a luxury good at a relative low level since the cost is between $50 and $250 (at this writing). A yacht would be a rather high-level luxury good pricing in between $750,000 to $10,000,000 (and up!).

12. I am, of course, assuming that strange situations do not pertain such as a person who needs to listen to music all the time or he will go into a coma or another such serious medical problem. The assumption here is that music is a pleasant (but nonessential) element to have available at all times. As such it is remotely connected to the ability to commit effective action.

13. The sense of "fairness" here relates to a theory of deserts. This is beyond the parameters of this treatment. However, it appears rather clear that no one chooses her race. Thus, being of a particular race should not be held against someone. It is unfair to penalize anyone for that which is not a direct consequence of some action she has committed. Discriminating against African Americans in the United States is thus unfair. Since the consequences of this discrimination are not life enhancing, it trumps all other secondary good claims. For a fine discussion of different senses of "desert" see Louis P. Pojman and Owen McLeod, eds., *What Do We Deserve? A Reader on Justice and Desert* (NY: Oxford University Press, 1999).

14. The line between basic and secondary goods is set by the ability of an agent to act in a very objective way within a society. The line between life enhancing, useful, and luxurious goods is less precise. It will probably vary over time and is certainly relative. Thus, this discussion must be a part of an ongoing examination that each society should continually update.

15. A more detailed argument for this is in my book *A Just Society*, Chapter 3.

16. In my recent writings I have begun with the following three premises: 1. Before anything else, all people desire to act—Fact/2. Whatever all people desire before anything else is natural to that species—Fact/Desiring to act is natural to *homo sapiens*—1, 2. I have used these premises in other contexts because I have not broadened my perspective to human nature (as I have in this volume). Thus, I do not believe the two versions to be in conflict, but simply that one reflects a rather more narrow perspective.

17. "Embedded" in this context means the relative fundamental nature of the good for action. A more deeply embedded good is one that is more primary to action.

THE NORMATIVE NATURE OF WORLDVIEW

Our ability to value anything is inextricably tied to our personal worldview. This is because worldview forms the context for all of our normative and factual judgments. It is only through an exploration of worldview that we can come to know fundamentally what valuation is all about and how it can be used correctly or not. This process forms the basis of inter-subjective dialogue about value. Thus, we begin with: (a) individual investigation into the foundation of valuation itself, and then move to (b) group consensus about such standards of valuation. These standards, in turn, allow social groups to discuss individual values of ethics, religion, and aesthetics along with their resultant social institutions.

Consider the following depictions of personal worldview:

Group A

> The World was all before them, where to choose
> Thir place of rest, and Providence thir guide:
> They hand in hand with wand'ring steps and slow,
> Through Eden took thir solitary way. —Milton, *Paradise Lost*[1]

18

This is the way the world ends
This is the way the world ends
This is the way the world ends
Not with a bang but with a whimper. —T.S. Eliot, "The Hollow
Men"[2]

Group B

Little Lamb, who made thee?
Dost thou know who made thee? —William Blake, "The Lamb"[3]

That bit of filth in dirty walls,
And all around barbed wire,
And 30,000 souls who sleep
Who once will wake
And once will see
Their own blood spilled. —Hanus Hachenburg, "Terezin"[4]

Above are two groups of paired poems. In each is a definite *point of view*. Group A begins with an optimistic view of a tragedy (the human fall in the Garden of Eden—at the beginning of the world according to the *Torah*) followed by an angst-ridden view of the end of the world.

Group B presents an innocent vision of gentle questioning about the causes of life from the mind of a carefree rural child, followed by the queries of a soon-to-be Holocaust victim about the nature of life in death and death in life.

In each passage there is a different set of donneés that surround each writer. In literature we call this *voice*. As a writer of poetry and fiction (and occasional reviewer of literary novels) myself, I can attest that the ultimate judgment that we make when reading a piece of fictive literature revolves around the voice of the author. Charles Dickens did not achieve fame on his stylistic writing. In fact, his sentences are often clumsy, and he uses some words improperly. His characters are often wooden and his plots predictable. What sets Dickens apart from others in his century (who were his superior in these departments) is his voice.

The voice of Dickens is that of a champion *for* children's rights, for the rights of the oppressed and *against* those who through their machinations seek to overreach themselves and grasp goods meant for others. When one reads a Dickens novel, he is impressed with the clarity of moral vision that suffuses the pages. This sense of literary voice is what I will call the worldview or *Weltanschauung*.

Voice is what demarcates the world we enter when we open the covers of a fiction book. This world is an escape and we assent to it or not, according to a myriad of factors. The act of reading is a knowing "suspension of disbelief." We willingly enter into the author's worldview and "test" how it is like to be there. This is more than merely becoming a "murderer" (in a mystery story) or a "member of the opposite sex" or a "person of a different race, religion, or culture"—it is the acceptance of a network of beliefs that together are expressive of values concerning the critical concerns of life: ethics, politics, religion, aesthetics, and so forth. When the world we enter is welcoming (meaning that it *accords* to some deeply held tenets within our own worldview), then we feel comfortable and react positively. When this world is foreign and hostile (meaning that it does not accord to our deeply held tenets within our own worldview), then we are uncomfortable and we react negatively.

The composition of this worldview-web-of-beliefs is not the same in everyone. For some (probably very few), the worldview may be driven by a purely logical system. These are the "Mr. Spocks" of the world.[5]

For others (a more common structure), the worldview is driven by a number of different considerations. These considerations include compassion, love, sympathy, fear, bravery, and so forth. These various components of the self are called upon as the situation dictates. This means that particular problems dictate which part of the self is most appropriate to respond. Such a problem-oriented approach is called *aporitic* (after the Greek word for "difficult problems").

These aporitic constructs often exist in isolation from one another. Thus, it is not uncommon for a person to be kind, caring, and compassionate in one context and ruthless in another. Such individuals defend their conduct by citing the particular circumstances of the situation. It is the difficult problems of the situation that bring out this or that aspect of their personality.

This fragmented approach to human action is dangerous. Not only does it make one's actions dependent upon external circumstances (thus rendering the agent "un-free" and "not responsible"), but it also destroys any holistic conception of the agent. If the agent is entirely dependent upon exterior circumstances to determine who he is, then there really is *no* real abiding person at all. Both the genetic and logical priority nod to the circumstances and not to the person as the prior and primary entity.

Therefore, it is important for the position I am defending that it be possible for one to evaluate one's worldview and life plan in a holistic fashion with reason being one of several key components. This holistic approach means that one cannot separate worldview from philosophy. Some analytic philosophers have suggested that somehow it is possible for philosophy to work independently of any worldviews.[6] For example, Rudolf Carnap (a prominent logical empiricist) has argued that it is possible to isolate "observation sentences" (empirical facts about the world) and "theoretical sentences" (objective statements which reveal relationships between the facts).[7] Both are really independent of anyone's "subjective" interference, the underlying assumption being that there is a hard distinction between doing analytic philosophy and introducing anything of one's *Weltanschauung* into the process. This notion of analytic method believes that philosophy is only a tool and is separate from its practitioner as well as being separate from the subject matter that is under investigation.

A somewhat similar position was developed from a different point of view by Wittgenstein in his doctrine that philosophy "leaves everything as it is" (*Philosophical Investigations, 124*). For Wittgenstein, philosophy should exist as a neutral tool that does not disturb the subject matter that it studies. This is unlike science that engages itself and interacts with its subject matter (not too unlike Carnap's notion of theoretical statements). Philosophy thus approaches its subject matter in a different way than science does. When philosophers try to imitate the method of science, they are "led into complete darkness" (*Blue Book, 18*). Instead, the philosopher becomes a sort of historian employing a tool that does not interfere with the subject matter nor does it involve the worldview of the practitioner: "philosophy may in no way interfere with the actual use of language; it can in the end only describe it. For it cannot give it any foundation either" (*Philosophical Investigations, 124*).[8]

These various views of analytic philosophy depict it as an objective tool that can be employed by anyone without taking on any of the characteristics, values, or worldview of the practitioner. This position seems wrong to me. I believe that the philosopher always brings his or her worldview along with him or her. This is not a position of epistemological relativism, but merely an admission that the subjective and objective don't neatly segregate.[9]

In creating an amalgam of the objective and the subjective interacting with each other, one very well imagine creating some sort of twin that possessed a both an objective and a subjective element (Thomas Kuhn and Paul Feyerabend could be cited as philosophers who did just this—albeit in different ways).[10] Consensus and logical argument appeal to the common body of objective knowledge resident within. But at the same time it is necessary to acknowledge the other aspects of *Weltanschauung*. This is especially true in moral philosophy.

Though they are subjective in nature, these worldviews are themselves subject to evaluative criteria. These criteria are similar to the criteria mentioned earlier concerning justice. They are formal and logical principles that are virtually devoid of empirical content. Together, these criteria can be put together to form what I call the **personal worldview imperative**: *"All people must develop a single, comprehensive and internally coherent worldview that is good and that we strive to act out in our daily lives."*[11] It is my conjecture that every agent acting or potentially acting in the world falls under the normative force of the personal worldview imperative. An examination of a few aspects of these can be found in the next section.

PERSONAL WORLDVIEW

The personal worldview imperative really features four key points: (a) **comprehensiveness**, (b) **coherence**, (c) connection to a theory of the good, and (d) a requirement of personal action. Let's examine these each in order.

COMPREHENSIVENESS

This requirement is also called "completeness." It is often said of any logical theory—especially those that apply to the world—that completeness is an important formal component. A personal worldview that is complete could confront novel situations in life and present an action recommendation. An incomplete worldview would be at a loss and would have to hoist up the white flag of surrender.

It seems to this author that the best way to ensure completeness in a personal worldview is by developing **goodwill**. There are at least two senses of "goodwill" that I would like to highlight here: a rationally based goodwill and an emotionally based goodwill. I believe that both are necessary for achieving completeness in our personal worldview.

The rationally based goodwill requires the agent to sincerely adopt a commitment towards living a life that takes reason into account. In cases of ethics this would mean using one's deductive and inductive powers in order to make sense of the situation confronting us, and then to allow this reason to inform upon our action decision.

The standpoint of rationally based goodwill suggests that a large part of who we all are as *homo sapiens* is rational. It is a dominant property of who we are. To fail to recognize and act upon this is to degrade ourselves. This is no small thing. Because of the assumed comprehensive nature of reason itself, agents so committed will never be at a loss of what to do. Completeness will be maintained.

But we are not totally rationally based beings. We are also emotionally based. There may be some overlap between these, but for our purposes let us assume that the ethically relevant aspect of our emotional being begins in *sympathy*. Sympathy is the connection between the emotions of two different people. Now some sympathy is of a superior looking at an inferior: "I feel so sorry for you." This is a form of sympathy, but it is not as morally relevant to the emotional goodwill. In the emotional goodwill there must be an even-handedness. This means one puts one's self on the level of the agent with whom we are emotionally connected. We are equal. There is no looking downward or upward. I call this disposition openness.

It is my conjecture that sympathy that is open yields caring. Caring is an action response by one agent to another to remedy pain or need within one's capacity. I believe that unless one is at the ends of the Bell curve in psychological normalcy, all normal people who connect with others in sympathetic openness will care for the object of their concern. This triad, (sympathy + openness => care) = philosophical love. When one has philosophical love for another, there will never be a case in which one will be at a loss for what to do. Completeness will be maintained.[12]

COHERENCE

There are at least two ways to understand coherence in this context: (a) deductive coherence and (b) inductive coherence. Deductive coherence has to do with simple contradictions. We should act contradictorily in our actions. Why is this? It is because even though we both embrace reason and emotion, reason trumps. Emotion is often contradictory. I want to buy the ice cream cone but I also want money for the movie ticket. I can't have both. Or I contend that I will not use recreational illegal drugs such as Ecstasy. However, though I say this in my Bible study group, when I'm with my "player" friends I take all that I can get. This is a clear case of deductive incoherence.

i. Jon says, "I will not take any illegal drugs." — Context 1 (Bible study group)

ii. Jon says, "Give me some of that Ecstasy drug." — Context 2 (at a rave)

If Jon believes in taking the illegal drug ecstasy, then his belief should show forth in all contexts. If Jon does not, then that, too should be evident. One's opinions of possible actions (that have ethical content) should not be context driven.[13]

In short, deductive incoherence asks you to be consistent with what you espouse and do between various contexts in which you are presented with action choices.

Inductive incoherence is very often not thought about in this context. Inductive incoherence is also called a sure-loss contract. It refers to a situation in which a betting house will always lose. For example, if I were to open the Boylan betting house on whether there will be a human on Mars by 2015 and I offered 5:1 odds yes and 5:1 odds no. Unless I have an infinite amount of money, I'm out of business. This is because the contradictory odds must be complementary to the primary odds. Otherwise, anyone could bet both ways and be sure of a positive pay off.

But what has this to do with ethics? Many people have personal life strategies that are inductively incoherent. Take this example:

i. Ms. X says she wants to be a good mother and wife.
ii. Ms. X also wants to have serial affairs with Mr. Y and Mr. Z.

In inductive incoherence the very qualities that would enable you to be successful in I will make you a failure at II. For example, a good spouse should be honest and supportive. A good parent should be there when the child is in need and be generally supportive in actions and attitudes. In II, a good cheat is adept at turning off her conscience. She must be able to lie well and to suit herself in all circumstances. The traits necessary to be successful in I will make one a failure at II and vice versa. If she were to set out to do both, she would be involved in a sure-loss contract.

It is the contention of this piece of the personal worldview imperative that she should not be deductively or inductively incoherent if she wishes to become the best person she can be.

CONNECTION TO A THEORY OF GOOD

This book presents several theories of the good. These include ethical intuitionism, ethical noncognitivism, ethical contractarianism, virtue ethics, utilitarianism, and deontology. She may also appeal to her religion or aesthetics in giving her a foundation for her ethical values. The point to all this is that she must have *reasons* for what she does. Some of these reasons should connect to a theory of being good: an ethical theory. Those who dismiss this part of the process are not in accord with the personal worldview imperative. The dictum gives leeway to various ways to fulfill this requirement. But not up for compromise is the requirement that one is sincere (a striving for the ethical) as well as authentic (the situating of the striving within a legitimate context). Obviously, the first requirement is more in our power than the second. We can strive because of a passion within our soul. But the object of our striving is ultimately an artifact of our reason. To strive for an improper goal would be to combine sincerity and an inauthentic goal (such as a person who wants riches at the cost of unfairly hurting others).

This is often the rub. Very few of us actually contemplate the best way to achieve our goals. We simply accept the social givens. This is unacceptable. We need to be responsible for the direction of our lives. The personal worldview imperative enjoins us to do just that.

A REQUIREMENT OF ACTION

How little is gained by someone who proclaims a position but never really lives it in his life. Sinclair Lewis' novel *Elmer Gantry* is one clear example of this.[14] In the novel, a charismatic Baptist preacher converts many and attains national prominence while really practicing actions that are contradictory to what he advocates. This is hypocrisy. Under the personal worldview imperative we are enjoined to do what we say. In the current colloquial jargon in the United States this is often described as "walking the talk."

A second key point refers to what we are enjoined to walk. Some ethical theories prescribe impossible outcomes. For example, the Shakers (a Protestant religious sect in the nineteenth century) told followers not to have sexual intercourse. This was based upon some sort of idea of extinguishing desire as a road to salvation. However, if everyone in the world did this, the world would cease to have humans in less than one hundred and fifty years.

For clarification let us describe ethical theories that prescribe unattainable ends as **utopian**. Utopian theories are to be discarded on the grounds of the personal worldview imperative.

Rather, we should adopt models challenging us to be good in the world that are possible—though they may be rather difficult to achieve. Let us call this, **aspirational** ethics. For example, the Reverend Martin Luther King, Jr.'s example of commitment to social justice is rather difficult for most of us to achieve, but it is possible. His life showed us so.

Ethics should be about what is aspirational and not what is utopian.

COMMUNITY WORLDVIEW

Community worldview is similar to personal worldview except that it is not so exact. This is because there is inevitably more diversity in a group than there will be in any single individual. The rough similarity between the two is mirrored in the **shared community worldview imperative**: *Each agent must contribute to a **common body of knowledge** that supports the creation of a shared community worldview (that is itself complete, coherent, and good) through which social institutions and their resulting policies might flourish within the constraints of the essential core commonly held values (ethics, aesthetics, and religion).*

There are several key elements to this imperative. First, there is the exhortation to create a common body of knowledge.[15] The *common body of knowledge* is a set of factual and normative principles about which there is general agreement among a community or between communities of people. This includes (but is not limited to) agreement on what constitutes objective facts and how to measure them. It also includes (but is not limited to) what counts as acceptable values that will be recognized as valid in the realms of ethics, aesthetics, and religion. This is an essential element in order for positive group discussion to proceed.

Second, there is a dialectical process of discussion among members of a single community and between members of various single communities that are united in another larger heterogeneous community. This discussion should seek to form an understanding about mission of the community within the context of the common body of knowledge and the commonly held core values held by members of the community. These values will include ethical maxims, aesthetic values, and religious values. Of course, there will be disagreements, but a process is enjoined that will create a shared worldview that is complete, coherent, and good.[16]

Third, the result of this dialectical creation of a shared community worldview is to be employed in the creation (or revision of) social institutions that are responsible for setting policy within the community/social unit. It should be clear that this tenet seems highly inclined toward democracy. It is. However, it is not restricted to this. Even in totalitarian states the influence of the shared community worldview is significant. One can, for example, point to the great differences among Communist states in Eastern Europe, the Soviet Union, China, North Korea, and Cuba from the 1960s to 1980. All were Communist. Yet there were great differences in the way the totalitarian regimes operated in each instance. This is because, even without the vote, the shared community worldview casts a strong influence upon the operation of society's institutions and their resultant policies.

Finally, it should be noted that the actions of those institutions must always be framed within the core values of the people who make up the society. Whenever the society veers too far away in its implementation of the social worldview from the personal worldviews of the members of the society, then a realignment must occur. In responsive democracies this takes the form of installing a new government as the result of the next election. In totalitarian regimes, change will also occur, but generally by coup d'état or by armed revolution.

Many people are more inclined to take seriously the personal worldview imperative because it makes them more effective at achieving the prudential and ethical ends that they hold. It allows for clear coherence and direction. However, one's community standpoint should not be discounted. This is because we all live in communities. Often the help and assistance we receive from them goes largely unnoticed by us. We only become aware of the community when it asks something from us.

Then we dig in our heels and cry, "Why should I help the community? What has the community ever done for me?" Many make this common complaint when the community solicits volunteers for community service and when the community orders us to pay taxes to support various community initiatives. It is inconsistent on the one hand to accept the assistance of the community via schools, police, fire, roads, bridges, Internet infrastructure, a fair business environment in which to compete, and so on, and on the other hand to deny to a reciprocal duty to give back to that community. Community membership is both a great enabler of personal liberty and a hindrance on personal liberty. One cannot have the one without the other.

Of course, there are the **free riders**. The free riders only want to accept the benefits of society and let others pay the bill. This one-sided approach is one of the greatest threats to building a fair community for all. From the community's point of view the free rider must be stamped out. However, how many community resources should be devoted to this? Every dollar spent on expunging the free rider is a dollar that isn't being spent on the core policy objectives of the community. Most communities will write off the free riders until they reach a significant threshold (often between 5 percent and 10 percent of a given population). At that point normal order will be significantly impacted by these renegades.

The last piece of the shared community worldview imperative is the tolerance that it commands. All individuals whose actions are in accord with the personal worldview imperative are to be tolerated. Behind this dictum of toleration is a belief that social diversity is a good thing. We are all different and that difference is good. That diversity will make the community stronger and happier because as times change there are more possible resources to draw upon. Homogeneity is *not* the desired social end. Certainly there are standards to which all must adhere—such as the personal worldview and community worldview imperatives that dictate *ceteris paribus* that all community members will be cooperative team players within an acceptable framework—but beyond these standards there is great latitude for personal and social expression of cultural diversity and its appreciation. In the end of the day, social diversity within these constraints is a future goal for us all to develop our communities to their potential as pleasant places to live. The manner in which the reader embraces this principle (or not) constitutes a response to one of the basic questions in ethics.

Key Terms

- personal worldview imperative
- comprehensiveness
- coherence
- goodwill
- utopian
- aspirational
- shared community worldview imperative
- common body of knowledge
- free riders

AN EXERCISE ON WORLDVIEW

Directions: Write two essays.
Essay One:
Go through the personal worldview imperative. Write out all of your strongly held beliefs about facts and values of the world. Then take a red pen and connect those that work together and with another color pen connect those that conflict. Be sure to state which color works with each.

Use this work sheet to construct a one-page essay discussing the synergies and conflicts of your own worldview (in light of the personal worldview imperative). What might a more satisfactory personal worldview look like (from your own standpoint)?

Essay Two:
Go through the shared community worldview imperative. Write out the principal communities to which you belong and other communities in the areas in which you live but which you don't belong. Use the two-color pen method to indicate points of synergy and difference.

Use this work sheet to construct a one-page essay discussing the various social groups in your community (those to which you belong and those to which you don't belong) and then comment on how these various communities adhere to and diverge from the shared community worldview imperative. What might a more satisfactory community worldview look like (from your own standpoint)?

NOTES

1. John Milton, "Paradise Lost" in *The Poetical Works of John Milton.* Ed. Helen Darbishire vol. 1 (Oxford: Clarendon Press, 1952).
2. T.S. Eliot, "The Hollow Men" in *The Complete Poems and Plays 1909–1950* (New York: Harcourt, Brace, and World, 1952).
3. William Blake, "The Lamb" in *Jerusalem and Selected Poems.* Ed. Hazard Adams (New York: Hold, Rinehart and Winston, Inc., 1970).
4. Hanus Hachenburg, "Terezin" in *I Never Saw Another Butterfly: Children's Drawings and Poems from Terezín Concentration Camp (1942–1944).* Ed. Hana Volavková, Tr. Jean Nemcová (New York: McGraw Hill, 1964). Hachenburg died shortly after this poem was written in 1944, at the age of 14, in a Nazi concentration camp.
5. For those who never watched the television show, *Star Trek,* I will identify Mr. Spock as a character totally driven by considerations of logic. He was devoid of emotion or any other considerations.
6. Kai Nielsen has discussed this briefly in his article, "Philosophy and *Weltanschauung,*" *Journal of Value Inquiry* 27 (1993): 179–186.
7. Rudolf Carnap, *An Introduction to The Philosophy of Science* (New York: Basic Books, 1966), part 5. Max Weber made a similar sort of argument in his classic article, "Value-judgments in Social Science" in *Weber: Selections in Translation,* ed. W.G. Runciman (New York: Cambridge University Press, 1978), 69–88.
8. Ludwig Wittgenstein, *Philosophical Investigations.* Tr. G.E.M. Anscombe, 3rd Edition (New York: Macmillan, 1958), section 124.
9. This is similar to Quine's insistence that analytic and synthetic truths don't easily segregate. See "Two Dogmas of Empiricism" in *From a Logical Point*

of View (Cambridge, MA: Harvard University Press, 1953).

10. Thomas S. Kuhn, *The Structure of Scientific Revolutions* 2nd ed. (Chicago: University of Chicago Press, 1970) and Paul Feyerabend, *Against Method* (London: Verso, 1975) and *Realism, Rationalism, and Scientific Method* (Cambridge: Cambridge University Press, 1981) have prominently called into question the dispassionate objectivity in science. Their work owes a debt to Willard Quine who wrestled with finding ways to try and express a "give and take" developmental process in which the individual and the world interact with each other. In the end Quine's amalgam seeks to emphasize the objective. See "Natural Kinds" in *Ontological Relativity and Other Essays* (New York: Columbia University Press, 1969). Kuhn and Feyerabend, on the other hand, set out an analysis, which emphasizes more strongly the force of the subjective.

11. Some might contend that my depiction of this imperative places an over reliance upon form over content. It is a "procedure" and thus cannot have normative "content." Against this attack, I would reply that though the prescription *simpliciter* is procedural, it will result in some content. And, if taken in the Socratic spirit of living an examined life, then the force of the normativity is toward participation in a process which must be sincere because it represents each of our very best versions of the "good, true, and beautiful." For a more rigorous examination of the personal worldview imperative see: Michael Boylan, *A Just Society* (Lanham, MD and Oxford: Rowman and Littlefield, 2004), Chap. 2. For my exposition on the relationship between the good, the true, and the beautiful, see my book: *The Good, The True, and The Beautiful* (London: Continuum, 2008).

12. In those rare cases in which the two goodwill standpoints disagree, the rational goodwill standpoint should supervene (Boylan 2004, Chap. 2).

13. I am assuming that the context does not change the description of the event involved. The generic description is invariant between various descriptions.

14. Sinclair Lewis, *Elmer Gantry* (New York: Harcourt, Brace, 1927). Sinclair Lewis was also the first American to win the Nobel Prize in literature.

15. I discuss the common body of knowledge in greater detail as it pertains to logical argument in *The Process of Argument* (Englewood Cliffs, NJ: Prentice Hall, 1988), Chap. 1.

16. I discuss an example of how this shared community worldview might arise in my essay, "Affirmative Action: Strategies for the Future," *Journal of Social Philosophy* 33, no. 1 (2002): 117–130.

RELATIVISM

- ❖ Cultural Relativism
- ❖ Moral Relativism
- ❖ What's at Stake?
- ❖ Key Terms
- ❖ A Thought Experiment: Finding Out What You Believe

CULTURAL RELATIVISM

Do you take sugar in your tea? Would it offend you if someone ate his hot dog with his left hand? Should married men grow beards? What do you think about veils and headscarves? These are just a few examples of customs that have real meaning to various societies on earth. The tendency to allow such differences in behavior flows from the freedom of human action (supported in Chapter 2, when it's in accord with the personal worldview imperative). Basic freedoms are a level-two basic good on the table of embeddedness. It would seem that some sort of flexibility in dealing with others within the context of their social traditions is a good thing. One must have a more embedded reason if one wanted to trump this prima facie right to **autonomy**. On this level (because of the prima facie right to autonomy), barring other factors, it would seem that all people whose actions do not violate the personal or community worldview imperatives should be allowed to do what they desire. Let us call this **legitimate cultural relativism**.

However, not all people have always thought that cultural relativism was legitimate. Many European Christian missionaries in the age of colonization and conquest tried to change indigenous peoples, who were under their power, to European ways—from religion, to language, to dress, and general behavior. These Europeans didn't like the native peoples and the way they lived their lives. These conquerors (and the missionaries who followed) thought that converting the conquered to Christianity was a more embedded reason. This is not a case of ethical embeddedness, but rather a religious reason (see the discussion in Chapter 6).

It is assumed that those cultures that have developed within the context of the shared community worldview imperative should be allowed to act and practice as they like (on the principle of autonomy just enunciated).

Now it should be stated here that there are also many similarities between cultures. For example, I don't know of a single culture that says that character traits of wisdom, justice, self-control, and courage are not virtues. However, what should count as fulfilling these abstract categories and how they match up against each other, is rather contentious.

Two features that are often brought forward to legitimate cultural practices are (a) the voluntary nature of the act and the compliance of the parties, and (b) the historical heritage of the practice—has it been an integral part of that culture for some time?

But often there is confusion on just what a practice is and whether it really falls within the bounds of morality. Some of this confusion may be linguistic and thus involve misunderstanding. An example of linguistic ambiguity is in the Islamic term *jihad.* Among Islamic believers, *jihad* has traditionally been concerned with concentrated attention and renewal at the personal and social level. It has often been a part of one's Ramadan schedule or the theme of one's visit to Mecca. However, because of our war-torn world today, it is often associated with high-pitched declarations of violence. This latter usage is an atypical usage seen in the larger historical context. But it is easy to see how a term or phrase from one language to another can evoke reactions that may not be entirely accurate.

At other times, there may be some real concerns. For example, the practice of female genital mutilation (sometimes mistakenly called female circumcision) has a deep cultural past in some North African societies. The practice is performed by older women on the younger women. It is done with the apparent consent of the young women. The purpose of the practice is to render sexual intercourse as painful so that wives are not inclined to cheat on their husbands (though there is no analogous practice that is performed upon men).[1] Female genital mutilation has a long cultural history. Does this mean it's a valid instance of legitimate cultural relativism?

At the writing of this second edition, most women in the world do not enjoy the same civil rights as men. These practices also have a cultural history. For example, in some countries young girls are denied primary education because the culture says that literacy is only the province of men. Does this mean that it is a valid instance of cultural relativism?

This sort of problem is often confused with the **blind prejudice problem**. In the blind prejudice problem people assert culturally based preferences that are not functionally tied to the phenomena they are describing. For example, someone might have a culturally based bias against gay men and a culturally based bias against pink shirts on men. When one puts these together, then whenever someone with these two prejudices confronts a man with a pink shirt, he or she first assumes he is gay. Second, she or he assumes he is evil (and may assault or kill him). Are such prejudices a part of valid cultural relativism?

It is obvious that we need some guidelines are in order to sort these issues. For that we turn to ethics.

MORAL RELATIVISM

In order to be clearer about these issues, we need to define the moral realm. Earlier, it was asserted that ethics was the science of the right and wrong of human action. Other accounts soften this claim to something like the perceived or recognized right and wrong of human action. This *latter* claim really accepts **moral relativism**. Moral relativism is often a feature of the normative theories mentioned in part 2: Chapters 8 through 10 (see especially the "open question" test in Chapter 8). This sort of position is depicted as **moral antirealism**.[2] The antirealist is committed to some variety of moral relativism (at least in the intersocietal realm).[3] The hooks for this approach basically appeal to what *seems right* within a society. The imperative is to ascertain the cultural landscape via language and perceived practices and then to adapt to the landscape.

The *former* claim is a rather stronger one based upon **moral realism**. It is here that the word *science* comes to play. If the groundwork of moral imperatives has a factual basis, then its discovery is a science — rather than a guess or intuition or social study that is the province of the antirealists.

Let's briefly look at the attraction that each theory has (more detailed analyses occurs in part 2). The antirealists believe that we cannot get beyond the normative givens in our culture. These cultural trappings include language and established practices. The task of the individual is to discern what her culture approves of and then to do it. Ethics, in this context, is a rather descriptive exercise. The ethicist is on par with the cultural anthropologist. The normative function comes from the givens of the society and are not really subject to change (unless there are contradictory imperatives existing side by side incoherently).[4]

The realists, on the other hand, think that we can supercede our particular culture, historical era, or other social descriptions. For example, in the United States from around 1830 onward there was a growing popular abolitionist movement against human slavery. These individuals fought against what was an accepted state of affairs in the United States for over two hundred and twenty years and an accepted state of affairs in Europe for even longer. (Most of the decision makers in the United States during this time period came from Europe or European descendants.)

How was it that abolitionists rose up to be a major social force? The advocates of slavery pointed to the same cultural documents (such as the Bible) to make their point. The abolitionists cited the same passages but interpreted them differently based upon a community worldview that created a different hierarchy of primary ethical principles than the advocates of slavery. For the advocates of slavery it was simply a matter of different readings of the Bible. Each side was equally valid. As such, the problem became a political problem.

For those who do not believe in moral realism, the end result of disputed questions about human action frequently devolves into who has the stronger political hand: **might makes right**. If you can control the political climate, then in a descriptive sense *you are right*. "Right" means what is anthropologically accepted due to conditions of social and political power dynamics.

It is important to separate this question from the one that says, "Who controls the rules in the society?" For the antirealists, it's all about power dynamics. When you are in power, then whatever you do is right. This is because right is the same thing as having the laws and the police on your side. In the case of slavery, with the Fugitive Slave Law (1850) and the Dred Scott decision (1856), it was clear that the power was on the side of the slavery advocates. The power structure supported their claims. Did this mean it was *right*? Does the concept of *right* have any meaning apart from what is the status quo?

The abolitionists believed that slavery was not a matter of historical tradition, linguistic, or cultural givens. No, it was an issue that could be debated upon the factual merits of the place of liberty in the hierarchy of legitimate claims that people may make against the society in which they live. For the abolitionists, they were passionate that slavery anywhere at any time was *always* evil. The argument could be based upon various arguments that cited facts about the world (such as the nature and structure of human action).

Each reader of this text must come to the table and decide whether moral realism or moral antirealism is correct. It will really determine their answer to the moral relativism question.

WHAT'S AT STAKE?

So why are we talking about this? Why is this an important issue? What difference does it make?

These are some important questions. Let's address them in order.

WHY ARE WE TALKING ABOUT THIS?

Well, this author would say that the moral relativism debate is one of the two strongest challenges to a functioning morality and social philosophy in the world today. If moral relativism is correct, then no country is in a position to criticize another for its actions. The offending country can merely say, "This is the way we do things here. Who are you to tell us naught?" Thus, when the world saw the atrocities in the Nazi concentration death camps against Jews, the general response was that the Nazi leaders should be punished. But why did the Allies think this? If they were moral realists they would claim that the Nazis broke universal moral laws against murder (the unjustified killing of an innocent at will). The Nazis clearly murdered innocent people. The slaughtered souls committed no crime. Thus, (the moral realists) would say the Nazis are guilty of murder on a wide scale and should be punished.

The moral relativists might take two stances.

Stance one: This is a different culture. The Germans have always had strong anti-Semitic behavior—as evidenced by the Passion Plays at Oberammergau in which various prejudiced stereotypes against the Jews have been depicted for centuries. Moral relativists would contend that in each culture one must accept the culture's givens if there is a general social acceptance and it is historically situated. Both conditions held in the case of the Jews in Germany so the moral relativists must let the Jews be murdered. The moral relativists might pose the question "Who are we (any non-German) to disagree?"

Do any readers really believe this (no matter their cultural heritage)? I think not. Ethical relativism doesn't cut it here.

Stance two: Hey, the Germans lost World War II. If they had won, then that would be different. But because the Allies won, then the Allies can dictate the terms of right and wrong and various sorts of punishments and humiliations (as they had done in the *Treaty of Versailles* that ended World War I). The spoils go to the conquerors. That's a fact. There is nothing more to it.

Some readers might agree. Others may demur. This second stance truly gets to the issue of *might makes right.*

WHY IS THIS AN IMPORTANT ISSUE, AND WHAT DIFFERENCE DOES IT MAKE?

The world today is becoming increasingly integrated. We increasingly live in a global community that is connected by communications and by international business (companies that transcend nation status). Because of these new realities, it is imperative that we have the tools to evaluate what is happening in the world. For example, recently Google and Yahoo have tried to get a foothold into the Chinese Internet market. The problem is that China does not operate a free and open society. When Yahoo offered an e-mail service, one person using it was identified from key words under government data mining and later sent to jail for five years.[5] Google was also requested to voluntarily monitor key words so that those key words would not be available on search engine requests—words such as "Tiananmen Square" or "human rights." If the directors of Yahoo and Google were moral realists, then they would demur at giving in to a totalitarian regime that suppresses human rights (a level-two basic good) no matter what the financial payoff (either a level-two or a level-three secondary good). Basic goods trump secondary goods; therefore both companies should have said they would pass on the commercial opportunity given these conditions.

However given the same scenario from a antirealist perspective, one would be inclined to accept the given values of Communist China and say something like this: "There has never been a human rights tradition in China—going back for thousands of years. They use language and culture in such a way that entrepreneurial forays trump everything. We cannot force our values upon them."

Since this is a rapidly changing world (economically and politically) we need to know whether the moral realist (i.e., **moral absolutism**) stance is a preferable strategy to the moral antirealistic (i.e., moral relativism) stance.

How the nations of the world act from here on out depends upon the decision about whether there are universal moral values. Herein lies the importance and the difference of this issue from a practical perspective. If we are moral relativists, then each and every problem of human interest will fall to the power of the ruling institution (governmental or economic) to make its call based upon conventional interests. Now these institutions may claim that there are historical and voluntary elements in what they do, but it is not clear how such claims are relevant to whether the action is right or wrong. Just because people continue in the society without causing violent revolution, and the practice has occurred for a long time, does this mean that it is legitimate?

If one is an advocate of a set of universal moral values, then each society (including our own) must be held up to this universal standard. The probity of our actions is about more than our power to change events. There are real standards that should determine the *oughts*. For those of this persuasion see Chapters 12 and 13. In the end, each reader must decide her own answer to this basic question of ethics.

KEY TERMS

- autonomy
- legitimate cultural relativism
- the blind prejudice problem

- moral relativism
- moral antirealism
- moral realism

- "might makes right"
- moral absolutism

A THOUGHT EXPERIMENT: FINDING OUT WHAT YOU BELIEVE

The claims of the moral realists and the moral antirealists are important in the context of legitimate cultural relativism. How should these issues be sorted out? The following exercise should make this clearer for each reader.

Step One:
Go to a news source—newspaper or online traditional news outlet. Then find two stories. The first story is meant to show a legitimate instance of cultural relativism. The second story is meant to be a controversial instance of cultural relativism. Now, make your choice and cut them out/print them out.

Step Two:
Write a paragraph (100 words or more) on why the first story is a legitimate instance of cultural relativism (citing criteria and reasons).

Step Three:
Write a paragraph (100 words or more) on why the second story is a controversial

instance of cultural relativism (citing criteria and reasons).

Step Four:
Write a long paragraph (150 words or more) projecting yourself as a character in the second story. How would you feel being a part of this situation? Would it make a difference if you were a part of those wielding the power or those subject to the will of others? Be clear about who are in the story and the reasons for your opinions.

Step Five:
Write a long paragraph (200 words or more) on whether you think that that there are universal ethical principles that supercede controversial cultural norms. Base your reasons upon your work in step three and step four (plus any of the key concepts set out in this chapter).

NOTES

1. There is a linguistic spin here. The practice of deactivating the female clitoris for sexual function is often described as "female circumcision." This is to bring it into a familiar context to male circumcision (a Jewish custom that many Christians also observe). The difference is that the male circumcision does not impair function. Only the foreskin of the penis is removed. No function is impaired. This is an example of linguistic confusion in cultural relativity.

2. For a brief introduction to some of the issues in the moral realism v. antirealism debate see the antirealist folk — Simon Blackburn, *Essays in Quasi-Realism* (Oxford: Oxford University Press, 1993); Gilbert Harman, "Moral Relativism Defended," *Philosophical Review* (1975): 3–22; and R. M. Hare, *The Language of Morals* (Oxford: Oxford University Press, 1952) compared to the moral realist folk — Christine Korsgaard, *The Sources of Normativity* (New York: Cambridge University Press, 1996); Alan Gewirth, *Reason and Morality* (Chicago: University of Chicago Press, 1978), Christian Illies, *The Grounds of Ethical Judgement* (Oxford: Clarendon Press, 2003); and Michael Boylan, *A Just Society* (Lanham, MD and Oxford: Rowman and Littlefield, 2004).

3. There is, of course, the response that the moral antirealist does *not* deny that there may be universal moral principles across time and space, but merely that it would be impossible to *know* that these exist. It would not be unfair (based upon their own terms of discourse) to move to the conclusion that such universals do not exist unless there is some empirical base to which said claim could be verified.

4. Of course, even if one were to discover that incoherent premises existed side by side, it would not solve the problem of which one to choose.

5. This alleged event occurred on February 8, 2006. See http://money.cnn.com/2006/02/08/technology/yahoo_china_b20/ (accessed September 26, 2007).

CHAPTER

4

EGOISM

INTRODUCTION

After ethical relativism, the second greatest challenge to morality is the doctrine of egoism as the basis of action. The reason that this is a challenge is that it asserts that everyone will act on the basis of whatever suits his or her own **prudential advantage**. Prudential advantage means the advantage of one's own personal interests based upon the principle of happiness (or perceived happiness). It is the contention of ethics that there are occasions in which one might be forced to act not for one's advantage or perceived advantage, but because the agent perceives that it is the proper course of action based upon principles (without regard for personal advantage).

There are two principal varieties of egoism: psychological and ethical. This chapter will set out the arguments for each within the context of the possibility of altruism. At the end of the chapter the reader will be invited to engage in a thought experiment meant to clarify her own views on the subject.

PSYCHOLOGICAL EGOISM

Basically, **psychological egoism** says that we only voluntarily do what we think will satisfy our own perceived interests. A straightforward rendition of the argument for psychological egoism goes like this.

Argument 4–1: An Argument for Psychological Egoism

1. All of us are hardwired to act according to our own perceived interests in all cases — Assertion
2. People have an imperfect ability to ascertain their real motivations for action — Assertion
3. People often mistake their real motivation for action (due to ignorance of the real underlying causes) — 2
4. When people attribute altruism as their underlying motivation for action they make a mistake — 1–3
5. Cases of falsification of premise #4 fall prey to the caveat in premise #2 — Assertion
6. People always act according to their perceived self-interest — even if they are convinced otherwise — 4, 5

In Argument 4–1 there are several key premises that warrant examination. The first is premise 1. It asserts a statement of human nature that has a biologically determinate basis. This is stated in the form of a scientific law. There are two forms of scientific laws: assertoric and contingent. An assertoric law must always be true. One counterexample will falsify the law. For example in physics the claim that force equals mass times acceleration ($F = ma$) would be falsified by an experiment in which this were shown not to be the case. The strength of premise one suggests an assertoric law. In other words, if we could find a single instance in which one acted not out of perceived self-interest, then the law would be rendered invalid.

But perhaps this is too hard. A weaker version of a scientific law is the contingent law, found in biology and the social sciences[1] (where a law means "for the most part": proving the null set from 5 percent to .5 percent, i.e., being true 95 percent to 99.5 percent of the time).[2] Those are the limitations of such a contingent law. If there were more than 5 percent of human action that did not conform to this rule, then it would be invalid.

The gauntlet is laid forth. If it is the case that more than 5 percent of people (in the most generous standard) feel that they did not act for their perceived self-interest, then the contingent law would be rendered invalid.

Let us also assume that in the first case there are more than one single case (the hard scientific law) and even more than the threshold of 5 percent. Then what is the response of the advocate of psychological egoism?

Premise 3 gives us the answer. Individuals don't know what makes them act. Only psychological scientists can undertake this exercise via empirical studies that will directly or suggestively point to an outcome. Under some theories of psychology ultimate motivation can be a hidden or suppressed cause. Such causes are unknowable to the subject and not precisely measurable to a scientist. What is not precisely measurable to a scientist is not empirically falsifiable. As such, these inscrutable causes seem more like posits of religion than of science: no matter what the data show, premise 1 is the fact. It cannot be shown to be otherwise.

What is one to do when there are no clear empirical criteria to decide the matter? Now this may be a case of the **rationality incompleteness conjecture**. Rationality seeks demonstrably to prove all propositions. However, in cases in which there is no empirical, non-question begging, test for verifying a principle, the best that reason can do is to offer various plausible alternatives. The resolution can only come about through appeal to the personal worldview imperative and its application in the way we confront novel normative theories. A recourse to the rationality incompleteness conjecture is the **most plausible hypothesis maxim**: in those situations in which the rationality incompleteness conjecture holds, one may employ the most plausible hypothesis based upon all relevant information given to the agent (relevance here is defined via the personal worldview imperative in concert with inductive logic).

In the end, this is a difficult problem. One possible further clarification can come from the following counterargument.

Argument 4–2: A Counterargument to Psychological Egoism

1. There is a difference between these two propositional descriptions of psychological egoism: (a) we only voluntarily do what under the circumstances we want to do or dislike least; and (b) we only voluntarily do that which we think will satisfy our own perceived interests—Assertion
2. 1-a is definitionally true—Fact
3. 1-a does not imply 1-b—Fact
4. There are many counter examples to 1-b—Assertion
5. Only 1-b defines psychological egoism—Fact
6. 1-a is true; 1-b is false—3–6

According to Argument 4–2, premise 1 there is a significant difference in the sort of claim that might be put forth as describing psychological egoism. Premise 1-a suggests a definition that really amounts to a description of voluntary action. Such a definition would be unacceptable because it is too broad. One cannot use a definition that applies to all voluntary action and claim that such a definition is synonymous with psychological. Such a move would be begging the question. Rather, something more specific is needed. Premise 1-b is the definition offered in this chapter. The counterargument suggests that there might be exceptions that are so prevalent that they falsify premise 1-b. Such exceptions might be on the model of the atheist man who gives up his seat in the lifeboat of the Titanic to a younger person. Because he is an atheist, the man who gives up his seat does not do so for a future reward. He sees that his choice will mean his death. Nonetheless, he does it.

Another sort of example might be a physician who feels a duty to work in a subsistence society or in dangerous situations (like Doctors without Borders). These individuals give up comfortable incomes and social status for physically dangerous working conditions and very low pay. When one talks to these medical heroes they often use language that reflects their sense of duty to the cause of suffering people. They do not employ terms such as "happiness."[3] This would be the general tone of objections to psychological egoism (see also ethical egoism and altruism).

ETHICAL EGOISM

Ethical egoism is a rather different approach. Whereas psychological egoism seems to clearly indicate that one is seeking to satisfy one's own perceived interests, the ethical egoist believes that striving after personal interest is an ethical duty. According to ethical egoism, if everyone is buzzing about acting after his own personal interests, then like the beehive, there will be order and happiness for all. This is rather like Mandeville's beehive (a foundational document in the formation of classical capitalism).[4] If it were the case that a society of self-interested people really brought about social harmony and happiness, then there might be a compelling argument for the theory. It certainly is simple and seems easy to apply. The problem is that the success of this doctrine depends upon whether it is really true that self-interested people will form such a cohesive whole. Much of the plausibility of this depends upon whether people are inherently good or bad (see Chapter 5). Barring such supportive evidence, it seems to be an unproven conjecture that may border upon utopian thinking.

If people have a duty to act in their own self-interest, then we need to examine what this self-interest might be. Unlike the psychological egoist, the ethical egoist has a more robust sense of free will. We can act in our own self-interests or not, and we can choose the way that we act. For our purposes there are two senses of "one's own perceived interests." On the one hand, acting in one's self-interest might mean that one always seeks *the immediate gratification of pleasure*. Or, on the other hand, it might mean one seeks what will give *the most personal satisfaction in the long run* of one's life. These aren't always the same. Let's look at two types of cases.

CASES

Case 4–1   **CONSIDERING HEROIN**

Your name is Sam. You have gotten into a crowd that is doing drugs. In a series of stages the group has become a group of codependents. They are increasing the strength of the drugs they are using. You are getting worried. You know that the next level being discussed, heroin, is a one-way ticket to self-destruction. Your life expectancy and general health will be severely compromised. Yet, they say that the high experienced when you take heroin is like no other. Should you hang with your mates or take this opportunity to split? Why or why not? ■

In Case 4–1 we are confronted with a classic case of short-term pleasure versus long-term misery. In this case the pleasure is an easy drug fix. The short-term pleasure is intense yet the long-term pain is irksome: addiction, shortened life expectancy, social ostracism, possible jail time, and other side effects. Most scales of quantitative cost-bene-fit analysis would fit the problem into the following scale:

Pleasure is measured on a scale of 1 to 100/
Pain is a negative value of –1 to –100

This cost-benefit chart is very simplified. It is set out to make a par-ticular point. If we are only considering pleasure and pain for ourselves alone, then according to the assumptions in Case 4–1 taking the heroin for five years will be far more painful in the total span of one's life than abstaining. If one were an ethical egoist of the sort that said that he was not considering initial pleasure but long term self-interest, then there is no contest. However, we all know that this is not the way many people see things. They are so focused upon the immediate gains and gratification that they minimize the severe long-term pain for the intense short-term satisfaction. Most ethical egoists would say that tak-ing the heroin option is really not the most pleasurable (all things con-sidered). Thus, they would advocate a long-term approach.

This additional cognitive factor is what separates the ethical egoists from the psychological egoists. In the former case there is a rational

CASES

CASE 4–2   THE OLYMPICS

Your name is Yvette. You are a 20-year-old international-level swimmer. At a recent orthopedic checkup it showed that you have advancing osteoarthritis in your right and left shoulders. In addition, it demonstrated severe lower back disorders at lumbar 4–5. The prognosis is if you keep up with this swimming through the Olympics (you have a shot at a medal), then you will become crippled by the age of 40. What do you do? You have a chance to achieve what few people can: an Olympic medal (or more than one medal counting the relays). This is a short-term gain. On the other hand, you will be a cripple by the age of 40. Age expectancy for an eighteen-year old woman in the United States is around 80. Thus, half of your life you will be a cripple. ■

calculation on what will bring the most happiness while in the latter case it is a hardwired disposition towards the pleasurable in each choice situation. This means that the psychological egoist may be biologically inclined toward immediate gratification. One must always choose the pleasurable because of deep-seated inscrutable motivation factors.

Ethical egoism presents more liberty. It says that we should strive to optimize our general *flourishing* that is heavily weighted toward long-term calculation. On the grounds of ethical egoism, one should not take the heroin. Cut out of the group and join the drama club.

Case 4–2 is more complicated than Case 4–1. In this situation the short-term gain is a valued, significant accomplishment. The achievement of a high-level physical goal that is intersubjectively recognized is far different from the dim haze of a drug-induced high. What this means in the cost-benefit calculus is that instead of the short-term pleasure that only lasts as long as the drug-induced high (Case 4–1), the pleasure lasts *before* the event (in anticipation), *during* the event (the action), and *forever after* in fond recollection. Thus, it might be possible to create the following cost-benefit scale (see page 44).

In Case 4–2 one may suffer some long-term pain for a short-term pleasure, but the pleasure is of the sort that it is a valued, significant accomplishment. This is the basis of the long-term fond memory that ensues. When one acts in a way that is consonant with their aspirational personal worldview imperative, then there is the real chance that forever after one's satisfaction over that accomplishment will sustain one— even though there are severe painful consequences.

Case 4–2 is more difficult for the ethical egoist because it is not so clear-cut what is the best course of action. Would the boring life be better than one that entailed the achievement of a worthy goal but with

A COST-BENEFIT ANALYSIS
OF CASE 4–1

Option one:
Taking heroin over some period—say five years. $100 \times 365 \times 5 = 182{,}500$ if taken daily over five years. Assuming the person is 18 years old, then the integrated pain interval would be from 18–72 (assumed lifespan). Let the pain (on the most generous hypothesis exist on a decreasing scale)— 54 years $\times$ (80–10 decreasing) = (689,850) on a daily accounting. Net accounting for using heroin = (507,350) total/ (9,395.38) per year/ (25.74) per day of pain for the rest of one's life of pain versus 182,500

total pleasure/ and no pleasure after five years.
Option two:
Not taking heroin. Say Sam has a boring life and there are no real upsides = 0/ but from this aspect of life by itself there are no downsides = (0).
Results option two: 0 > (507,350)
Option three:
Not taking heroin. Boring life, but happy for having made the abstinence choice—2 + per day = 39,420 > (507,350) ■

A COST-BENEFIT ANALYSIS
OF CASE 4–2

1. The Before: five years in anticipation—at $65 \times 5 \times 365 = 118{,}625$
2. The Event: $100 \times 1 = 100^5$
3. The After: (60 years of life expectancy and fond memories) $35 \times 60 \times 365 = 766{,}500$
4. Total Positive = (1 + 2 + 3) = 825,225

Option one:
The negatives are 40 years of progressive pain from 20–80 integrated to a continuum at = (876,000)

The net loss is (50,775) which over 60 years is (846.25) per year or (2.32) per day.

Option two:
Doing nothing 0 > (50,775)

Option three:
Dropping out of your sport and having regrets about this. Regrets are variable between 2.5–5.0 per day, which either creates a pass or a slight positive gain. ■

a significant price tag? Let me make it perfectly clear that I am not advocating athletes use steroids or other life-threatening drugs in order to achieve their ends.[6] Case 4–2 is rather describing the permanent pain that one might suffer in legitimately achieving a valued, significant accomplishment. There can be pain associated with personal gain. It is not enough to say that one will never aim at a single event because of long-term pain. Rather, one must specify just what is the short-term pleasure and what is the long-term pain and how each relates to the perceived personal advantage of the agent. There is no mechanism for this. This is why ethical egoism is not a full-blown normative theory and set in part two of this book. Rather, the general disposition of aiming at personal advantage under a normative ought creates a particular characterization of the agent and her moral motivation. Ethical egoism is most compatible with various versions of classical capitalism (an economic and not a moral theory).

Another way to think about our various choices from the ethical egoist model is to consider Plato's tripartite soul. According to Plato, the soul has three parts: *thumos*—spiritedness; *epithumos*—directed spiritedness or desire; and *sophia*—wisdom. For Plato, the task of the individual was to keep each in balance, with wisdom leading the other two parts. This is a general prescription to individual happiness that will also lead to an ethical person. If the three parts act in harmonious concert under reason's lead one will be happy and moral at the same time. Like Mandeville's beehive, the vision is a fair one; however, is it realistic? To get a better handle on this, let us consider the strongest objection to both sorts of egoism: altruism.

EGOISM AND ALTRUISM

Since we have outlined two sorts of egoism, let us examine how altruism is an objection to each. First, let us consider psychological egoism.

Let's define **altruism** as a person acting from the motivation of principle or duty rather than from the motivation of any personal advantage. This definition sets the advocate of altruism squarely against the psychological egoist. There is a deep disagreement here (as per the Titanic or socially motivated physician examples). Those advocates of altruism will bring forth such cases. However, the psychological egoists will counter with their hidden motivations and personal ignorance dictums. As mentioned earlier, the possibility of altruism (at least one case) and especially the widespread possibility of altruism (more than 5 percent) would be devastating to the psychological egoist. Such foundational disagreement causes us to recognize the rationality incompleteness conjecture and employ the most plausible hypothesis maxim (see the thought experiment at the end of the chapter). It will be on these grounds that the question will be answered.

Second, consider ethical egoism. The strongest argument against ethical egoism from the standpoint of the altruism is that ethical egoism ignores community sensibilities. Since one is obliged only to maximize his own personal interests, there is no need to consider oneself within a social environment. Without the consideration of the social environment, then what makes ethics special? Why do we need ethics apart from economics and decision game theory? Ethical egoism (altruists would contend) has no answer for this. If we are only engaged with the personal worldview then why should the shared community worldview matter? Altruists contend that it is this very social sensibility that is the most plausible hypothesis to explain why there are so many empirical cases of people whose behavior seems only to be explicable on the basis of altruism.

There is a significant body of people every day who seem to act on principle or duty due to a social sensibility that on the face of it seems to support altruism. There are, of course, other accounts of the behavior. However, the debate is important. The egoism versus altruism dilemma is one of the basic questions of ethics.

KEY TERMS

- prudential advantage
- psychological egoism
- rationality incompleteness conjecture
- most plausible hypothesis maxim
- ethical egoism
- altruism

A THOUGHT EXPERIMENT: FINDING OUT WHAT YOU BELIEVE

Step One:
Find a current news event (from the newspaper, Internet, e-news sources, etc.) and cut it out/copy it. The sort of artifact you want to choose should be a case in which there is apparent altruism.

Step Two:
Write a half-page argument on why your artifact demonstrates psychological egoism.

Step Three:
Write a half-page argument on why your artifact demonstrates ethical egoism.

Step Four:
Write a half-page argument on why your artifact demonstrates altruism.

Step Five:
Choose your favorite alternative among steps 2 through 4 and write a one-page short story or narrative scene showing why your choice is the right one.

NOTES

1. Of course, the sense of weaker applies to us. Presumably the law or some cadre of supporting laws *always* hold, but this particular version of a quasi-universal generalization is not quite precise. We will allow the given parameters to set the standard on what ranges we think are acceptable in imprecision.

2. One may also apply Bayes Theorem here; see Ian Hacking, *An Introduction to Probability and Inductive Logic* (Cambridge: Cambridge University Press, 2001).

3. I invite readers to visit the website of Doctors without Borders to verify the tone of social duty that is set out: http://www.doctorswithoutborders.org/ (accessed 26 September 2007).

4. Bernard Mandeville, *The Fable of the Bees and Other Writings* (Indianapolis, IN: Hackett, repr. 1997).

5. Here I am assuming that the athlete only approaches the generally recognized levels of unbearable pain—8, 9, 10 (times ten on a one-hundred scale)—for the last third of her life. This is highly structured. As this author is a former athlete who knows these issues firsthand, I believe this is a reasonable assumption "for the most part."

6. For an extreme case see Robert Goldman, "Bad Sports: Olympics 2000," *Current Events* (October 27, 2000): 1–4.

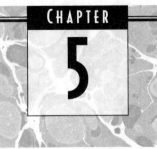

CHAPTER 5

ARE PEOPLE GOOD OR BAD?

❖ Introduction
❖ Humans Are Bad
❖ Humans Are Good
❖ What Difference Does It Make?
❖ Key Terms
❖ A Thought Experiment: Finding Out What You Believe

INTRODUCTION

The question of whether people are, by nature, good or bad depends upon various understandings of genetics and of the nature of human beings, as such. There have been intelligent writers who have taken different sides on this question. The point of this chapter is not to determine the question, but to set up what is at stake and the critical issues from which readers might make their own decision.

HUMANS ARE BAD

The first worldview standpoint to be examined is that humans are, by nature, bad. Why would one think this? There are a number of proponents of this position. They come from several camps: (a) **psychological egoists**; (b) Hobbsians; and (c) religious thinkers. Let's look at these in order.

48

First are the psychological egoists that we have encountered earlier. These individuals would demur at the tag of "bad." They would simply say that people are self-interested in what they do in all cases. This tendency is a hardwired genetic expression. It can be explained in evolutionary terms via the survival advantage of phenotypes who act for their own benefit versus those who do not. For the most part, all animal species act for their own advantage. This allows them to be more successful at reproduction and passing on their genes to the next filial generation. There are some exceptions to this, such as crows in which seemingly altruistic behavior of a clarion crow that announces an attacker and sticks around a bit to make sure that the other crows leave. But the sociobiologists contend that this represents the second-best strategy for survival: if you cannot get your own genes into the next filial generation, then getting the genes of those close to you is the next best action. More so-called second-level genes are passed on if virtually the whole flock escapes (save the clarion) and this more than makes up for the loss of the single clarion. What, at first glance, appears to be altruistic behavior is really an instance of the **selfish gene strategy**.[1] If the selfish gene strategy is correct, then various exemplifications of the selfish gene strategy in humans might include competitiveness to the point of getting or exceeding the level of available social goods that others possess. Since, on this account, strategy origins are biological, then there is a strong tendency to do whatever it takes to garner the most goods possible. One's only check is the threat of other humans who may retaliate. The agent wants the most without paying an undue price for it. When others are upset, they merely up the price for that behavior; it's all about a cost/benefit egoistic calculus.

If this account is correct, then one should not expect anything more from anyone. All there is, amounts to the individual trying to get as much as he can with a minimum of penalty. If this is the way things are, then it should be no surprise if your employee steals from you when you have not created a very efficient theft-detection system. Why wouldn't the employee steal desirable goods when he has a low chance of getting caught?

The second camp comes from **Thomas Hobbes**. Because Hobbes wrote in the seventeenth century, he is not inclined to swing his argument toward genetics. Instead, he talks about human nature (however that is accounted for). Hobbes believes we are competitive and ambitious within an environment of limited goods and unlimited wants. This is a very capitalist view of things. He adds the posit that people are essentially equal. This means that if person A is superior in traits x, y, and z, over B, then B is superior in traits e, f, and g, such that the ultimate scores balance out. Some may say this is a very generous balancing of things, but what is the result? If everyone is essentially equal in the total summation of things, then that leaves a playing field with equally qualified competitors vying for a limited number of prizes. It is much like the childhood game of musical chairs. There are twelve members at the birthday party and eleven chairs. When the music stops one is without a seat. Tough luck. The quiet and cooperative children are dominated by the overly aggressive. Is this a proper metaphor for adult society? Hobbes thought so.

What follows from this is that the achievement of the prize is everything. There are no door prizes for also-rans. The only thing that counts is being one of the winners. But what does this mean about the way we characterize people in society vis-à-vis the way we construct social policy? Of course, it means that we think of people as being self-interested to the highest degree and that the only way to control them is to put into place clear controls that will curb their wayward tendencies.

The third perspective is theological. From the perspective of Christians, all people are born with original sin (the sin of Adam and Eve) such that they need the redemption of Jesus Christ to make them whole. Most other religions take a different tact. Judaism and Islam consider the agent to be pure until he or she proves otherwise. This is the general standard for most of the major world religions. Thus, from the Christian perspective, humans are inclined to evil unless they make a conscious choice to turn their lives around to be altruistic and beneficent.

The bulk of other religions suggest that each person also make such a choice for the good. But they frame the decision as one from a morally neutral standpoint.

In the end, the religious take on all of this is that unless people make a conscious decision to formulate their worldview toward what they take to be the good, then they will fall into a category that exhibits the list of competitive excesses toward personal self-absorbed obesity.

On all three grounds a coherent and plausible account can be made supporting people as bad.

How does one evaluate these claims? One way is to go to the newspaper, or the Internet, and cut out/copy a half-dozen stories of bad behavior. Now think about these vis-à-vis the thesis that people are bad. What would such an explanation look like? Do you think that it is correct?

HUMANS ARE GOOD

The second perspective to be examined is that people are good. As in the first take on the subject one must determine what characteristics might be viewed as good. For our purposes let us interpret these proponents as: (a) altruists, (b) Lockians, and (c) religious thinkers.

In the first case, some sociobiologists argue that there may be an evolutionary advantage to being open to altruism. This is because altruism breeds cooperation that may enhance social frameworks. Those who live in a robust functioning social framework may be more likely to pass on their genes to the next generation than those who do not. Thus, cooperative behavior may be evolutionarily advantageous to the agent.

This argument seems to fly in the face of a similar argument on people being basically bad. One way to think about this comes from the influential book *Unto Others: The Evolution and Psychology of Unselfish Behavior.*[2]

Argument 5–1: The Biological Basis of Altruism

1. Genetic determinism asserts that every single action is determined by biology—Assertion, p. 298
2. Behaviors are only broadly determined by biology—Assertion
3. Strict genetic determinism is false—1, 2
4. Cultural interactions also determine the agent—Assertions, p. 299
5. Agents are determined by a mixture of nature and nurture (as understood as group biology and group nurture, culture)—3, 4
6. Mixing theories is an example of methodological pluralism—Fact
7. Methodological pluralism is the way to understand human behavior—5, 6
8. The behavior of parents caring for their children is a prime example upon which to test the struggle between hedonism vs. altruism (aka pluralistic motivation)—Assertion, p. 301
9. The criteria used for this evaluation are availability, reliability, and energy efficiency—Assertion, pp. 305–308
10. Hedonism is a less reliable mechanism for providing for child care than is altruism or pluralistic motivation—Assertion, pp. 312–319
11. Altruism is just as available and efficient (with insignificant differences) as hedonism—Assertion, pp. 321–324
12. Altruism/pluralistic motivation is a more plausible model for human behavior than is monistic hedonism—8–11
13. Altruism/pluralistic motivation and methodological pluralism are the proper ways to understand human behavior—7, 12

This argument from Sober and Wilson is a good example of a biologically-based position that does not necessitate egoism or hedonism (233–247). This is supported by the prominent sociobiologists, E. O. Wilson.[3] The Sober and Wilson argument sets out that even from the program of two determined philosophers of biology, that in the case of childcare (premise 8), either altruism or a pluralistic motivation is a more plausible explanation (inference at 10). This is a result of premise 2 that only gives general (and not complete) reign of human behavior to biology. If these authors are correct in their argument, then altruism stands as a plausible candidate for human behavior—at least in part. If altruism is possible, then the possibility of humans being good may have a biological basis (assuming that not acting for self-interest is indicative of being good).

Another way to look at this is via an argument from **John Locke**.[4]

Argument 5–2: The Limits of Force: Self-Defense

1. In the state of nature man lives for the most part with others cooperatively according to reason—Assertion
2. In the state of nature some people will try to steal another's property or to enslave another—Fact
3. An attack against my property is the same as an attack against my person—Assertion
4. When an individual is attacked by another seeking to subjugate him, the alternatives are to become a slave or to fight back with power—Assertion
5. No one must yield to becoming a slave—Assertion
6. In the state of nature when someone attacks one's property or person he may fight back with power—2–5

The key to this argument from our perspective is that premise 1 contends that the natural state of nature is cooperative and not competitive. This is a very positive spin on human nature and directly contradicts Hobbes. Locke is no simple dreamer. He knows that people cheat and pervert their natural inclinations. But what does this mean? It means that though person X exhibits behaviors of being an "over-the-top competitor," this phenomenon can have different explanations. One is that people are naturally bad (meaning competitive at all costs); the other that though people are naturally good, they can still do bad things. In the first case (Hobbes), the individual is merely exhibiting his human nature, while in the latter case (Locke) he is perverting his human nature. Though the individual behaviors may be the same, it is important to note that the reasons for these are different. (See more on the significance of this in the next section.)

Religious thinkers are split on this. Some think that because God creates us, and because God is good, that we (also) are good. Our goodness under this account relies upon the principle of heritability. If any x has property ϕ, then all theorems proven from x also possess ϕ. This means that if God is good and if God created the world, then everything in the created universe is good.

Of course, there are some religious perspectives that engage God in bad as well as good. This is either (a) the God who is all and thus contains good and bad or (b) the God who is a trickster and does bad periodically to test things out or (c) the God who does bad as part of an inscrutable plan.

On all three grounds a coherent and plausible account can be made supporting people as good.

How does one evaluate these claims? One way is to go to the newspaper, or the Internet, and cut out/copy a half-dozen stories of good behavior. Now think about these vis-à-vis the thesis that people are good. What would such an explanation look like? Do you think that it is correct?

WHAT DIFFERENCE DOES IT MAKE?

I would suggest to readers that it makes a great deal of difference whether we believe people to be good or bad. This is because it affects the community worldview. Let's review two sorts of situations in which one attitude or the other will make all the difference: job supervisor and policy maker.

JOB SUPERVISOR

I would guess that every reader of this book has had a job before. In your job you had a supervisor (hereafter called the manager). Now let's look at life in the ABC insurance company among CSRs (customer service representatives who are also licensed insurance agents). In ABC the New York sales manager is named Cruella De Ville. She believes that people are basically bad. At a recent senior staff meeting there was a complaint that her staff were not handling enough customer phone calls and that productivity was not increasing as it should. Cruella told the senior staffers that she believed the reason was that too many CSRs were sending personal e-mails and shopping on the Internet while they were at work. What she proposed was a twofold solution: (a) she would tell all CSRs that all their e-mails and computer activity would be monitored by "Big Brother," a new management software that can give you reports on everything an employee does on their computer. "Big Brother" will keep the employees on edge because nothing anymore will be private. (There is a supplemental package that will monitor land-line calls and any cell phone communication within the building to a five hundred foot radius outside—called "Big Brother Enforcer.") In addition to these measures, Cruella will make surprise raids upon areas of the office that she believes are cheating the company by engaging in personal activities on company time. Cruella declares that she stamp out abuses and move productivity and profit margins toward those envisioned by the strategic plan.

In ABC the San Francisco sales manager is named Jemal Washington. He thinks people are basically good. At a recent senior staff meeting there was a complaint that his staff were not handling enough customer phone calls and that productivity was not increasing as it should. Jemal told senior staffers that he thought that the work paradigm that was presented to workers was not creative enough and did not reward those who exceeded expectations. Jemal suggested that they create a performance bonus system. Everyone would be paid their normal hourly wage no matter what. However, those who met certain production goals would be given more pay. "When they meet these goals the whole company makes money so why shouldn't we share it with them?" says Jemal. "I think that if we create an environment that is responsive to their natural urges to help the company, and that we are willing to compensate them fairly for this, then we will achieve the profit margins envisioned by the strategic plan."

WARM-UP EXERCISE 5–1: PEOPLE AS GOOD OR BAD

Answer the following three questions:

1. So who would you like to work for: Cruella De Ville or Jemal Washington?
2. A second question (not necessarily connected to the first) is which manager do you think will get the best results?
3. What do your answers to questions 1 and 2 say about whether you believe people are basically good or bad? ∎

POLICY MAKER

You are a member of the House of Representatives. You have brought forth a bill aimed at lessening poverty in the United States. The essence of your bill is this: (a) You will pay unemployed men or women for job training and living expenses for up to five years while they look for work. This stipend includes rent, clothes, food, daycare, and tuition to community college. (b) The program will be relatively unbureaucratic without a lot of checks and balances.

An opponent to the bill, Mr. B, says that the bill is doomed to failure because it encourages people to cheat because: (1) it gives up to five years of support, and (2) there are minimal checks on people to ensure that they are actually enrolled in community college. What's to stop these folk from using this money to buy drugs and relax into the life of iniquity?

WARM-UP EXERCISE 5–2: PEOPLE AS GOOD OR BAD

1. What are the strong points of the bill's sponsor?
2. What are the strong points of Mr. B?
3. Whose position is stronger, and how does one's understanding of whether people are good or bad fit into all of this? ■

Warm-up Exercise 5–2 is meant to focus the reader upon what difference it would make for policy decisions if one believe others to be either basically good or bad. Obviously, the net result is significant. It could make the difference in passage or not.

Whether people are considered to be good or bad is not an abstract question wafting in the wind. The way we answer this question is crucial to the way we act in the world. Both from the sample discussions of business management and government politics, the final outcome can sometimes depend upon this. Intelligent people have answered this question differently. Where do you sign in?

KEY TERMS

- psychological egoists
- selfish gene strategy
- Thomas Hobbes
- John Locke

A THOUGHT EXPERIMENT: FINDING OUT WHAT YOU BELIEVE

Sometimes the best way to test one's own beliefs is via directed self-reflection. Let's step back a moment and consider whether people are good or bad in a thought experiment.

Step One:
Bring forward some of the news stories you have already collected. Focus on those that make an assumption as to whether people were good or bad. Choose two.

Step Two:
Examine the arguments or assumptions each article makes. Write a paragraph defending and then attacking the assumption made in the article on whether people are good or bad in this instance.

Step Three:
Try to isolate several key points in your expositions (step two) that would point in one direction or the other.

Step Four:
Interpret the plausibility of each pivotal claim and choose one over the other.

Step Five:
Write a one-page defense of step four as being the way things really are.

This exercise should assist readers in finding out for themselves which position they hold. It can also be a useful device for class discussion. The key to making it work well is by the detail in the causal account of one solution versus another.

NOTES

1. The author most often associated with this position is Richard Dawkins, *The Selfish Gene* (New York: Oxford University Press, 1976).
2. Elliott Sober and David Sloan Wilson, *Unto Others: The Evolution and Psychology of Unselfish Behavior* (Cambridge, MA: Harvard University Press, 1998), Chap. 10.
3. Edward O. Wilson, *Sociobiology* (Cambridge MA: Harvard University Press, 1975).
4. John Locke, "On the State of War," in *An Essay Concerning the True Original, Extent and End of Civil Government* (London: Awnsham & John Church, 1695): II.3.

CHAPTER

6

MORALITY AND RELIGION

INTRODUCTION

This chapter seeks to address some of the traditional difficulties that theists and nontheists face when they seek to justify moral theories. After examining a few positions and their consequences, I employ my view about personal worldview that seeks to move in the direction of establishing a solution that both theists and nontheists can live with.

THE ORIGIN OF THE PROBLEM

As you will see in part 2, moral realists define ethics as the science concerning the right and wrong of human action.[1] However, when we ask the question, "What justifies one theory over another?" it is often the case that there are dual answers. On the one hand, it is possible to give one *sort* of explanation utilizing only aspects of the "natural" realm.[2]

For the individual who is satisfied with the natural realm, the traditional theories that support moral realism may be sufficient.

On the other hand, some may say that all purely natural explanations are metaphysically deficient because they do not take the question to its proper starting point. These individuals ask for more than a merely natural explanation. They want to inquire into the ground of the natural explanation. Why do they do this?

The answer is that they are convinced that there is an independent source of goodness that exists in some other (supernatural) realm. This entity is the ground for everything in the natural realm.[3]

This is the basis of one of the arguments for the existence of God that Aquinas sets forth, namely, that if ethics asserts that something is "good," then there must be a final cause (goodness) toward which all things strive.[4] In the philosophy of religion this is often termed to be an issue concerning "creation." Within the three Middle Eastern religions (Judaism, Christianity, and Islam), there is an acceptance of a supernatural ground for the natural. This ground is often depicted as "creation." Whether this is a logical or a genetic creation is a matter of some dispute, but the principal point here is that there is an invocation of something beyond the natural.

From this position one would have to say that any of the purely natural justifications given for the major ethical theories are incomplete because they do not reflect this supernatural ground.[5]

Now the advocates of a nonreligious grounding of ethics will say that they can offer an account that is both coherent and consistent; therefore, why should they consider anything else? When one offers one account that is complete and sufficient, any others will be mere duplication. If one assumes that nature is simple, then such duplication will not only be aesthetically unpleasing, but it will also be false. (This is because under such an account truth is simple and the given account is a duplication, ergo; the second account is an unnecessary appendage—code language for being in violation of the doctrine of simplicity.)

It is interesting that even if one held such a view about the status of redundant accounts, the natural account is always accorded the first place of consideration—relegating all subsequent accounts as redundant. What if one began with the supernatural account and then declared that the natural account was redundant? Why begin with the natural account? Some might refer to Aristotle who said that all knowledge begins with empirical apprehension. It is genetically prior to all other sources of knowledge.

But being *prior* does not necessarily make such knowledge *primary*. In fact, it may be the case that knowledge, which is genetically prior, is logically posterior. Thus, even an empiricist such as Aristotle could be brought forth to support a position that would allow redundant accounts.

Of course there are some who will rail at any reference to a supernatural because it smacks of religion. Such critics do not believe in religion and anything beyond the natural.

Others will point to the fact that there are many religions and each proposes a different understanding of the Divine. If one were to encompass religion into ethics, then (in principle) the ideal of a single ethical theory that applies to all people at all times and places might be hopelessly muddled.

Perhaps this is a practical problem. But if any exposition of ethics *must* contain a reference to religion, then there can be some fundamental difficulties that arise from the different religions' view about the nature of God. For example, if one views God as a loving and forgiving entity who guarantees forgiveness for *any* sin if only the agent performs a true and contrite confession, then one might establish one sort of ethics. On the other hand, if one viewed God as a truly just figure who did not forgive, as such, but meted out perfect justice (occasionally tempered by dispositional mercy), then one would have a supernatural basis for an entirely different sort of ethics.

Since Christianity and Islam (along with Judaism) differ on some of these issues (as well as many others), then the difficulties regarding incorporating religion as a *necessary* component of any ethical system become apparent.

With so many practical problems, why would anyone want to incorporate religion as an integral component in an ethical theory? Many nontheists would say, "There is no reason to do so—except as a descriptive, sociological exercise." The theists will say, "You can talk all you like about the 'natural' or 'philosophical' justifications for adopting a theory of ethics, but the truth is that God is the author of all that is, and any theory of right and wrong that does not include God is incomplete."

Such is the problem of ethics and religion in a nutshell.

ABSOLUTE GOOD

Absolute good is a concept most aligned to virtue ethics and its proclivity to "perfectionism" (see Chapter 11). Other conceptions of good are either functionally or conventionally based. Why is something good? This is an issue that we have broached earlier. Both G. E. Moore and R. M. Hare have written extensively on this subject.[6] There are many senses of saying of some x that "x is good." Whether it turns out that something is thought to be good because of one's immediate grasping of an unnatural property or because of certain linguistic usages, the question can still be asked (by others) whether any of these senses of good depend upon there being something which possesses a natural property goodness, and whether "goodness" as a property really exists independently from good things.

Such speculations can be approached from many directions. One direction would be to examine how it is that we mean anything in language. Under this approach the question of absolute goodness translates into one of linguistic meaning. The result such analysis could prove either point depending upon what one takes to be the operation of "signs" and the mechanics of sense and meaning.

Another approach might focus upon how we come to know (epistemology) and a third upon the ontological status of particulars and universals. It seems to me that none of these get us very far, because the philosopher is either inclined toward theism or not. If he is, then he will find an argument to support his case. If he isn't, then the conclusion will be that there is no absolute goodness.

In each instance the worldview of the philosopher informs upon the truth of this issue and inclines him toward a position and the arguments necessary to support it.

I put it to the reader whether you think it is necessary for there to be absolute goodness for one to meaningfully refer to some x as being good. Is there some "deep" sense of goodness that resonates beyond a mere conventional or functional starting point? For a simple depiction of the problem let us consider Warm-Up Exercise 6–1.

WARM-UP EXERCISE 6–1: ON THE STATUS OF GOODNESS

A. "X is good" means that x's goodness is a consequence of our depicting certain things or properties as good and that this x before me shares those properties. The reason that certain things or properties have been designated as good is purely conventional. We will simply all agree to it.

B. "X is good" means that x's goodness is a consequence of how x operates in some natural or artificial system. Whenever things or properties contribute to efficient operations they are good because efficient workability is taken to be a *per se* positive value.

C. "X is good" means that x's goodness is a consequence of x sharing in or resembling some aspect of absolute goodness. In this way all goodness is alike in its origin. This is because it is somehow known (in a nonlogical manner) that absolute goodness really does exist. ■

Statements A, B, and C all offer accounts of why something might be good. Which seems most attractive to you, the reader? Persuasive arguments can be offered for each, but I would suggest that no single rational argument will satisfy everyone (the rationality incompleteness conjecture). This is because the answer to this question follows from another aspect of one's personal worldview, namely, whether there is a God and whether such a God is the repository of absolute goodness. If one says, "yes" to such a query, then certain consequences will follow. If one says, "no," then other results will obtain.

This obviously can cause some problems with creating an ethical theory. Let us examine one popular option among those who wish to acknowledge the place of religion in ethics, and then we will conclude this chapter with a suggestion of how to resolve some of these difficulties.

DIVINE COMMAND THEORY

Divine command theory is a very old theory of why we should be moral: because God commands us to do so. An early form of this theory occurs in the book of Genesis in the Torah. Adam and Eve were *commanded* not to eat of the Tree of Knowledge [of Good and Evil]. It was a command—pure and simple. They could have no means to judge this command because that would beg the question, that is, they would have needed knowledge of good and evil to judge the command—but they lacked this because they could not receive such *unless* they had already eaten of the Tree. Such a situation is a pure instance of following a command merely because one in rightful authority dictates it. (Obviously, such a question has vexed Talmud scholars for eons since the agents are punished for disobeying a command they could not properly evaluate.)

Another example of this theory also comes from the Torah. It is the revelation of the Ten Commandments to Moses. God gave to Moses these dictums of how to behave. The orders applied to human behavior toward God and toward other people. These commands contain both prohibitions (Thou shall not do x) and obligations (Thou shall do x). As a metaphor of their supreme importance, these commands were writ in stone. One obeyed these orders because the author was the ruler and creator of everything, God.

Plato examines a version of divine command theory in his dialogue *The Euthyphro*. In this case the question is asked whether "x is holy because the gods love it" or whether "the gods love x because x is holy." In other words, one is asked to choose between an extrinsic and an intrinsic account of x's value. In the extrinsic account, x becomes holy merely because the gods love it. One can imagine one point in time (t_1)

in which x was not holy. Then at (t_2) the gods notice x and declare (at t_3) that they love x. In this case x is only holy at (t_3 and after). If at some moment in the future (t_n) the gods should fall out of love for x, then it will no longer be holy again.

This points to some of the shortcomings of command theory as Plato has characterized it, namely, that the extrinsic view seems to relegate the moral agent to a diminished status. He must merely follow the orders of another. This seems to go against the principles of autonomy discussed in the introduction. The moral agent is a mere servant or slave to another. This seems to undermine the very foundations of ethics.

However, those in favor of such an approach will say that it is not merely *anyone* who you are submitting to, but the Ruler of the entire Universe. This makes things different. Besides, there *is* a conscious, autonomous decision to follow God's dictates—whatever they may be. Thus, one exhibits his or her autonomy in the decision to abide by the commands of God. The subsequent action of automatically following those commands carries with it the autonomy exhibited in the original decision.

This turn of the issue moves us toward the modern interpretations of this question. Philip Quinn has framed the dialogue in terms of modern moral philosophy.[7] Quinn distinguishes between two understandings of the theory. On one reading a person's moral obligation to do x depends upon a command from God to do x. This is very similar to Plato's formulation from the *Euthyphro*. A second reading would make person's moral obligation to do x dependent upon God's will that the person be morally obligated to do x.[8] This second version shifts the origin of obligation from being the respondent of a command (a passive position) to that of ferreting out the will of God, in order to discover what is best to do (an active position).

The difference between these two formulations is striking. The "command formulation" makes God very much like humans—ordering them to do this or that. (One might imagine a capricious God even capable of asking someone to do something awful, such as murdering one's son [for example].) If one focuses upon merely the "ordering" act, then it sets God in an anthropomorphic context that may conflict with other aspects of God's character such as his/her/its perfect knowledge, goodness and power. Since these properties are so nonhuman-like, it would suggest that anthropomorphic characterizations of God are not fruitful research strategies.

There is also the issue of whether speech acts within conventional contexts really imply moral obligation. John Searle and John Rawls have argued that in the case of promise making (one example of a speech act), the resulting obligations may be more a function of their institutional rather than their moral character.[9] Therefore, if God's commands are construed as speech acts, and if speech acts do not confer moral obligation, then God's commands do not confer moral obligation.

Objectors to this position might argue that God is a special case—or at least that it is different in kind than anything that Searle and Rawls are talking about.

Another problem with the command theory is that only one sort of revelation is allowed, a command. If there were such a command, it would fall upon some prophet who would then have the task of interpreting this command to others. Objectors could contend that all forms of revelation are equal. Commands are no more genuine than other signs that indicate the "will of God." In this case, what is primary is the will of God and not the specific form of that revelation.

A command is merely one form of revelation. As such, it is a vehicle to express the will of God.[10] What is primary in this instance is obeying God's will.

Further, if we are getting the command secondhand (via the prophet), then it is possible that (a) some embellishment or omissions might occur, (b) some applications and examples might come from the prophet herself, and (c) there may be some ambiguity in the range of application.[11] Because of these practical problems in transmission, some believe that God offers several simultaneous forms of revelation so that the principal issue, that is, determining him/her/its will, might be accomplished.

These arguments for the "will" over the "command" formulation are often countered by the issue of *obligation.* One may understand in a more primary fashion and with greater clarity that some action x is good, but what links such understanding to the obligation to act? A great advantage of the command formulation over the will formulation is that contained within the command formulation is the obligation to *obey* the command. It is one thing merely to know "x is a good action," and another to feel obliged to "do x." Robert Audi has attempted to bridge this distinction by making the command morality to be a set of internalized moral standards that is compatible with autonomy-based ethics.[12]

The student of these positions must determine whether the will formulation can be understood in such a way that it also enjoins action to the same extent as the command formulation, and whether the command formulation can be modified in such a way that clarity and ethical voluntarism are not lost.

Further, an argument that could be brought against both forms of divine command theory refers back to the last section on absolute goodness.[13] It can be remembered that absolute goodness is often depicted to be a property of God that grounds all our understanding of day-to-day imperfect goodness. However, if God's commands and/or God's will are what makes anything good, then "good" is only an outcome of actions that God commits (or wills). This would seem to go against our previous attribution of absolute goodness to God. This is because "goodness" is simply what God does or wills. The origin of goodness is in an activity—not in the independent existence of an intrinsic property (compare again to the *Euthyphro*). In this instance it would seem that those who attribute the property of absolute goodness to God (as many religions do by dogma), are mistaken. God is not good *per se*, but is only good *per aliud* through his/her/its actions.

This is obviously an important issue that defenders of divine command theory must answer.

AN ETHICS WITH AND WITHOUT RELIGION

In the first section of this chapter the problem between philosophical and theological ethics was outlined. In my presentation of this problem two major difficulties were discussed. First, there are the problems concerned with justification. Is a purely philosophical justification sufficient? Are redundant explanations bad? Which account best explains why we should act ethically?

Second, there is the problem of creating a practical language of morality through which all may communicate about ethical issues.

Let's address these questions together. As in the case of philosophical feminism, my interpretative device will be the personal worldview imperative. When we apply the personal worldview imperative to the issue of justification we face two types of agents: (a) those who are theists, and (b) those who are nontheists (the atheists and agnostics).

The worldview of the theists contains God. Since this entity is responsible for everything that is, it would be wrong to have a theory about the right and wrong of human action without reference to that being. This is because the personal worldview imperative enjoins us to develop both a comprehensive and internally consistent vision of the world. If one accepted the existence of God as the creator of everything, and then left him/her/it out of the account of the right and wrong of human action, then such an agent would either fail to be comprehensive (because it left out a key element) or it would fail to be internally consistent (because for everything save ethics there is reference to God, and for ethics there is not). In either case, the personal worldview imperative would require those who believe in a God that is the supreme creator and ruler of everything to be included in the exposition of a moral theory.

By the same argument the nontheist would not want to include God in an ethical theory because it would be employing an entity that the agent does not believe exists. To import a nonexistent entity into one's worldview would internally inconsistent. For these individuals it is absolutely necessary to have a theory justified without recourse to supernatural entities.

But what of the theory that the nontheists have justified? If it has been well justified, then what should be the position of the theists? This is really the important turn of the question. The answer lies in the common body of knowledge. Since theists and nontheists must live and work together, they must not only create a body of agreed-upon "facts about the world" and "how to talk about these facts," but they must also create a common worldview that may differ from their individual worldviews in several respects.

The shared community worldview is a common vision of what life is and should be. It is absolutely essential for trust and esprit de corps to develop between people. When formed in accord with the shared community worldview imperative, it will prevent aberrant and evil community visions to emerge.

In the case of the relationship between an **ethics with and without religion,** the theists and nontheists would, as a community, have to work out a common worldview that includes as much of their individual worldviews as possible so that some accord might be reached. This accord would constitute a shared community worldview by which both sides could judge the right and wrong of human action. It is almost a certainty that such a common worldview would *not* include God. This is because among the nontheists the absence of God in any accepted worldview is paramount. It is a deal point.[14]

It is hoped that the theists could disassemble the various traits/actions they believed were truly good (such as loving others, forgiveness—or any number of other religiously based virtues) from the source of those traits (i.e., God). In this instance, the theists could create a common worldview with the nontheists. There might be no mention of God, but many of the most essential aspects of the theists' worldviews (i.e., the derivative traits without the source of those virtues) might be able to be accommodated.

Such a common worldview would be consistent with philosophical ethics (which is justified without reference to God). It would be created through the common body of knowledge with reason being afforded the trump card in cases of dispute (because of its universal intersubjective character).

Obviously, this sort of ethical formulation has the advantage of allowing the theists and the nontheists to find common ground for their moral judgments. This can permit reasoned discourse instead of mere contending among interested parties who have no common ground. But there is also an advantage to the theists themselves. Such a system affords *them* a common ground for ethical discussion without getting into various theological disputes that often characterizes interfaith dialogues. By leaving God out of the formulation they are able to forego the wrangling about their various interpretations of who God is and what is his/her/its nature.

However, this situation I am describing does not disallow a theist from holding *two* theories of ethics. The first theory is the common theory that person shares with his or her society. This is the shared community worldview discussed above (philosophical ethics).

The second theory might be a theological ethics that the agent wills upon all those who share a worldview that includes God (in the particular fashion that such a theist understands the nature of God to be). In such a case philosophical ethics (without God) would be said to apply to all people. This is because philosophical ethics has eliminated that which is a "deal point" to the nontheists. It has also created a common worldview among theists who do not share a common understanding of God.

Among those with a common understanding of God, there would also be the opportunity to accept theological ethics that includes God and is consistent with that person's or group's understanding of who and what God is. Theological ethics would contain everything within philosophical ethics, with the addition of a different metaphysical superstructure and its accompanying justification as well as some additional duties that might ensue from one's religious orientation. For example, in the Roman Catholic Christian tradition it is thought to be a duty to perform some level of fasting after Maundy Thursday and extending until sundown on Saturday before Easter. This is a religious duty that Catholic Christians might believe is "good." But it would certainly be meaningless to non-Christians. Likewise, keeping the Ramadan fast is good for Muslims but cannot be a duty for nonbelievers in Islam.

Jesus made an interesting observation in this regard. He replied to a query about the custom of carrying a Roman Centurion's coat a mile upon request by saying that the truly religious person would fulfill his or her moral (in this case civil) duty and then carry the coat another mile (symbolizing the fulfillment of a spiritual duty).

What could be commanded of everyone is to carry the coat one mile. This is the dictate of the common worldview (philosophical ethics). But among a coherent religious subgroup an extra duty may obtain. For these individuals there is a duty to carry the coat for an extra mile (due to theological ethics). This second duty is moral because it pertains to judgments about the right and wrong of human behavior. But it may only be commanded of those who accept such a spiritual model.[15]

This "solution" to the two parts of the problem listed at the beginning of the chapter will not completely satisfy either the advocates of philosophical ethics or of theological ethics. However, I believe it is the only way to give full weight to the worldviews of the theists (in their many forms) and the nontheists. We live in a heterogeneous world. It is imperative that we establish a common worldview that embraces values that we can all make reference to as we try to endorse the good and eschew the bad. To add extra layers for particular views of the Good, the True, and the Beautiful should threaten no one if it is executed in this manner.

KEY TERMS

- absolute good
- divine command theory
- ethics with and without religion

A THOUGHT EXPERIMENT: FINDING OUT WHAT YOU BELIEVE

Create a fictional village of 2,000 people. Five hundred people in the town are Christians, five hundred are Jews, five hundred are Moslems, and five hundred are atheists. The town gets together in a general town meeting to debate the new town charter that gives direction for an overhaul of the legal code and town ordinances. Each group will want to represent their own interior interests but must accommodate the new-shared community worldview.

In 750 words, write a scenario that you think would work at allowing each party to be true to their beliefs and yet to forge a group consensus. Make sure you offer concrete examples. ■

This thought experiment should assist readers in finding out for themselves which position they hold. This can also be a useful device for class discussion. The key to making it work well is by the detail in the causal account of one solution versus another.

NOTES

1. The main focus here is upon moral realism because the antirealists do not hold there to be moral facts in the natural world—much less the supernatural. See part 2 for more on antirealism.
2. The natural realm is the realm of empirical, intersubjective verification. One contrast to the natural realm might be the supernatural realm. This later arena concerns religion.
3. This depiction is especially true for advocates of the Middle Eastern religions (Judaism, Christianity, and Islam). However, there is also some applications in Hinduism (depending upon the sutras one quotes) and some

sects of Buddhism (such as Pure Land and the followers of the Amida Buddha). In these cases, *what is,* is grounded in some *other* force. Names are not important. If there is a supernatural foundation to "what is," then any natural explanation will be incomplete. [A similar sort of argument may be made concerning so-called "primal" religions.]

4. *Summa Theologica* I, q.2, a.3

5. Some critics might contend that we need an "autonomy of ethics" argument prior to accepting religious claims about the goodness of a certain deity. If this argument were correct, one would be involved in a hopeless circle that supported the goodness of God upon an independent ethics of goodness and the existence of goodness in ethics upon the goodness of God. Most theists would argue for the primacy of God's goodness (and thus avoid this difficulty).

6. G. E. Moore, *Principia Ethica* (Cambridge: Cambridge University Press, 1903) and R. M. Hare, *The Language of Morals* (Oxford: Clarendon Press, 1952).

7. Philip Quinn, *Divine Commands and Moral Requirements* (Oxford: Clarendon Press, 1978). Quinn prefers will formulations over command formulations. Another supporter of this strategy is Edward R. Wierenga, *The Nature of God* (Ithaca, NY: Cornell University Press, 1989). For the opposite side see Robert Merrihew Adams, "Divine Command Metaethics Modi-fied Again," *Journal of Religious Ethics* 7 (Spring, 1979): 66–79.

8. There is perhaps a third formulation of this latter category as set out by Mark C. Murphy, "Divine Command, Divine Will, and Moral Obligation," *Faith and Philosophy* 15, no. 1 (January, 1988): 3–27.

9. John Searle, *Speech Acts* (Cambridge: Cambridge University Press, 1969), 54ff. and John Rawls, *A Theory of Justice* (Cambridge, MA: Harvard University Press, 1971), 344ff.

10. This sense of a command being expressive of the will of God is developed by Philip Quinn, "An Argument for Divine Command Ethics," in *Christian Theism and the Problems of Philosophy*, ed. Michael Beaty (Notre Dame, IN: University of Notre Dame Press, 1990), 293ff.

11. Of course, in some religious traditions, such alterations are thought to be impossible. In Islam the prophet is the "rasul" or mouthpiece of God. In this way what the prophet says is thought to be identical to what God says.

12. Robert Audi, "Divine Command Morality and the Autonomy of Ethics," *Faith and Philosophy* 24, no. 2 (2007): 121–143.

13. Linda Zagzebski holds that all value comes from God—in particular from God's motives. See "Morality and Religion," in William J. Wainwright, ed., *The Oxford Handbook of Philosophy of Religion* (New York & Oxford: Oxford University Press, 2005): 359.

14. The theists may counter that "belief in God" is a "deal point," too. If this is insisted upon, then dialogue between the two groups will be severely limited. It is probable that it will degenerate into mere political infighting between special interest groups. This would be unfortunate because it would mean that real rational discourse on these issues would become impossible.

15. Of course among the "universalistic" religious models such as Christianity, Judaism, and Islam, there is an appeal that these dictums *do* apply to all people and those who fail to recognize this are damned. Such a statement is an

epistemological belief on their part and may or may not be so. Still, the fact remains that there are many that will not share in that vision of religion either because they are nontheists or because they are theists with a different understanding of the nature of God. Since it is a practical necessity that we all live together in cooperation and peace, there needs to be a mechanism for creating a morality that can be applied to all—even if it is not as pure as one's religiously based ethics.

FEMINIST ETHICS

INTRODUCTION

This chapter will explore some aspects of feminist ethics and the ethics of race. It will be the goal of this chapter to stretch the reader to think about alternate visions of what is important in life and what is just. This examination can be useful in setting out one's personal worldview and as a component in the construction of the shared community worldview.

GENDER: ARE MEN AND WOMEN DIFFERENT?

We all have anecdotal stories about how men and women think and act differently. Deborah Tannen claims it goes beyond the anecdotal.[1] She points to how men and women have different linguistic strategies and that this suggests substantial differences in personal worldview.

Another way to get at this is to turn to moral psychology. A famous pioneer in this field is Lawrence Kolhberg. Kolhberg decided to study stages of moral development using a sample space of New England male prep school students. He developed a test based upon the **Heinz dilemma** and from student responses he created a hierarchy of moral development. The Heinz dilemma is a moral case. In the Heinz dilemma there is a man called Heinz who considers whether or not to steal a drug that he cannot afford to buy in order to save the life of his wife. Heinz's wife will die unless she has this drug and this drug *will* save her life. The druggist has refused to lower his price. The question is, "Should Heinz steal the drug?" Kolhberg catalogued the responses of the prep school boys and came up with a scale of moral development in Case 7–1.

CASES

CASE 7–1 KOHLBERG'S STAGES OF MORAL JUDGMENT

LEVEL ONE: PRECONVENTIONAL MORALITY

Stage One: Heteronymous Morality

(The agent is egocentric; one acts rightly only to avoid punishment.)

Stage Two: Individualism

(The agent has a concrete individualistic perspective; one acts rightly to serve his own needs only.)

LEVEL TWO: CONVENTIONAL MORALITY

Stage Three: Mutual Interpersonal Expectations and Relationships

(The individual views him/herself in relationships with other individuals, therefore; one acts rightly to seem good in one's own eyes as well as in the eyes of those with whom one has the relationship.)

Stage Four: Social System and Conscience

(The individual differentiates various societal points of view from interpersonal relationships. One acts rightly to keep societal institutions going as a whole—"If everyone did such and such," what would happen to these institutions?)

LEVEL THREE: POSTCONVENTIONAL OR PRINCIPLED MORALITY

Stage Five: Social Contract Morality

(One can imagine herself and others logically prior to being in a society and then in the society. She takes this dual vision of a person and sees acting rightly as often creating conflict between natural, moral rights and legal rights. This conflict is unresolved.)

Stage Six: Universal Ethical Principle Morality

(One views him/herself as a rational individual among other rational individuals. Because of this point of view, differences in race, gender, religion, culture, or history become meaningless. To act rightly one is to be committed to universal, abstract moral principles that absolutely impose duties.)[2]■

What is striking about Kohlberg's scale is that men score markedly higher than women do. One can draw at least two conclusions from this: (a) men are ethically better than women, or (b) there's something wrong with the scale.

Option (a) seems to have no biological or social foundation. That leaves (b). Harvard educational psychological psychologist Carol Gilligan decided to explore the latter alternative. This led to a conjecture on two aspects of being moral: care and justice.

CARE AND JUSTICE

Gilligan believes there is a unique voice that is expressed in some women, but is rarely expressed in men.[3] This unique voice she calls "care." Care is generally characterized as emphasizing *relationships* and *emotive connection* (sympathy). It is contrasted with "justice" that focuses upon abstract principles of equality and fairness. The way one expresses herself from the care perspective includes terms that evoke relationship: "I understand . . . I want to understand you," "They ought to listen, and try to understand." The emphasis is upon care and responsibility—particularly following from interpersonal relationships.[4] Feelings of empathy and compassion are cogent, and selfishness is eschewed.

In contrast to this, the language of justice expresses itself as: "I have a right," "This principle supervenes that principle . . . therefore I will act guided only by these considerations."

Gilligan contends that too often the perspective of care has been ignored as a legitimate moral point of view. She argues for her position through evaluating a Kohlberg's chart of moral development. It is clear from this chart that what Gilligan is characterizing as "care" seems to be relegated to stage 3 on Kohlberg's chart. Obviously, Gilligan would not share this low priority given to care. This difference in evaluation standards is drawn by Gilligan in the analysis of Kohlberg's Heinz dilemma.

From the point of view of "justice" one might respond with some of these insights: (a) a human life is worth more than any amount of money; (b) the druggist is not justified in his refusal to lower his price; (c) Heinz's wife has a right to the same medical treatment rich people get because they can afford it; (d) theft is bad, but allowing someone to die is worse; (e) Heinz should steal the drug. These arguments are meant to appeal to level three postconventional moral reasons. From the justice point of view this is the most highly developed moral viewpoint.

From the perspective of care one might respond with some of these insights: (a) there might be other approaches besides stealing the drug—maybe Heinz could borrow the money; (b) if Heinz should get caught, then where will that leave his wife? (c) if Heinz is successful at stealing the drug this time, who is to say that he will be as successful in the future? His wife will continue to need him. Is theft really a good long-term strategy for allowing their relationship to continue and for the husband to maintain giving his spouse the nursing she desperately needs? (d) perhaps Heinz could talk to the druggist more thoroughly and show him—make him understand—that his wife needs this drug to live. How could the druggist refuse Heinz's wife the drug if he *really* understood the situation? (e) Heinz should act in these other ways in order to best help his wife.

The justice viewpoint is concerned with abstract, universal principles. The care viewpoint is concerned with particular people living together in the here and now. These two standpoints are different. Logically the first covers a general perspective. The universe it describes is universally quantified so that it covers generic people who are representative of all.

Logically the second resists universalization into abstract laws and principles because the focus is upon individuals and their unique interrelationships. The bond that exists between any two people has a special dignity that defies general characterization. If Gilligan is correct, this second viewpoint is prevalent among many females (30%) and is virtually absent among males. Given this empirical data, then to exclude this perspective from moral reasoning might be tantamount to gender discrimination.

If we accept the premise that the care viewpoint can be linked to women, then the answer to the question, "Why a feminist ethics?" can be answered by referring to the ethics of care and the lack of serious discussion of this topic in the history of philosophical ethics. A feminist ethics is required to rectify this omission.

Is it true that care (as I have described it) is really gender linked? This is certainly an important point to Gilligan (as well as others, such as Nel Noddings).[5] Gilligan cites her own research and that of others to support her conclusion. However, the empirical research is mixed in this regard with other studies showing no gender link associated with moral reasoning.[6] I am not a psychologist and not professionally competent to examine these various studies, but some general, critical issues can be raised.

First, there are many traditional groups that emphasize interpersonal relationships and the obligations they entail above abstract principles of rights and justice. These groups contain men and women, suggesting that it is the group membership rather than gender which fosters caring. Let us examine three of these: 1) teachers; 2) religious groups; and 3) police officers and soldiers. I have chosen these examples to represent (a) occupational groups which require caring [medicine and social work would be further examples]; (b) worldviews that are oriented toward caring (peace activists, civil rights workers, and the Green Movement might also fit in here); and (c) primal bonding groups which highlight one-on-one commitment above all else.

Teachers are often very caring. Whether male or female, teachers choose their field because of their concern for young people. Indeed, the entire *raison d'être* of becoming a teacher is to foster and nurture growth in another. One gives himself up to his students for *their* good. Thus, personal caring and commitment among these individuals is common whether they be male or female.

The second example concerns religious groups. Again, I draw on examples from my own experience. I have been involved in volunteer work with people of various religious persuasions (Christian, Jewish, Islamic, Buddhist, and Hindu). I have found that many of these people genuinely cared for others and sought to form lasting relationships of value with all sorts of people. In fact, in all of these religions the establishment of genuine, authentic loving relationships is promoted (at least in theory) by their holy scriptures.

I have been nurtured by many gentle and loving individuals who were (as often as not) males. These individuals were not "hellfire and damnation" people (who might be associated with the pure "justice") but those who resonated an inner peace due to their religious orientation. I would submit that these people also offer a counterexample to those who contend that it is "very rare" for men to be caring. In this case it is the internalization of a worldview that is responsible for the caring — not one's gender.

The final example is a group I have less experience with. I bring it up largely from secondhand experience. These are the police officers and soldiers of the world. Now on the face of it, this would seem to be just the sort of group that philosophical feminists should want to oppose (most do). These occupational groups are not known for their nurturing of others. But I would raise the following issue for consideration.[7] These individuals extol the virtue of personal relationship. "Always faithful" (*semper fidelis*) means for these people "establishing firm interpersonal bonds which will supervene all else." This is why soldiers will jump on grenades, attempt impossible feats, and risk their lives. They create strong interpersonal bonds (albeit based upon a hierarchy of rank). These bonds often supercede considerations of justice. This is why both good actions can occur (such as heroism) and why bad actions can also occur (such as the massacre of a civilian village due to following the command of another person—with whom you had formed a relationship of trust).

Similarly with the police: how many novels have we read about police partners who acted contrary to the ethics of justice in order to be true to the ethics of relationship? Certainly these can conflict. Do you "sell out" your partner just because she is "on the take"? Do you "rat" on him/her? The ethos of this sort of job seems to be that you don't. Relationship trumps the abstract concepts of justice and rights.

Since the military and police are heavily male, and since it seems that they value (perhaps overvalue) relationship and the particularity of circumstance, then it would seem that care alone is not sufficient to properly describe the feminine voice.

In each of these three examples it has been asserted (on the basis of anecdotal evidence [examples one and two] and secondhand evidence [example three]), that perhaps something more than "care" alone is needed to define feminist ethics.

There are several responses that could be made to this analysis. First, one can say that not all relationship-driven ethical decisions can count as counterexamples. Like the U.S. Supreme Court test of pornography, "one knows it when one sees it." But what would this mean? Certain cases may be obvious to all. But what of difficult cases? Such instances require a refinement of criteria. One does not want to fall into the trap of saying that one simply "knows" the proper application of care without any objective criteria (unless of course one were an intuitionist).

A second response posits that care should be viewed in a context of oppression. Women have been oppressed in most of the world's cultures throughout history. This means that men have minimized their opinions and intelligence. This means that men have limited their career options. This means that their political and legal status has been less than that afforded to men.

The context of oppression illustrates that care be viewed as both a *reason for oppression* (in a contest between an aggressive egoist and a caring nurturer, the latter is generally dominated by the former) and a *future remedy* (if men can be "improved" to form true and authentic relationships with women, then the men will cease their domineering ways). Behind this is the assumption that if one forms a legitimate human relationship, then he will not seek to domineer or exploit the other.

This is an interesting proposition. I believe it is true. But how do we know whether a relationship is authentic? Hegel set out certain criteria in his master/slave dialectic.[8] The communitarians and the Marxists have similarly structured criteria. What is there about establishing a relationship that insures equality and reciprocity? This has been a foundational issue of interpersonal relations at least since Plato and Aristotle.[9]

Some might contend that this begs the question. To beg the question one must assume what she is trying to prove. If one makes the oppression argument from the vantage point that if there had been an authentic relationship, then the problem of oppression would not have occurred, then one is assuming that, in fact, the only relevant cause for the effect of oppression *must* be an inauthentic relationship. But this may not be the case. There may be other causes such as personality changes due to growth or personal problems, or the development of some personal goal that does not include the other person, and other reasons.

A third issue may question whether dependence or dominance are per se evils. If I am involved in a relationship and something happens *to* me (either by an exterior force or by my own agency) that makes me less capable for action, then is it always bad for my friend/spouse to take a dominant role (temporarily or permanently)? This is a question of maternalism/paternalism. Often, it is *because* of one's relationship that one contemplates diminishing autonomy.

What if we modify this and say that my character requires my partner/friend be maternal/paternal to me? This may be due to some defect in me, for example, I am bad with spending money, therefore I need someone who will pay my bills for me and help me restrain my spendthrift inclinations. Should my partner refrain from giving me assistance because violations of autonomy are always wrong? Does the answer change if the person needing help is a man or a woman? Is such a question asymmetrical according to gender? Are examples of maternalism/paternalism ever examples of care? Can care, itself, breed inequality?

These questions lead us to examine the relationship between **justice and care.** In my initial presentation, I set care out in contrast to principles of justice (following Gilligan). Justice was aligned to traditional, timeless, abstract theories of morality and care was tied to relationship-oriented, situational, emotionally laden reasons for acting. Though this characterization of the theories seems to suggest some considerable difference, it is possible that the two might be linked in a variety of ways.

A focus upon care alone may not be enough to demarcate feminist ethics. It may be that some sort of amalgamation with justice will be necessary in order to create a full-blown moral theory. Let's examine some possible problems that might occur if we neglected the justice pole entirely.

First, if one is entirely focused upon relationships, situations and emotions, then there may be a tendency toward moral relativism (see Chapter 3). This is because particulars are not principles, themselves — but are the empirical ground of general principles. Principles that govern the right and wrong of human action are structurally necessary for moral absolutism. Thus, when one completely eschews moral principles in favor of particularism, she is committed to some sort of moral relativism. The disadvantages of moral relativism have been outlined earlier. They include a severe limitation on the context of moral discourse that may turn the creation of national laws and international behavior into mere political and power posturing.

Second, if someone truly cared for another, wouldn't it be more reasonable to assume that she would wish justice, rights, and equality of opportunity for that person, also? Without a link to justice, have we not really created a "power bond" rather than an authentic interpersonal relationship? Might not this be some of what jars from the soldier/police officer example cited above? When all that matters is a bond between people (and there is not commitment to justice as a restraint on this bond), then there is the potential for all sorts of evil acts to occur. Justice can restrain this.

And what of justice without care? Are we really going to say that X is a totally good person just because she woodenly performs good deeds or joylessly and without emotion performs good works? I, for one, would contend that it is equally insufficient for justice to exist without care. This insufficiency can be described differently depending upon the moral system one adopts (see the next section).

If this is true, then the dichotomy between justice and care is a false one. A number of feminist authors agree.[10] Really, care and justice must occur together in practice (though they may be conceptually separated for the purposes of analysis). Both in interpersonal relationships and in the broader political environment, justice is enhanced by care, and vice versa.

RACE: WHAT IS RACE AND WHY IS IT AN ISSUE?

Another way to envision the scope of the feministic ethical standpoint is to examine race and **the position of the "other."** The positive response of the care ethic comes from the result of being an oppressed group. It is in this second way that those of oppressed groups can find expression in feminist ethics. So often the practice of ethics in a community/society follows laws of economics and political expedience rather than ethics. In these cases minorities or those less powerful are relegated to the roles of being oppressed. The shared community worldview of the ruling class is imposed upon all — even when aspects of that worldview are absurdly out of place.

Many times, the ruling class is ignorant of this. They do not even see that they are oppressing others. It is a transparent event to them. The rulers are doing well. They work hard. Thus, the conclusion the rulers come to is that anyone who isn't successful is a failure due to a personal defect. But this is generally not the case. Often luck plays a big role. Luck can be understood via one's starting point in life, the socioeconomic group to which she is a member, her upbringing, and other factors.

The standards used for judging others have increasingly assumed homogeneity. In fact, the trend to homogeneity in society and in the way we structure norms is counterproductive. If one were to adapt models of biological evolution onto the social realm, then the same postulates that rule biology would apply to human society. The postulates that interest us are:

- There is racial/ethnic variation in a society (such as the United States)[11]
- The environment of the United States (the intrastructure and the exostructure)[12] is constantly in flux
- Populations that are robustly diverse will survive changing environments better than those that are not
- Countries that do not empower their diverse populations are virtually the same as homogeneous populations

From these four principles we can infer that homogeneous populations and those that are virtually the same as homogeneous populations, namely, those that do not empower their diverse subpopulations, will be functionally less fit for performing excellently in a diverse world. This is because each subpopulation can be described by a set of character traits. No trait is good or bad by itself, but merely effective or not within a certain environment. For example, if there were a robust population that was heterogeneous and within the population there were individuals who were excellent at tracking several problems at the same time and quickly moving their attention from one task to the next, then these individuals (in an "information age" [environment one]) will help the population succeed. In this event the existence of quick-thinking, frenetic individuals will be prized within the population.[13]

However if we take these same individuals and pattern a new technological society (environment two) in which quick decisions cease to be important, but slow-thinking pondering of a single problem is the critical factor for success, then the population will need some slow-thinking individuals who can stay on a single problem for extended periods of time. The frenetic individuals so prized in environment one will become losers in environment two.

So is it "better" to be quick thinking or to be slow thinking? The answer is that neither are better per se, but only relatively better given certain environmental factors. This is why the most successful populations are those that will be the most diverse and welcome, honor, and support this diversity.[14]

Yet, when we look at the reality of life in America (or virtually any other country we've heard of) it seems that the aim of public policy is to only allow diversity if it means to bring in more janitors, farm workers, or other underpaid "semi-slaves." This servitude mentality is meant to preserve preference against the model of merit (see the next section). Under the model of social evolution this is a prescription for social disintegration.

Since it's a given that social environments (as well as biomes) will change, unless the population has groomed a representative cross-section of its population to carry on its professions, these professions (arguably the backbone of society) may (probably) functionally degenerate under these new conditions and the society will suffer.

OPPORTUNITY AND DESERT

Objectors to feministic ethics (broadly construed as per this chapter) often put forth the argument that the individuals who do not make college admission, professional school admission, or hiring in desirable jobs do not merit it. They are losers in the competition of life. They *deserve* to fail. Those promoting this position often say that merit[15] must be based upon past actions and not upon some sort of social, utopian goal. Who do you want holding the scalpel (in the case of medical school admissions)—a person whose actions have shown his excellence or some other individual that acquired his position based upon some sort of legalistic quota? For simplicity sake, let us label this position as $merit_1$ (m_1).

Proponents of **desert**-based criteria agree that merit should be based upon past actions. However, how are these past actions measured? M_1 asserts that they are interested in actual work performed to judge an individual's merit. However, it seems to some advocating the broad feminist position that this is not the case. Really what m_1 wants to assert is that some sort of positioning on the majority population's grid, marks work performed. This is not necessarily indicative of merit.

In order to explain this, let us examine the argument via the model of the puzzle maker.[16] In this thought experiment, any given period of life (a subcategory of life—such as preparing for one's life profession as an orthopedic surgeon—or the whole of one's life) can be thought of as putting together a puzzle. Now anyone who has worked at puzzle making knows, the early stages of puzzle creation are the hardest. One has to assemble the border and then organize the thematic and color combinations in a general, holistic fashion. This is very time consuming. Most aspiring puzzle makers fail during this stage.

As one progresses in the puzzle-making process things become easier. The final 10 percent is really a breeze.

Now, what if life were really like puzzle making? Some people enter life with very little if any of the puzzle completed for them. In these situations, most fail. Others are given a 40 percent, 60 percent, or even an 80 percent completed puzzle. This dynamic means that for those individuals they must only complete the rest. Now, let us try to compare two individuals at the extremes. Person A was given only 10 percent of her puzzle at birth and when she finished high school she had completed 50 percent of the puzzle. She is up against Person B who was given an 80 percent completed puzzle at birth. B had a calm and supportive domestic life, two hard-working, supportive parents, comfortable income, and a biological makeup that was free from chemically imbalanced mental afflictions. With so much oversight and environmental and natural advantages, it's no wonder that B went from 80 percent to 87.5 percent in his pre-college years. However,

FIGURE 7.1   Merit Measured by the Puzzle-making Thought Experiment

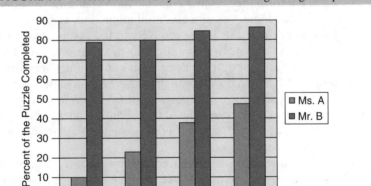

when evaluating the two candidates, which one really *did* more? See Figure 7.1.

The m_1 group would say Mr. B. They would point to the differential between 50 percent and 87.5 percent on society's grid. However, some proponents of feminist ethics broadly construed would suggest that Ms. A has demonstrated greater merit because she went from 10 percent to 50 percent. This indicates that by her own actions alone she accomplished 40 percent. Whereas B, by his own actions, only achieved 7.5 percent.

Obviously, this is a case at the extremes. However, it is put forth to make an abstract point about merit. Some people have natural advantages of environment that can include some or all of the following when it comes to the ability to enter a profession:

- Adequate food, clothing, shelter, and protection from unwarranted bodily harm
- Basic educational opportunity
- Being treated with dignity and love for who you are
- A nurturing home environment
- Parental models for patterning behavior (that the society views positively)
- Freedom from disabling disease whether it be mental or physical
- Inside connections affecting admission to universities and to the professions
- Affluence

Obviously, this list could go on and on. But when Mr. B speaks with hubris about how he has become a partner in the accounting firm, it may be important to know that Mr. B's father is the senior partner in the firm and got B his job in the first place (and has been holding B's hand all his life). This is the life of preferment that allows parents to present to their children, ceteris paribus, a puzzle that is 80 percent complete. All the child has to do is not to screw up too badly and he's set for life.

This preferment list need not merely include socioeconomic factors. Race and gender are also factors. For example, in a profession that is not representative of society's diversity, one will (by definition) find an overrepresentation of some other group. Let it be assumed that this overrepresented group is comprised of white males. And let it further be assumed that unreflective members of that group, without actual malice, simply imagine that the typical member of said profession is a white male. In this case, a clique is created that seeks its own continuation (as all cliques do). Thus, the practitioners of the profession put up barriers that create "old boys' club" expectations that have the effect of excluding all others outside of that model. If such assumptions are correct, then in the puzzle maker example, being a white male seeking to enter that profession is to possess (whether one seeks it or not) a preferment: a significant part of the puzzle completed for him. Feminist ethics (here interpreted) would say that this is *not* success by merit; it is success by unmerited preferment.

KEY TERMS

- Heinz dilemma
- justice and care
- the position of the other
- desert

A THOUGHT EXPERIMENT: FINDING OUT WHAT YOU BELIEVE

You are on a hiring committee for an attending physician at a major hospital in the United States. Percival Johnson, a white Anglo-Saxon Protestant who held the job for 35 years, died. Now you have to fill his spot. Dr. Johnson was well respected in his tenure. You have 50 resumes before you and some of them are from women and from minorities. The hospital is dedicated to equal opportunity for all applicants, but you really don't know how to apply this concept in this case since these "other" candidates are nothing like Dr. Johnson. Every applicant you have received is board certified. However, some have come from much "better" programs than others. Your assistant, Sarah, says that you should use the care ethic to emotionally connect to the life story of the applicants involved in order to determine the "short list." You aren't so sure.

In 750 words, present an opinion on whether you should take life experiences (the road traveled to here) as a criterion for merit and desert in this position.

This thought experiment should assist readers in finding out for themselves which position they hold. This can also be a useful device for class discussion. The key to making it work well is by the detail in the causal account of one solution versus another.

NOTES

1. Deborah Tannen *You Just Don't Understand: Women and Men in Conversation* (New York: Ballantine Press, 1991).
2. Lawrence Kohlberg, *The Psychology of Moral Development* (San Francisco: Harper and Row, 1984), 174–186.
3. Carol Gilligan, "Moral Orientation and Moral Development," in *Women and Moral Theory,* ed. Eva Feder Kittay and Diana T. Meyers (Totowa, NJ: Roman and Littlefield, 1987). Gilligan is citing her own research statistics.
4. Carol Gilligan, *In A Different Voice: Psychological Theory and Women's Development* (Cambridge, MA: Harvard University Press, 1982).
5. Nel Noddings, *Caring: A Feminine Approach to Ethics and Moral*

Education (Berkeley, CA: University of California Press, 1984).

6. This literature has been surveyed by Marilyn Friedman in "Beyond Caring: The De-Moralization of Gender," in *Science, Morality and Feminist Theory*, ed. by Marsha Hanen and Kai Nielsen (Calgary: University of Calgary Press, 1987).

7. The point of such an example is to highlight one feature of the definition that we are examining in order to view its adequacy. Since most feminist ethical theorists would distance themselves from this sort of example, one should ask, "What further principle is needed to support this position?" One cannot randomly accept one sort of bonding over justice over others *simpliciter* without begging the question. There must be additional criteria added to exclude such examples.

8. G. W. F. Hegel, *Phenomenology of Spirit*, trans. A. V. Miller (Oxford: Oxford University Press, 1977), 111–119.

9. Key texts for Plato in this regard would be the *Lysis* and the *Symposium*. Aristotle's treatment of friendship in the *Nicomachean Ethics* books 8 and 9 are also instructive.

10. See Rosemarie Tong's presentation in *New Perspectives in Healthcare Ethics* (Upper Saddle River, NJ: Prentice Hall, 2007) and Alison M. Jaggar, "Caring as a Feminist Practice of Moral Reason" in *Justice and Care: Essential Readings in Feminist Ethics*, ed. Virginia Held (Boulder, CO: Westview Press, 1995).

11. One variant upon this argument is the position that "race" is not a robust social or biological classification. The authors of this essay tend toward this direction with the caveat that among most of American society this is certainly not the case. For this reason, we will assume the existence of race for practical purposes. However, in reality, *homo sapiens* is the only robust category for a species (under the traditional definition: capable of interreproduction). Other accidental differences exist for the artificial purpose of subjugating another for selfish purposes.

12. By "intrastructure" it is meant the social landscape of what it means to exist in America during the present age. For example, the rise of computer applications during the 1990s made a big difference in the intrastructure of the United States. Those plugged into the information economy profited mightily. Those without these resources became poorer. By "exostructure" it is meant the social landscape of what it means for America to exist in the world. When the communist Soviet Union fell in the late 1980s the international climate changed radically. The same might be said about the terrorist attacks of 9/11/01 in New York and Washington, DC.

13. This argument is made in more detail in Michael Boylan and Richard E. Grant, "Diversity and Professional Ethics," *Journal of the National Medical Association* 96, no. 10 (October, 2004): 188–200; and Michael Boylan, "Culture and Medical Intervention," *Journal of Clinical Ethics* 15, no. 2 (Summer 2004): 187–199.

14. This point is often argued from different vantage points. For a range of these see: Elliot Sober and David Sloan Wilson, *Unto Others: The Evolution and Psychology of Unselfish Behavior* (Cambridge, MA: Harvard University Press, 1998); Piet Strydom, "Sociological evolution or social evolution of practical reason: Eder's critique of habermas" *Praxis International*, 13, no. 3 (2993): 304–322; Patricia Fara, Peter Gathercole, and Ronald Laskey (Eds.), *The Changing World* (Cambridge, MA: Cambridge University Press, 1996).

15. The reader should note that "merit" (often referred to in the literature of philosophy as 'deserts') refers to a theory of what agents can justifiably claim on the basis of their achievements; a further expansion of this argument can be found in Michael Boylan, *A Just Society* (Lanham, MD and Oxford: Rowman and Littlefield, 2004), Chapter 7.

16. By "puzzle maker" we mean the person who puts a puzzle together, not one who manufacturers it.

PART

2

THE BASIC ANSWERS

It's All about Your Intuition: Ethical Intuitionism

SNAPSHOT

One can generally describe ethical intuitionism as a theory of justification about the immediate grasping of self-evident ethical truths. Ethical intuitionism can operate on the level of general principles or on the level of daily decision making. In this latter mode many of us have experienced a form of ethical intuitionism through the teaching of timeless adages such as, "look before you leap," and "faint heart never won fair maiden." The truth of these sayings is justified through intuition. Many adages or maxims contradict each other (such as the two above), so that the ability to properly apply these maxims is also understood through intuition.

THE PROBLEM THIS THEORY ADDRESSES

Ethical intuitionism may be the oldest (and most widely used—though often not acknowledged) of all theories of ethics. Most of our earliest writings on value cite various moral maxims or aphorisms that are accepted directly without logical argument (see below). In the ancient Greek world Aristotle and others appealed to *endoxa* or common opinion of what constituted moral behavior. This was the starting point for ethics. Such a starting point became the standard for acceptable conduct. Certainly, ethical intuitionism predates recorded history. For this reason it is probably imbedded in all of us in one form or other (whether we consciously practice it or not).

In the seventeenth century, René Descartes offered a powerful argument for epistemological intuitionism that was carried over to ethics by the Cambridge Platonists. Later, in the nineteenth century, Thomas Reid took a strong intuitionistic position in response to some of the criticisms of another Scot, David Hume.

In the twentieth century, G. E. Moore, W. D. Ross, R. M. Hare, and John Rawls have made explicit use of ethical intuitions in the construction of their theories. As we will see, their usages can be very different.

Ethical intuitionism is and *has been* very widely practiced. Though often unacknowledged, it has been appealed to by many in applied ethics and in moral education. This is because of its ease in application. In this chapter a variant of ethical intuitionism will be presented that seeks a moral absolutist standpoint. In the next chapter, a second sort of intuitionism will be set out that is descriptive in nature as it seeks to uncover the descriptive action-guiding force of moral discourse. These two forms of ethical intuitionism have various similarities, but in the end the version presented in this chapter is, itself, prescriptive in a way that the emotivist version presented in the next chapter is not.

THE ARGUMENT FOR THE THEORY

Before beginning our analysis of ethical intuitionism, it is instructive to examine intuitionism in general. This is because the foundations of ethical intuitionism are found in the general structure of intuitionism, per se.

INTUITIONISM

Intuitionism is the immediate grasping of truth. Let's unpack this definition. First, intuitionism is *immediate.* This is to be contrasted to *mediate* knowledge that relies upon a mode of mediation such as another term or some scientific, logical, or mathematical theory. A classical example of mediate knowledge is given in the following argument:

Argument 8–1: Mediate Syllogistic Knowledge

1. All humans are mortal (All M is P)
2. Socrates is a human. (All S is M)
3. Socrates is mortal. (All S is P) — 1, 2
   Key: Middle term (M) = humans; Subject of the conclusion (S) = Socrates; Predicate of the conclusion (P) = Things that are mortal.

In Argument 8–1 we say we know that S connects to P (Socrates is mortal) because the middle term is attached to both S and P in a valid syllogistic figure. Our knowledge that "S is P" in the conclusion is thus mediated by: (a) the middle term connecting to each extreme; and (b) the system of logic that dictates the rules of valid syllogistic argument forms. Both (a) and (b) act to give us mediate knowledge that "S is P."

From this example we can see that mediate knowledge often contains mechanisms or conditions under which we can say we "know." In the absence of a mediating term or a system that provides definitions, causes, inferences, and other internal justifications, we say that we grasp directly, immediately.

Second, intuitionism is the *grasping of truth.* This leads us to the question, "truth of what?" This is a somewhat controversial topic, but I would put forward that the truth we grasp is of two sorts: (a) it is the truth "that x is," and/or (b) it is the truth that "x possesses property f". The former calls for us to apprehend some entity, x. An example of this might be the mystical grasping of God's existence or the independent existence of "Good."

When we have nonpropositional apprehension of an entity one may appeal to this sort of intuitionism to grasp the entity. In other words, our apprehension is necessary if we are to be able to formulate any justified beliefs about the nature of that entity. As Aristotle said in the first chapter of *Posterior Analytics II,* the apprehension of "thatness" precedes our knowledge of "what-ness." Thus, intuitions in sense (a) can form the basis of further knowledge that may utilize prior intuitions in consequential inferences.

Another example might be the apprehension of universals, such as employed by Kant in his transcendental aesthetic (from *The Critique of Pure Reason*). Kant believed that we directly grasp Space and Time. For Kant, Space and Time cannot be justified with reference to any other entity or system. They are immediate primitives that are apprehended directly. These concepts are necessary assumptions in order for there to be any knowledge at all. Following Newton, Kant believes that Space and Time really exist. We know directly that "Space is" and that "Time is." Upon later reflection we notice that we grasp these directly both in the genetic order in which they are presented to us and in their status as objects of our minds.

This is important, because it might be possible for something to be given to us directly in the genetic order (as a principle of developmental psychology), but not in the logical order. Psychoanalysis is full of cases in which that which is presented directly as a brute given to children may be susceptible to later foundational analysis when the subject becomes an adult. By reviewing these apprehensions in light of some psychoanalytic theory, one can gain mediate knowledge of x (a feeling, attitude, or perception). Thus, there is "in principle" mediate knowledge of x even though it wasn't first understood mediately. In these cases the genetic order is merely an accident of our human developmental processes. However, in the cases of Space and Time, the genetic order is also the logical order. No amount of analysis can create a prior inference by which we might derive Space and Time. They are primitives whose existence must be grasped immediately in order for any other knowledge about the world to develop.

Sense (b) calls for us to apprehend x "as situated." This could take the form of primitive sensation (it is true that the thing before me is red) or a propositional truth not preceded by an inference ("p or not-p" is true). In this case we apprehend immediately the truth *about* some thing, proposition, or state of affairs.

One example of this can be found in Aristotle's *Posterior Analytics* I.1 in which he says, "All teaching and all intellectual learning arises from pre-existent knowledge. This is evident if we consider all the cases. For the mathematical sciences are had through this way and each of the other arts. Similarly too with arguments: deductive and inductive."[1] When we examine the structure of systems of mediate knowledge we find that we can only push the starting points back so far. There comes a time when we have to stop. These *principles* are grasped by an intellectual power of the mind (intuition or *nous*).

Another example can be found in Descartes. In the *Meditations on First Philosophy* Descartes begins by doubting everything. Then he considers his own existence. "There is no doubt that I exist . . . 'I am, I exist' is true necessarily each time I utter it or conceive of it in my mind."[2] Descartes does not "prove" his existence mediately, that is, as the conclusion of a deductive argument. To do so would involve begging the question (the so-called Cartesian Circle). But if the *cogito* ("I think") is taken as an instance of immediate intellectual grasping, then it is a stronger argument. In *Meditation III* the conditions of something being presented to the mind as "clear and distinct" are presented. "In the first level of knowing there can be nothing else except a clear and distinct perception of my affirmation" (p. 35). Thus, if some connection is grasped with forceful vividness, it is grasped *clearly*. If it is apprehended as a unique proposition with recognizable boundaries, then it is *distinct*. If a proposition is both clear and distinct, then its truth or falsity is immediately grasped.[3]

Certainly there are critics of this sort of intuitionism,[4] but our task here is not to enter into an extended discussion of intuitionism per se, but to set it out in general so that we may turn our attention to *ethical* intuitionism.

The word *grasping* is used to differentiate the mental state of belief that is not mediately justified. When we justify a belief mediately, we say we "know" (as in the example given in Argument 8–1). There may be other requirements for mediate knowledge depending upon one's system of epistemology, but these are not pertinent in this context. Our attention is directed toward the immediate grasping of truth.

One sort of example that has often been put forth follows in the Cartesian tradition. It asserts that mathematical and geometrical principles can be grasped immediately and a fortiori so can other principles (such as ethical principles). This position was held very strongly by the Cambridge Platonists.[5]

Certainly, there are many applications of intuitionism in general. Ethics, religion, and mathematics are only three areas. These are by no means exhaustive, but they give the general direction of such inquiries.

ETHICAL INTUITIONISM

I have spent some time talking about intuitionism in general, because this is necessary for understanding how it applies in ethics.[6]

Picking up from the end of the last section I would say that **ethical intuitionism** as a theory may aspire to several things: 1. Ethical truths are objective and apply to all people; 2. These universal truths can be apprehended immediately; 3. The distinction between good and evil does not depend upon passions and the inclination to do such and such, but is rooted in a basic grasping of fundamental verities of good and evil.

This fundamental declaration of truth was espoused indirectly by Descartes (above) and by the Cambridge Platonists, as well as Richard Price and Thomas Reid (pre-twentieth century philosophers).

It is very important in ethical discourse to pay attention to the level of application. I will distinguish two levels of application: level one which deals with the principles, themselves, and level two which concerns the operation of ethical decisions.

LEVEL-ONE INTUITIONISM

On **level-one intuitionism** a person grasps the truth or existence of the principles. Principles are the starting points of systems of knowledge. When one works deductively from a theorem to its proof, one is forced to employ mediate knowledge. However, when one examines those truths that do not admit to anything prior (in a logical sense), then one cannot infer the truth of said principle. If it is to be grasped as true *simpliciter*, it must be grasped immediately. Thus, proponents of ethical intuitionism offer various maxims that are said to be known immediately.

Examples of these maxims might be: A1, "One ought not lie;" A2, "One ought to act with compassion towards others;" A3, "One ought to respect another's autonomy;" and A4, "One ought to act to protect others when they cannot protect themselves."

As one can see these maxims may have overlapping domains. As W. D. Ross states these moral maxims impose a duty on all people to obey them.[7] The nature of this duty and its exceptions will be discussed shortly.

However, it still could be argued that we do not need to resort to immediate grasping to obtain ethical maxims at the level of principles. Mill believed that "good" could be defined as maximizing pleasure for the greatest number. Herbert Spenser thought good could be defined in terms of being "more evolved." Aquinas appealed to the created laws of nature. These philosophers pick out natural criteria as the basis for judging something to be good. If *these* naturalistic philosophers are correct, then intuitionism is incorrect. This is because naturalism allows the justification of ethics [what is good] to be mediate. The mediating agency is nature and the scientific methods for examining nature. Thus, intuitionists and naturalists are philosophical enemies.

At the beginning of the twentieth century, G. E. Moore (an intuitionist) presented his famous "open question" argument to demonstrate what he took to be the "naturalistic fallacy."[8] To see how this works let us examine the definition of good that the naturalistic utilitarians offer, "Good is defined as maximizing pleasure for the greatest number."

To begin we must make certain assumptions. First, there are only two sorts of definitions: those that are analytic and those that are synthetic.[9] *Analytic propositions are those in which the predicate term does not enlarge our understanding of the subject term.*[10] Two examples of this would be: B1, "All black ravens are black" and B2, "All bachelors are unmarried males." In B1 the predicate term (being black) does not enlarge our understanding of a black raven. Similarly, in B2 the predicate term (being an unmarried male) does not enlarge our understanding of a bachelor. If we understand the subject term in each instance (B1 and B2) we already understand what is given to us in the predicate term.

Synthetic propositions are those in which the predicate term enlarges our understanding of the subject term. Two examples of this are: B3, "All ravens are black" and B4, "The boiling point of water is 100 degrees centigrade." In B3 the predicate term attributes a property universal to the subject term. One could understand the subject (raven) such that you could pick one out when shown various species of birds without knowing whether *every* raven must be black. Thus, in B3 the predicate term (being black) enlarges our understanding of the subject term, raven. Similarly in B4 one can be able to identify water chemically as H_2O without knowing what its boiling point is. Thus the predicate term (the temperature at which the liquid state boils) enlarges our understanding of the subject term, water.

Obviously, analytic propositions are definitionally true. They do not tell us anything new about the world. Synthetic propositions enlarge our understanding of the world. Thus, the only propositions fit for the naturalists are synthetic ones.

Now if we are to apply the open question test (Case 8–1) we must first assert that if the definition turned out to be analytic, then it would not be naturalistic. Only *synthetic* propositions will do.

CASES

CASE 8–1   **THE OPEN QUESTION TEST**

1. Take the proposed definition and invert the subject and predicate terms—creating a question.
2. Take the altered proposition and examine whether the new formulation is "open" or "closed." If it is closed, then the definition is naturalistic. If it remains open, then is nonnatural.
3. Closed versus open is determined by whether we must still appeal to criteria outside the definition to provide completeness. ■

Following the instructions above we will take our original proposition, "Good is defined as maximizing pleasure for the greatest number," and invert it—creating a question, "Is maximizing pleasure for the greatest number good?"

Second, we will examine whether the altered proposition is open or closed. Moore says it is still open. We have not satisfied our understanding of good by the definition. In other words, it is still an open question whether maximizing pleasure for the greatest number is good. This is not self-evident.

Compare this to B3 and B4. "Is being 'black' a property of all ravens?" and "Is 100 degrees centigrade the boiling point of water?" These questions can be shown to be true without being analytic (because they can be empirically tested). Thus, these questions become closed upon application of the test.

If we agree with Moore's analysis, then "good" is not a natural quality and can only be known by immediate grasping, intuitionism.

LEVEL-TWO INTUITIONISM

Level-two intuitionism deals not with abstract principles but with principles situated in the context of life. At this level we are dealing with what we need to make actual ethical choices. In order to understand this operation let us concentrate upon two functions in level two: (a) recognition and (b) application.

By "recognition" I mean the process by which we decide whether the act before us is of a particular character. For example, if a woman is pregnant and considering an abortion, is this an instance of someone exercising autonomy or someone contemplating murder? The answer to this query can obviously go a great ways in determining what we are morally permitted to do.

In the above example there are certainly some mediate steps that can be made vis-à-vis what we know about murder and autonomy. These terms have their own definitions, which, in most instances would prove to be decisive. However, when two maxims seem to overlap there is an apparent ethical dilemma. An *ethical dilemma exists when the agent finds him/herself in a moral situation that is not his/her fault in which all the choices presented are instances of ethically impermissible actions.*[11] In elementary logic a dilemma is often presented in the form of a question that offers two unacceptable options such as, "Have you stopped beating your wife?"[12] If you say, "Yes," then it seems as if you were beating your wife and have now stopped. If you say, "No," then it seems as if you are *still* beating your wife.

In the case of an ethical dilemma one is, through no fault of one's own, faced with the necessity of doing a morally impermissible action. If morally overlapping maxims had no further means of adjudication, then one might find himself in a moral dilemma. It is at this point that intuitionists may invoke a level-two act of recognition and decide that the action in question falls more correctly under one or the other overlapping description and its attendant moral maxim. Thus, in our example above, the agent may through an immediate grasping decide that this situation of possible abortion falls more appropriately under autonomy than under murder (or vice versa).

However, there are other times when one cannot avoid the conflict of moral maxims. In this case level-two recognition is not sufficient to adjudicate the conflict. What is needed is level-two application. When intuition comes to play in this mode we have a situation of one maxim actually superseding another in its force. It is not the case that one maxim more correctly *describes* the situation. That is level-two *recognition*. Rather we have an instance of genuine conflict that has to be resolved.

To help explain this better, let us turn back to W. D. Ross and his discussion of duties:

> I suggest *"prima facie* duty" or "conditional duty" as a brief way of referring to the characteristic (quite distinct from that of being a duty proper) which an act has, in virtue of being of a certain kind (e.g., the keeping of a promise), of being an act which would be a duty proper if it were not at the same time of another kind which is morally significant . . . [there is] *a prima facie* rightness of certain types of act . . . [this] is self-evident; not in the sense that it is *acting for one's self-interests* evident from the beginning of our lives . . . but in the sense that when we have reached sufficient moral maturity and have given sufficient attention to the proposition it is evident without need of further proof.[13]

Most duties are prima facie and not absolute duties. This means that they can be overridden by other duties when a situation arises in which there is a conflict. If we go back to the duties we illustrated earlier we can illustrate this via an example.

Al: One ought not lie.
A2: One ought to act with compassion towards others.
A3: One ought to respect another's autonomy.
A4: One ought to act to protect others when they cannot protect themselves.

Each of the above propositions would elicit a prima facie duty to follow his or her prescription. However, consider Thought Experiment 8–1.

THOUGHT EXPERIMENT 8–1: THE DEATH OF GRANNY

1. Your grandmother is dying.
2. Your grandmother is in great psychic and moderate physical distress.
3. Your grandmother has always had an intense fear of death and disease and has never handled "bad news" well.

4. The physician tells you that if your grandmother can maintain a positive attitude she can live another year and it will be relatively pain free. If she becomes overly agitated her condition will worsen and her death

will be much sooner and her physical pain will increase greatly.

5. You are sitting with your grandmother and she asks you whether she will be "all right" (meaning that she won't die and will get better). What do you say? ■

The various moral maxims A1 through A4 can all be applied to this situation. It is not the case that we are deciding just where to subsume this action under which ethical rule. All four do apply. The problem is they prescribe different actions. A1 and A 3 suggest that we tell Granny the truth and try to make it go as easily as possible. If she really knew that a positive attitude would help her live, then she could be a part of her own cure. This decision would make A1 and A3 supervene A2 and A4.

A2 and A4 suggest that Granny is not that type of person. She will never take it well. If you tell her the truth, she will be unable to handle the news. She has a history of handling illnesses that were much more minor as if they were fatal and as a result she has gotten worse. It is true that this time might be different, but you don't think so. You will act in Granny's best interests and conceal the information from her because she needs protection. This decision would make A2 and A4 supervene A1 and A3.

Which decision is the best to make? Which of these pairs of moral maxims ought to overrule the others? It's clear that they all can be properly ascribed to the situation, but since they dictate contradictory actions, it is necessary to choose one pair over the other. Since the duties involved are prima facie and not absolute, one duty may override another. The question is on what basis do we do this?

This is often called *the priority problem*. For ethical intuitionists the ultimate solution to which of competing maxims should supervene is decided by level-two intuition. John Rawls address this problem by putting certain restraints on the operation of intuition (considered judgments in reflective equilibrium), but in the end there is an appeal to intuition.[14]

Thus, in level-two application, intuitionism operates to provide a priority ordering among competing maxims, all of which can properly be ascribed as applying to the situation in question.

To review, then, ethical intuitionism can operate on two levels. Level one is concerned with the apprehension of the principles themselves. Level two operates both as the *recognition* of the appropriate moral maxim in a given situation, and, in cases that involve more than one competing maxim, intuitionism provides a priority in *application* by making one maxim the more important.

One further point should be made: it is not necessary to accept intuitionism at both level one and level two. Just because ethical intuitionism can operate on two levels does not mean that all of its practitioners will employ it on both levels. It is possible, for example to accept intuitionism at level one and eschew it at level two (choosing another theory that will solve the recognition and application problems). It is even possible to accept level two without accepting level one (though this is less common).

ARGUMENTS AGAINST THE THEORY

Intuitionism, in general, and ethical intuitionism are not without their detractors. I will summarize some of the criticisms that are made against both intuitionism in general, and ethical intuitionism using the basic structure of the preceding section as a guide.

ARGUMENTS AGAINST ETHICAL INTUITIONISM AT LEVEL ONE

There are three criticisms at this level that I will highlight: (1) Naturalism, (2) The Humian objection, (3) Logical empiricism.

1. *NATURALISM*

If the laws of ethics are to be found in nature—just as the laws of physics are—then *intuitionism* (which is a non-natural theory) is false. This discussion has translated in the twentieth century into the "Is-Ought" question. This supposed split is evidenced by the hunt for factual (scientific) criteria (the "is") by which ethical decisions might be made (the "ought"). For example, the laws of physics can, in principle, be confirmed or falsified by common experience with nature.

Naturalists such as Mill, Spenser, and Aquinas all held that there *are* ways of basing normative maxims upon facts in the world that can be arrived at through the scientific method. Mill believed that "good" could be defined as maximizing pleasure for the greatest number. Herbert Spenser thought good could be defined in terms of being "more evolved." Aquinas appealed to the created Laws of Nature. If they are right, then the intuitionists are wrong. Moore offers his open question test as an argument against the naturalists. However, naturalists do not take this test as decisive. Instead, they say that: (1) The open question test, at best, only illustrates the incompleteness of those definitions that are examined. Incompleteness is not the same as falsity. (2) Further, the open question test is not exhaustive either of all the possible naturalistic approaches that have been tried or of those that might be tried in the future. Thus, the naturalists do not take the open question test as decisive.

To counter this objection the intuitionist must show that the open question test is decisive or that some other device is. Another strategy might be to attack naturalism in another way. However, this may have the unintended consequence of not providing support for intuitionism, but some other theory, instead.[15]

2. THE HUMIAN OBJECTION

David Hume believed that the intuitionists represented by the Cambridge Platonists were putting forth a theory by which some act of spontaneous reason would determine moral truth. In opposing this theory Hume said, "reason alone can never be a motive to any action of the will . . . it can never oppose passion in the direction of the will."[16] This is because reason cannot move us to action except as it is in accord with a prior desire.

By itself reason only illustrates certain factual connections, but these connections "can never give them any influence; and 'tis plain, that as reason is nothing but the discovery of this connection, it cannot be by its means that the objects are able to affect us . . . reason alone can never produce any action or give rise to volition . . . reason is, and ought only to be the slave of the passions, and can never pretend to any other office than to serve and obey them".[17]

In short, Hume believes that morality is based upon *action*. "What moves us to act?" is the question we should be asking. Analysis and immediate grasping may yield truth (of a sort), but this is largely irrelevant to action. We may, in fact, judge some action to be good, and yet fail to act. What use is reason then if it cannot necessarily determine the will to act? At best, the intuitionists offer an epistemological insight into the possible origins of knowledge. Even if they are true about that (which Hume will also contend), they have not gotten us any closer to understanding how the will has been directed to act—why we act in one way and not another.

In response to Hume, ethical intuitionists have two courses: (a) they can deny that ethical intuitionism is about motivating people to act, or (b) they can attempt to refute the objection.

If the ethical intuitionist were to deny that ethical intuitionism is about motivating people to act, then they would be asserting that the province of ethical intuitionism is merely to justify ethical truth claims. This is a legitimate response since intuitionism in general and ethical intuitionism have been presented as primarily concerned with doing just that. In this case the ethical intuitionists would respond to Hume that he is asking more of ethical intuitionism (namely that it justify truth *and* motivate to action) than was ever intended. Under this response the ethical intuitionist could relegate questions of motivation to the "will" or some other aspect of the human psyche.

Other ethical intuitionists (such as the Cambridge Platonists) were interested in providing motivation for ethical action. These ethical intuitionists need to defeat Hume's objection. A common strategy for such a refutation is to adopt a Platonic psychology that would assert that "to know x-type action is good, is to do x." If this always follows, then Hume is wrong. However, this is a difficult task, at best.

3. LOGICAL EMPIRICISM

Earlier we talked about there being two sorts of propositions: analytic and synthetic. Not everyone agrees that this is a correct way of parsing propositions, but most of the logical empiricists, such as Carnap, held this to be essential to the program they were presenting.

In our discussion earlier, I mentioned that analytic propositions told us nothing about the world, but only about the closed system in which they operate. A perfect example might be mathematics. One can create all sorts of exotic mathematical systems and geometries that no one claims represent the world in which we live. These systems are created and judged in terms of coherency and completeness. Coherency and completeness are internal criteria. They judge the system from within. Thus, a system may be "true" if it satisfies these inward-looking conditions.

Since we expect any system of ethics to be "outward" looking and apply to the world in which we live, if ethical intuitionism offered truths that were merely analytic, then the maxims derived from these truths would be trivial. Their proximate justification and application are a function of the system from which they came. This is why I characterize them as "inward" looking. If this assessment is correct, then such principles would not be adequate for ethics as I have described ethics.

It is also true that from Plato onwards, many intuitionists used analogies to mathematics to illustrate how ethical intuitionism operated. The appeal was that we all had confidence in the truth of mathematics and its clear application to the world. If ethical intuitionism was akin to mathematics and if the foundations of mathematics were grasped immediately, then there was an added plausibility to ethical intuitionism.

However, if mathematics has now been relegated to a merely conventional device without synthetic truth, then maybe ethical intuitionism yields such truths, too. In this case immediate grasping of ethical maxims yields nothing important about acting in the world. If mathematics and intuitionism were merely statements of analytic truths, then their theorems and prescriptions would merely be a statement about a private universe that someone has created and which satisfies certain inward-looking requirements.

To refute such attacks the intuitionist must either (a) show that its maxims are synthetic and not analytic; or (b) s/he must deny the entire synthetic/analytic distinction. Either of these arguments might refute this challenge.

ARGUMENTS AGAINST ETHICAL INTUITIONISM AT LEVEL TWO

Level two is the realm of recognition and application. Both of these functions require the subject to make judgments in a more cluttered environment than in level one. Because of the level of abstraction present in level one, each competing maxim can be viewed on its own. However, at level two there is a comparative assessment built in. One must compare various descriptions of some given action and immediately grasp which is the most correct (recognition), or decide which given maxim will supervene others in directing our duty to act (application).

The major problems with this level are related: *subjectivism* and *relativism*. Since the agent makes a judgment based upon an immediate grasping, s/he is unable to *account* for his or her action to another except to say that "this action appears to be an 'x' to me" (recognition) or "this maxim 'y' is the one that ought to be used here to determine our duty" (application). But if queried by another agent why s/he thinks that this is the case, the first agent can only say, "It is immediately obvious to *me*. If you can't see it the same way, there is nothing I can say to you."

Thus, we are at an impasse. The first agent could resort to various persuasive devices in order to make the second agent acquire a "pro attitude"[18] toward accepting description x or maxim y. These devices will, by necessity, be nonlogical. This is because logic employs machinery that operates mediately. The propositions and inferences in logic are open to public intersubjective debate and resolution.

This is not true with immediate graspings. They are private and not available to public scrutiny and resolution. Either another person perceives it that way or s/he doesn't.

The obvious result of this might be a subjectivism in which each party declares their truth to be the only way. Since logical argument cannot be of use in this situation, power politics and propaganda/nonlogical persuasion will have to be provided.

Societies and subgroups within societies will assert their autonomy and ethical relativism will result (for how could anyone be in a position — using ethical intuitionism alone — to offer a refutation?).

Is this what we think ethics should be? Subjectivism and ethical relativism creating a cacophony of competing positions within an arena in which power is the only deciding factor?

This criticism is very strong. I see the types of responses to be:

i. One could deny that such disagreements really exist. Just because one cannot prove to another that a particular maxim supervenes, does not mean that discussion is impossible. Perhaps by careful Socratic discussions, the other agent can be made to see for him or herself the truth of some level two applications.

ii. Another reply might be that the realm of contention which is the unacceptable conclusion pointed to by critics is really the world in which we live. The world *is* pluralistic and we do resort to power, politics, and propaganda to solve our disputes. Intuitionism at level two is supported by an examination of how homogeneous societies and subgroups have diversified in today's world. By this argument, intuitionism is the most realistic of the moral theories because it offers a plausible explanation of today's moral pluralism.

iii. A final variety of response is to deny the operation of intuitionism at level two entirely. It is not necessary to accept ethical intuitionism at level two. If one were only to accept level one, then perhaps the refutations just outlined might not apply.

In the end each reader must decide for herself whether the advantages of this theory outweigh the disadvantages.

KEY TERMS

- intuitionism
- ethical intuitionism
- level-one ethical intuitionism
- level-two ethical intuitionism

A CHALLENGING CASE STUDY

Directions: Write a two-and-a-half page essay (750 words) on the following case. Be sure to first set out what you believe to be the moral maxims that apply to the case. Second, evaluate whether you agree with one or more of the maxims based upon personal worldview or community worldview tenets. Make your reasons very explicit. Be sure to make it clear whether you are referring to level-one or level-two ethical intuitionism in constructing your essay.

You are a student attending Major State University (in Anywhere, USA). You were at the library last night as you were preparing your "challenging case study" to turn in to philosophy class today. The trouble is that you observed Fred Football (a student in your class) copying his essay off the Internet in a "cut and paste job." This amounts to academic dishonesty. At Major State this is grounds for expulsion. However, you also know that Fred is the first member of his family to seek education past high school. His father died two years ago, and the family is counting on Fred (and his sports scholarship) to be able to get a high-paying job to support the family once their welfare payments stop in three years (five-year lifetime limit). If you tell on Fred, he may be expelled from college. If you don't tell on Fred, he is undermining the very academic institution that you attend. What do you do?

NOTES

1. 171a 1–6, cf. 71a 12–16. Translations are mine. Ross's and Barnes's commentary on this latter passage agrees with the classical Greek commentators that Aristotle is asserting some sort of intuitive knowledge; however this is complicated by the puzzle of the *Meno* (71a 29) which raises the problem about learning anything about x unless we already have this knowledge to begin with. Aristotle postpones his deeper reflections about *nous* (the power by which intellectual induction and intuition takes place) to *Apo.* II.19.

2. René Descartes, *Oeuvres* Charles Adams and Paul Tannery (Eds.), Vol. 2 (Paris: Vrin, 1976): 25. Translations are mine.

3. There is some complication in this example. The *act* of grasping clearly and the *act* of perceiving distinctly are instances of immediate grasping. However, the reflection that some proposition is true in virtue of its being "clear and distinct" is a mediate subsumption (viz., using the categories of clear and distinct as the mediating agents for the subsumed proposition). This merely means that what is grasped immediately can be used proximately in a logical subsumption or in the proof of a theorem (both mediate operations).

4. Two prominent critics of Cartesian intuitionism would be Gilbert Ryle in *The Concept of Mind* and Ludwig Wittgenstein in *Philosophical Investigations*. The former offers a behaviorist account as an alternative while the latter says that x's belief in the truth of a proposition reflects merely a social convention.

5. See my account of one of the more prominent Cambridge Platonists, Henry Moore, in "Henry Moore and the Spirit of Nature," *Journal of the History of Philosophy* (1982).

6. As I indicated earlier, there is no single version of this or any other major theory in ethics. I will present two versions of ethical intuitionism that operate at the level of principles and at the level of application. However, this division is not intended to be exhaustive.

7. W. D. Ross, *The Right and the Good* (Oxford: Oxford University Press, 1930), 19.

8. G. E. Moore, *Principia Ethica* (Cambridge: Cambridge University Press, 1903), 14.

9. This in itself is a controversial claim. It was first set out by Aristotle and more recently by David Hume and the logical empiricists, e.g., Rudolph Carnap, *The Philosophical Foundations of Physics* (Chicago: University of Chicago Press, 1951). Obviously, Quine's essay "Two Dogmas of Empiricism" found in *From a Logical Point of View* (Cambridge, MA: Harvard University Press, 1953), created a debate on this issue that is still unresolved.

10. There are a number of versions of analytic and synthetic propositions. The ones I offer are heavily Kantian, however; this should not affect the presentation of the open question test.

11. It is important to distinguish between a moral dilemma in which an agent, through no fault of his own, must commit a morally impermissible action, and a difficult moral choice in which the agent is confronted with an action s/he knows to be morally correct, but is

an action which will cost the agent a great deal (in practical terms). Morally difficult choices are not "fun" to make, but there is no question of what is the correct path of action. The only question is whether the agent has the courage to do what s/he thinks is right. See Chapter 11 on virtue ethics.

12. The dilemma question presumes that the respondent has never beaten his wife.

13. Ross, *The Right and the Good*, 25–27.

14. John Rawls, *A Theory of Justice* (Cambridge, MA: Harvard University Press, 1971), 40–45. Rawls's approach seeks to blend level-two intuitionism with some rational input; however it is intuitionism that decides the priority problem.

15. Certainly intuitionism is not the only nonnatural theory available. The "emotivists" and "noncognitivists" would count as two other alternatives.

16. David Hume, *A Treatise of Human Nature*, ed. L. A. Selby-Bigge (Oxford: Clarendon Press, 2nd ed. 1978), II.3, 413.

17. Hume, 414–415.

18. A "pro attitude" is generally associated with emotivism (see the next chapter). The point of the above example is that when intuitionism fails at this level (according to this potential refutation), then it disintegrates into nonlogical modes of discourse—one of which is emotivism.

CHAPTER

9

IT'S ALL IN YOUR ATTITUDE: ETHICAL NONCOGNITIVISM

- ❖ Snapshot
- ❖ The Problem This Theory Addresses
- ❖ The Argument for the Theory
- ❖ The Argument against the Theory
- ❖ Key Terms
- ❖ A Challenging Case Study

SNAPSHOT

Ethical noncognitivism is a theory that suggests that the descriptive analysis of language and culture tells us all we need to know about developing an appropriate attitude in ethical situations. Ethical propositions are neither true nor false, but can be analyzed via linguistic devices to tell us what action-guiding meanings are hidden there. We all live in particular and diverse societies. Discerning what each society commends and admonishes is the task for any person living in a society. We should all fit in and follow the social program as described via our language/society.

THE PROBLEM THIS THEORY ADDRESSES

Proponents of noncognitivist ethics believe that there are two difficulties with most of the universalist, moral-realist theories: (a) these moral-realist theories incorrectly believe that one society or moral thinker can discover realistic criteria that foundationally dictate to all what is ethically true, and (b) moral realists rigidly adhere to outmoded standards that haven't kept up with social history (unlike language that is constantly evolving with culture). Ethical noncognitivism seeks to address both issues. By emphasizing descriptivism over moral realistically based prescriptivism, ethical noncognitivism seeks a social situatedness that is grounded in a social science sensibility of culture and language.

THE ARGUMENT FOR THE THEORY

Advocates embrace ethical noncognitivism because they feel that the groundwork of moral realism theories is flawed. This is because first they feel that the a priori assumptions about human nature and its structure are unproven. Second, they feel that independent empirically driven assumptions about pleasure, social interestedness, virtue, or human action are all based upon empty essentialism, that is, a false understanding of empirical data. Ethical noncognitivists believe essentialism and moral realism in ethical discourse are dead wrong. Essentialism is often associated with religion and its dualistic metaphysics. Moral realism suggests there are factual, empirical underpinnings to the grounds of morality. Those who think essentialist and moral realism justifications are just a bunch of nonsense may find strong attractions to ethical noncognitivism.

At its starting point, ethical noncognitivism is a variant of ethical intuitionism. The difference is that, on the one hand, ethical intuitionism accepts level-one intuitionism as an epistemological act that connects the seeker to *what is true*. This source of truth is played out in level-two intuitionism via application to the case at hand.

On the other hand, ethical noncognitivism *begins* at level two. There is no level one. All posits are purely conventional. No propositions about value judgments are ultimately true. We set them down to see what happens. They create attitudes in agents that are positive or negative (also termed "pro attitude" or "con attitude"). But though these attitudes that result don't convey a strong sense of independent truth,[1] they are nonetheless action guiding—but only in a conventional sense. This is because all of us live in a social context that uses language to express what we think and feel, then we must take this social context into account. I take this uncritical acceptance of the social context to be the position of the behaviorists/linguists.

For behaviorists[2] the statement that "X knows that p" is not about some mental capacity that X possesses, but instead is a statement that X is disposed to assert p in appropriate settings. This can be the case even if X cannot give any good reasons *why* he believes p. X's belief that p is (in this case) based upon public standards of what is reasonable to believe without further proof.

For example, how do you know that this thing before you is an apple? You might say it is an apple if it is red and has a certain sort of shape. In most societies this might be fine. We have a case of what is acceptable word usage. But if pressed further on why we call this sort of red thing an apple, there is no justification beyond it being a public standard to call these things apples. Thus, our identification of p as an apple is a statement about language usage within a particular society.

One could imagine alternate societies that would require a taste test in order to render a judgment on whether something is an apple. In that society we would have to enlarge what we take to be definitive criteria and what counts as a reasonable set of primitive posits. The only justification is that X is in a society that uses language in that way. Unlike the intuitionists who believe that there are private, introspective mental states, the behaviorists assert that this public criterion is the only acceptable account of noninferential knowledge.

Wittgenstein replies to those who are not satisfied that this approach is fully adequate by asserting that so-called private introspective acts do not signify anything. There is no answer to questions about primitives that are acquired and used without prior inference. This is because "meaning is use." Wittgenstein begins his *Blue Book* by asking the question, "What is the meaning of a word?"[3] This has been often expanded by commentators to include "What is the meaning of a sentence?"[4] This sounds like the structure of my depiction of the level-one intuitionists *grasping truth*. It is a similar set of questions, but the results are much different. Because here, the *meaning* is determined by its "use" (*Gebrauch*), or "employment" (*Verwendung*), or "application" (*Anwendung*). Meaning is seen in the context of the rules of the language game and those rules, by themselves, "hang in the air."[5] They only become rooted in actual cases. This creates a public basis for meaning. There can be no private language. Therefore the sort of experience that the intuitionists describe (an introspective, reflective assertion of "what is") is *meaningless*. This is because introspective, reflective acts are both intangible and indescribable. They require a public context to give them significance. This is because "to signify," means "to signify ⇒ to someone." Ergo, the nature of signification and meaning is public.

This is the foundation of a descriptivist posture. If there is no independent existence of truth, then the *true* is only what people say it is. The cultural/societal context determines it all. If we return to Chapter 3, then we would be deeply committed to a general relativism, then the robust boundaries upon this are within larger social and linguistic groups. For example, one might point to the Middle East as a social/religious/linguistic area. To describe this further, let's turn to Thought Experiment 9–1.

THOUGHT EXPERIMENT 9–1: LOYALTY AS THE HIGHEST VIRTUE[6]

As the head of school in a college located in Beirut, Lebanon, you are faced with a troubling situation. Your expelling a student, Ahmed X, from the university for selling drugs. The expelling of Ahmed X upsets the militias that are in your neighborhood. Your contention is that you are the chief officer in charge of the mission of the college. Selling drugs or any other illegal activity is prohibited. Their contention is that, sure, selling drugs is bad, but if you had to stack this against Ahmed's support of the local militia and the larger Hamas group, then this demonstration of loyalty outweighs Ahmed's drug sales. Ahmed should be readmitted to the university so that he might get his degree and continue on with the cause. You believe in both the mission of the university as an academic institution and in the causes represented by the militia and the larger group, Hamas. Which imperative should trump? ■

From the point of view of ethical noncognitivism if the culture in Lebanon values loyalty above all others then the various sentences that talk about value will put loyalty at the top. All the observer can do is to learn more exactly about how this is the case and fall in line.

Noncognitivism has a basic metaethical position of parsing sentences into: (a) sentences about fact—the so-called empirically based cognitive uses of language; (b) sentences about linguistic meaning within a social context, and (c) sentences about instrumental value that are noncognitive and are set within various social constructs and intuitively justified (at level two) by citizens within some society.

Sentences of the first type are like: "The boiling point of water at sealevel is 100 degrees centigrade." These sentences talk about the empirically observed nature of the world and are empirically falsifiable. Sentences of the second type are like: "Murder in the United States is wrong." Sentences of the third type are like: "Don't murder." The first sentence is about a state of affairs and can be falsified. The second describes a linguistic/social context—the language game within a particular context. There are linguistic and social constructs that are only quasi-factual in a social science sense because they describe a moving target. The third sentence is a command that is set out to persuade an audience. It is not factual. It only reveals the level-two intuitionism standpoint of the speaker. The speaker has a "con" attitude about murder.

Proponents of noncognitivism often talk about the **locutionary, illocutionary,** or **perlocutionary** force of a sentence.[7] This jargon flows from an understanding of the communication flow of the speaker making the sorts of statements that are empirically factual (locutionary) or a feature of linguistic/social analysis (illocutionary) or finally instrumental to persuasion or other effects (perlocutionary)[8]. For example consider the following: Jack says to Sean, "Do you want to look at my signed Henry Aaron baseball?"

The locutionary force of the statement would be that Jack actually has an autographed Henry Aaron baseball. *This is a statement of fact that can be verified or falsified on the basis of an inspection of Jack's treasure trove.*

The illocutionary force of the statement would be that Jack is asking Sean to look at his signed baseball. A baseball from the professional teams is an important social artifact for many young people living in the society. Thus his friend should look on this occasion with keen anticipation. *This is a consequence of the social/linguistic meanings of the terms of a question.*

The perlocutionary force of the statement is a performance by Jack to Sean that seeks to make Sean envious of Jack's treasure trove. *This is a consequence of Jack's understanding of Sean's value system about baseball players and the value of autographed paraphernalia.*

To solidify your understanding of these modes of expression, consider Thought Experiment 9–2.

THOUGHT EXPERIMENT 9–2: IDENTIFYING NON-COGNITIVIST CONSTRUCTS

Your name is Kiva. You have just met the most terrific guy. His name is Éamon. You really want to go out with him. Éamon is really good at music. He plays several instruments and is amazing at the piano and the clarinet. You say to him, "Do you want to go to the concert this Friday? I have two free tickets from my Mum. There is a key soloist from Russia on the piano who just won an international competition. What do you say?" ■

What are the locutionary, illocutionary, and perlocutionary forces operating in the thought experiment? How do they affect the outcome? In what ways are they descriptive? Do they carry any metaphysical weight behind them? What do you make of this presence or absence of this?

By working through thought experiment one, you should get a sense of how this system works and whether you are comfortable with this way of understanding moral discourse.

LANGUAGE AND METALANGUAGE

Another key distinction along this path is the distinction between statements and statements about statements (**metalanguage**). For example, one might say that a statement might be, "Joseph Stalin was a bad person." This statement can be described via the apparatus described above. It is a normative claim that has illocutionary force because it linguistically describes a negative attitude toward Joseph Stalin. It has no locutionary status since there is no scientific test to determine goodness or badness. It may have perlocutionary force in as much as the speaker has an instrumental point to make to his audience (such as being an avid anti-Communist).

However, when we change the statement to, "Ronald Reagan said, 'Joseph Stalin was a bad person'" then things change. The proposition now possesses locutionary force because it can be checked whether Ronald Reagan ever said this.

In this second instance, its illocutionary force changes from prescriptive (Stalin was bad) to descriptive (Reagan said Stalin was bad). The perlocutionary force also changes from being a true believer in anti-Communism to being an historian in describing history.

The first statement was a first-order linguistic statement while the second was a second-order linguistic statement (also called a metalinguistic statement).

The ability to differentiate between brute statements and metalinguistic statements is critical to being able to understand what people mean when they make moral claims. At the end of the day, understanding moral claims in a context is the target of knowledge.

EMOTIVE CLAIMS

The last reason to adopt noncognitivism is that it gives a clear place to emotion.[9] The place of emotion in ethical discourse in the modern philosophical western tradition begins with David Hume. Under this account Hume holds that one may judge an action to be good or bad based upon that observer's sympathy with the observation of what has happened. For example if Mary gives money to a beggar at the steps of the Metro station and the beggar exhibits gratitude for the action, then the observer will similarly assimilate the positive emotional interchange between these two and judge the action positively.[10] This sort of reaction is often called the *newspaper test*. According to the newspaper test a good way to evaluate whether something that you intend to do is good is whether you would be comfortable with the social judgment that others would make about your proposed action were it to be put onto the front page of the newspaper (or these days, across the blogs of cyberspace).

In Hume's later writings this approach is simplified in a way that is not too different than the approach of Wittgenstein discussed above. Hume seeks simplicity:

> Throughout this enquiry, we always consider in general, what qualities are a subject of praise or of censure, without entering into all the minute differences of sentiment, which they excite. . . . These sciences are but too apt to appear abstract to common readers, even with all the precautions which we can take to clear them from superfluous speculations, and bring them down to every capacity.[11]

In the context of modern feminist ethics, emotions are also highly regarded vis-à-vis the notion of care. Using either the basic connection of *empathy* (the ability to project one's self into the situation of another) or *sympathy* (the ability to emotionally connect with another), the moral agent can connect with the plight of another and this provides moral motivation for action.

The care ethic gives a high degree of particularity to moral evaluation.[12] This has the advantage of matching a theoretical approach to the way most approach moral situations: from the standpoints of the particular agents involved. If these proponents of feminist ethics are correct, then a sort of level-two intuitionism will be informed by the dynamics of the moment via *empathy* and/or *sympathy*.

A final proponent of emotion would be one who wishes to exhort the sorts of emotions that she feels are appropriate to the historical/social situation of that society. For example, if one were living in the Southern United States in 1850 during the abolitionist debate on slavery s/he might reasonably argue that the Declaration of Independence declares that all men are created equal and are endowed by their creator with certain inalienable rights, among these are life, liberty and the pursuit of happiness. This might be a document indicating social norms against slavery. Thus, one might use emotive words to convince others of this position.

On the other hand, one might say that Thomas Jefferson, the writer of the Declaration of Independence, was (himself) a slaveholder and a man who reputedly had a child with one of his slaves, Sally Hemming.[13] Thus, if the pattern of the icon of human rights accepted human slavery, then perhaps it could be advocated as a social norm using emotive language.[14]

Obviously, this section is full of divergent views. There are various sorts of ethical noncognitivists. Most find their motivation in their belief that language and its social analysis tells us descriptively what is the proper attitude to take in various social situations. Others enhance this with an overlay of emotion-analysis that seeks to wed this with a powerful force in human action: emotion.

The ultimate reason that some become ethical noncognitivists is that that some people are not comfortable with a worldview that purports that there are moral facts or that reality is dualistic: either religious or Platonic in asserting an independent existence of the truth of various propositions—such as the independent existence of the good (or even the realistic grounds for such).

In order to fulfill the criteria of authenticity and sincerity as dictated by the personal worldview imperative, these individuals will look to social science to provide models of what a particular culture professes to be good.

THE ARGUMENT AGAINST THE THEORY

There are two sorts of objections to this approach to being good in the world. The first comes from the theoretical doneés of the theory itself and the second comes from outside the theory.

FROM INSIDE THE THEORY: THE FREGE-GEACH PROBLEM

Peter Geach attacked ethical noncognitivism by noting that when combining statements (that are asserted to have no truth content) into linguistic contexts, that they yield results that, in fact, do appear to have truth content.[15] In this context Geach builds upon the philosopher Gottlieb Frege's distinction between assertion and predication, or in other words, between illocutionary force and propositional content, respectively. This seems to confute the mission of the noncognitivists who want to maintain that there is no truth functional content in moral discourse. For example consider the following argument.

Argument 9–1: The Frege-Geach Problem

1. If tormenting the cat is wrong, then getting your little brother to torment the cat is also wrong — Assertion
2. Tormenting the cat is wrong — 1
3. Therefore, getting your little brother to torment the cat is wrong — 1, 2

The use of the word "wrong" is used differently in premise 1 and 3. In premise 1 the use is purely descriptive. In the conclusion it is prescriptive. Somehow, within the context of the modus ponens structure of basic logic, the word takes on a different meaning. Why is this? Has some sort of magic occurred? Perhaps the problem is with premise 2? But this follows as a direct inference from premise 1. Somehow the context has created a change. What are we to make of this? Clearly the context contains only the logical operators and quantifiers. Wittgenstein said that this left everything as it is. Was Wittgenstein wrong? A problem seems to exist for proponents of ethical noncognitivism.

Simon Blackburn created his solution to this dilemma by arguing that conditionals are not so opaque as they might first appear.[16] In practice the space between the "if" and "then" various attitudes inscrutably appear. Since noncognitivism is all about the assertion of attitudes, this conjecture might be very enlightening. Blackburn asserts that hidden operators exist in exhortation (the H! or hooray operator) or condemnation (the B! or boo operator). These added factors act as illocutionary forces to account for the change in status between premise 1 and the conclusion in Argument 9–1. At the point of premise 2, the B! factor slips in so that it is no surprise that the conclusion changes the meaning of "wrong" from descriptive to prescriptive.

Alan Gibbard has put forth another popular response to the **Frege-Geach problem.**[17] Gibbard creates a context of possible world semantics. One possible world is the factual social world with its nonfactual normative attitudes. This standpoint inserts semantics of factual-normative worlds. This group of worldviews creates ordered pairs with (w = a set of facts, n = a set of norms). The norms in the second place of the ordered pair represent forbidden, obligatory, or indifferent — a very Kantian trio (though Kant was a moral realist). In this way Gibbard hopes to solve the dilemma. Thus, when some individual considers an action, then she is faced with both the factual and the normative data at once (though separately and sequentially).

Thus using the structure of Argument 9–1, we would say that the exposition of premise 1 includes both parts of the ordered pair. If this is true, then no magic occurs after all, because the normative component occurred all alone—albeit as the second component of an ordered pair.

There are detractors to this style of solution, such as Walter Sinnot-Armstrong who contends that the acceptance of this sort of solution is tantamount to accepting moral realism—which proponents of ethical noncognitivism are loathe to do.[18] Also, Gibbard's solution (dependent as it is upon possible world contexts) moves away from the standard of locutionary, illocutionary, and perlocutionary contexts. This may thus require a redefining of the whole problem in different terms.

FROM OUTSIDE THE THEORY: PROBLEMS WITH ETHICAL RELATIVISM

A second sort of criticism to ethical noncognitivism comes from those who focus upon the antirealism feature of ethical noncognitivism. Because the noncognitivist thinkers do not believe that moral premises are factual, but merely conventional, the result is moral relativism. At the end of the day, one's careful focusing upon the language of moral discourse seems rather like an attorney looking at the law. In the philosophy of law, there are generally two standpoints: positivism and natural law. In the case of positivism the law exists as an artifact that depicts society's values. There is not really a moral *right* or *wrong* with the law. The law stands as a sort of historical record of social/linguistic usage. It is the highest authority of what is a permissible attitude and its associated action within a society.

But when society changes, then so does the law. This principle is conservative. One must have a compelling reason to change in order for change to occur. Baring this, the status quo, under the doctrine of stare decisis, will always hold unless society has moved in a different direction. In this way, positivism defends the social judgments of society at its particular point in human history. There is no hyperrealistic context by which to judge the statute itself apart from its social/historical context.

Detractors from this sort of analysis point to the necessity of people to supersede the contexts of their social/historical contexts. One such advocate is the late Australian philosopher, Alan Donagan. Donagan cites the case of Franz Jägerstätter, a pious Austrian farmer who was pressed to serve in the German Army. Jäggerstätter understood (via moral realism) what was happening during Hitler's occupation of his country:

> [W]henever rulers have declared war against other countries [he wrote in a memorandum], they usually have not broken into their lands in order to improve them or perhaps give them something. Thus, if one is fighting against the Russian people, he will also take as much out of that country as can be put to use here. If we were merely fighting Bolshevism, would other things like iron, oil wells, or good grainlands have become such important considerations?[19]

Franz Jäggerstätter saw empirical facts that showed to him that Hitler and his program were a pack of evil lies. The social/historical context that was offered to the Austrian farmer was not true. But what did he mean by this? For Jäggerstätter there were true moral facts. It was not just a question of social history and its consequent relativism. No. Hitler was wrong. Even if you could show how the analysis of moral language justified the death camps as a part of the glorification of the Third Reich's completion of its historical destiny, this would *not justify it!* This is because there are objective moral data that confute the very program itself. These data are the basis of moral realism. As Jäggerstätter himself said,

> For what purpose . . . [he asked] did God endow all men with reason and free will if, despite this, we have to render blind obedience; or if, as so many also say, the individual is not qualified to judge whether this war started by Germany is just or unjust? What purpose is served by the ability to distinguish between good and evil?[20]

So what was the consequence of this moral objection to Hitler's war when the farmer was pressed into service in the *Wehrmacht?* The Nazis beheaded him.

It is this sort of moral example that proponents of moral realism (and thus detractors of ethical noncognitivism) do appeal. The history of ethical progress depends upon pivotal figures at the low level—like farmer Franz Jägerstätter (what farmer is not an empiricist?)—or at the high level—like Martin Luther King, Jr. and Mahatma Gandhi who connect to and address moral principles that supercede the social/historical context of the times. Such examples, detractors to moral noncognitivism contend, belie the truth of the quasi-precise social science that is at the bedrock of this ethical theory.

In the end each reader must decide for herself whether the advantages of this theory outweigh the disadvantages.

KEY TERMS

- Ethical noncognitivism
- locutionary
- illocutionary
- perlocutionary
- metalanguage
- Frege-Geach problem

A CHALLENGING CASE STUDY

Directions: Write a two-and-a-half page essay (750 words) on the following case. Be sure to first set out what you believe the deontological position to be. Second, evaluate whether you agree with this solution or not based upon personal worldview or community worldview tenets. Make your reasons very explicit. Be sure to make it clear whether you are referring to locutionary, illocutionary or perlocutionary analysis in constructing your essay.

You are the head of your college's school newspaper (a biweekly). Your college is a private college that has an association with the Roman Catholic Church. In the last issue, your faculty advisor censored an article written by an openly gay student. [The Roman Catholic Church, at the writing of this edition, does not endorse a gay lifestyle.] The reason given was that the administration did not want to give a forum to these views. However, you are confused. You thought that newspapers were to address all sorts of viewpoints. Your boyfriend is an ethical noncognitivist. You are a moral realist. You must write an e-mail to your faculty advisor about this. How do you make your case? What might your boyfriend say?

NOTES

1. For a discussion of these issues concerning truth and ethics, see my book *The Good, The True, and The Beautiful* (London: Continuum, 2008), Chapters 4–5.
2. As mentioned earlier I am depending upon Gilbert Ryle's analysis here. Gilbert Ryle, *The Concept of Mind* (London: Hutchinson & Co, 1949): 11–24. This position has been echoed by others, as well.
3. Ludwig Wittgenstein, *The Blue and Brown Books: Preliminary Studies for Philosophical Investigations,* preface by Rush Rhees (Oxford, 1958).
4. This expansion, however, is controversial.
5. Ludwig Wittgenstein, *Philosophical Investigations,* ed. G. E. M. Anscombe, Rush Rhees, and G. H. von Wright,

trans. by G. E. M. Anscombe (Oxford, 1953), sec. 198.
6. This is based upon an actual case related to me by Raja Nasr of Marymount University in Arlington, Virginia.
7. This sort of vocabulary comes from Hans Reichenbach, *Elements of Symbolic Logic* (New York: Macmillan, 1947) and R. M. Hare. *The Language of Morals* (Oxford: Clarendon Press, 1952) and expanded in *Freedom and Reason* (Oxford: Oxford University Press, 1963). This sort of approach to ethics has been further developed by J. R. Searle, *Speech Acts. An Essay in the Philosophy of Language,* (London, Oxford University Press, 1969) and J. Lyons, *Linguistic Semantics. An Introduction,* (Cambridge: Cambridge University Press 1995).

8. This is a term coined by Hare (1952) and developed by John Austin, *How to Do Things With Words: The William James Lecture delivered at Harvard University, 1955,* ed. by J. O. Urmson (Oxford: Clarendon University Press, 1962).

9. Contemporary accounts of the relation of emotion to ethics include: Annette Baier, "What Emotions Are About," *Philosophical Perspectives* 4 (1990): 1–29; *Moral Prejudices: Essays on Ethics* (Cambridge: Harvard University Press, 1995); Jonathan Bennett, "The Conscience of Huckleberry Finn," *Philosophy* 49 (1974): 123–134; Simon Blackburn, *Ruling Passions* (Oxford and New York: Oxford University Press, 1998); Donald Davidson,"How is Weakness of Will Possible?" In *Essays on Actions and Events,* (Oxford: Oxford University Press, 1980); 21–43. Simone de Beauvoir, *The Second Sex,* translated and edited by H. M. Parshley (New York: Bantam, 1952); Jon Elster, *Alchemies of the Mind: Rationality and the Emotions* (Cambridge: Cambridge University Press, 1999); Sigmund Freud, *Project for a Scientific Psychology.* Vol. 1 of *Standard Edition of the Psychological Works,* ed. and trans. James Strachey (London: Hogarth Press, 1895); Allan Gibbard, *Wise Choices, Apt Feelings: A Theory of Normative Judgment* (Oxford: Oxford University Press, 1990); Patricia Greenspan, *Emotions and Reasons: an Inquiry into Emotional Justification* (New York: Routledge, Chapman and Hall, 1988); Greenspan, *Practical Guilt: Moral Dilemmas, Emotions and Social Norms* (New York: Oxford University Press, 1995); Greenspan, "Emotional Strategies and Rationality," *Ethics* 110 (2000): 469–487; William James, "What is an Emotion?" *Mind* 19 (1884): 188–204; Anthony Kenny, *Action, Emotion and Will* (London; New York: Routledge and Kegan Paul, 1963); Martha Nussbaum, *Love's Knowledge* (Oxford: Oxford University Press, 1990); Nussbaum, *The Therapy of Desire: Theory and Practice in Hellenistic Ethics* (Princeton: Princeton University Press, 1994); Nussbaum, *Upheavals of Thought: The Intelligence of Emotions* Nussbaum, (Cambridge: Cambridge University Press, 2001); Justin Oakley, *Morality and the Emotions* (London: Routledge and Kegan Paul, 1992); Jean-Paul Sartre, *The Emotions: Outline of a Theory* (New York: Philosophical Library, 1948); Robert Solomon, *The Passions: The Myth and Nature of Human Emotions* (New York: Doubleday, 1984); Bernard Williams, "Morality and the Emotions." In *Problems of the Self: Philosophical Papers 1956–1972,* (Cambridge: Cambridge University Press, 1973); 207–29. Ludwig Wittgenstein, *Philosophical Investigations,* trans. G. E. M. Anscombe (New York: Macmillan, 1953); Richard Wollheim, *On the Emotions* (New Haven: Yale University Press, 1999).

10. The two key works to be considered here are Hume's, *Treatise on Human Nature (1740)* Book 3 and his *Inquiry.* In the first work, his interest is in moral psychology while in the second he consciously adopts a stance of simplicity.

11. David Hume, *An Inquiry Concerning Human Understanding,* ed. Thomas Beauchamp (NY: Oxford University Press, 2000), Appendix 4, note.

12. For an argument for this position see Jonathan Dancy, *Ethics without Principles* (Oxford: Clarendon Press, 2004).

13. For a discussion of these issues and sources see my entry: "Thomas Jefferson," in *The Encyclopedia of Philosophy* 2nd ed. Donald M. Borchert

(Detroit: Thompson Gale/Macmillan, 2006).

14. This style of emotivism can be found in A. J. Ayer, *Language, Truth, and Logic* (NY: Dover, 1952 [1936]); C. L. Stevenson, *Ethics and Language* (New Haven, CT: Yale University Press, 1944).

15. Some of this goes back to criticisms made by J. Jørgensen, "Imperatives and Logic," in *Erkenntnis*, 7 (1937–1938): 288–296. Geach's argument can be found in Peter Geach, "Imperative and Deontic Logic," *Analysis* 18, no.3, (1958): 49–56 and "Assertion," *Philosophical Review* 74 (1964): 449–465.

16. Simon Blackburn, *Spreading the Word* (Oxford: Clarendon, 1984).

17. Alan Gibbard, *Wise Choices, Apt Feelings: A Theory of Normative Judgement* (Oxford: Clarendon Press, 1990).

18. Walter Sinnott-Armstrong, "Some Problems for Gibbard's Norm-expressivism," *Philosophical Studies* (1993): 297–313.

19. Gordon C. Zahn, *In Solitary Witness: The Life and Death of Franz Jägerstätter* (New York: Holt, Rinehart and Winston, 1964), 223. I take this example from Alan Donagan, *The Theory of Morality* (Chicago, IL: University of Chicago Press, 1977), 15–18.

20. Zahn, *In Solitary Witness,* 233.

CHAPTER

10

IT'S ABOUT FREELY MADE AGREEMENTS: ETHICAL CONTRACTARIANISM

SNAPSHOT

The ethical contractarians assert that freely made personal assent gives credence to ethical and social philosophical principles. These advocates point to the advantage of the participants being happy/contented with a given outcome. The assumption is that within a context of competing personal interests in a free and fair interchange of values, those principles that are intersubjectively agreed upon are sufficient for creating a moral "ought." The "ought" comes from the contract and extends from two people to a social group. Others universalize this, by thought experiments, to anyone entering such contracts.

THE PROBLEM THIS THEORY ADDRESSES

So often moral theories *prescribe* without taking into account the interests of those involved. **Moral contractarianism** addresses this issue on the side of each and every person (and by extension) types of people who have particular interests. The extension of interests attracts those who will do what they will within the constraints of a negotiated settlement. This standpoint emphasizes individual empowerment. None of us are forced to accept an unacceptable contract. Thus, we will all be motivated to accept the deal that is presented because in one way we are involved: (a) directly in a personal contract (such as the case in marriage or friendship), or (b) directly in a contract of commercial sorts; (c) indirectly in participation within society (if we don't like it in some situations we can leave or check out), and (d) indirectly by voting in a democracy or by promoting any local influence in an autocracy for the effects that most benefit our families.

THE ARGUMENT FOR THE THEORY

Contractarianism in the Western philosophical tradition goes back at least as far as Socrates' famous argument in the *Crito*. In Socrates' trial he was found guilty of corrupting the youth and of advocating against the gods of Athens. The sentence given was death.[1] In the *Crito* Socrates' friends are trying to convince him to make a quick exit. The standard maximum punishment in the ancient Greek world (fourth century BCE) was exile. However, Socrates had been sentenced to death. Not even his accusers really thought that it would go this far. Socrates, in turn, offers the following argument.[2]

Argument 10–1: Socrates' Contractarian Argument

1. Man ought never act unjustly—Assertion/ 49a4
2. To repay injustice with injustice is unjust—1/ b10
3. To repay injustice with injustice ought not be done—1, 2/ b10
4. [To do harm is the same thing as doing evil]—Assertion
5. To do evil is unjust—Assertion/ c2
6. To repay evil with evil is unjust—5/ c4–5
7. To repay evil with evil ought not to be done—1, 3, 6/ c10

8. [Suffering is an evil and or an injustice]—Assertion
9. Suffering does not permit us to do evil or to act unjustly—3, 7, 8/ c11
10. A man must carry out just agreements—Assertion/ e5
11. A state to survive requires that laws have force and apply in all cases—Assertion/ 50b 3
12. Individual exceptions to the laws mean that the laws do not apply in all cases—Fact/ b5
13. Individual exceptions to the laws undermine and harm the state—11, 12/ b5
14. Each individual makes an agreement with the state to abide by its judgments—Assertion/ c4
15. This agreement is a just mutual transaction with give and take—Assertion/ d–e
16. To retaliate against the state is to harm the state—Fact/ 51a
17. To retaliate against the state is to do evil to the state—4, 16
18. To do evil to the state even when the state does evil to you ought not to be done—7, 9, 17/ 51a2
19. Retaliating against the state should not be done—17, 18
20. To seek individual exceptions to the law should not be done—4, 13, 18
21. To not abide by the judgments of the state is to break a just agreement—14–15
22. Man ought not fail to abide by the judgments of the state—14, 15, 21

23. Man has an obligation to abide by the judgments of the state and not to seek individual exceptions to the law—20–22

The form of this argument refers to a contract between an individual and the state (in this case, Athens). The contract is implicit. Socrates never signed any document nor made any explicit oral contract. Instead, he remained in Athens and accepted its benefits. He knew the laws of the state and who was in charge. He was free to walk away at any time and he hadn't. Thus, under the doctrine of implicit contract (actions that seem to imply the existence of a contract even when no formal contract has been executed), Socrates felt obliged to accept the judgment of the landholding men of Athens. Thus, the first point to note is that contracts need not be explicitly written or verbal acts, but may be implicit.

There is, of course, some difficulty with implicit contracts. They assume that everyone views and accepts the conditions in the same way. This can be displayed via the following example in Case 10–1.

CASE 10–1   SNOW SHOVELING AND IMPLICIT CONTRACTS

Mary Wilson approaches her neighbors, Mr. and Mrs. Smith with the following proposition: "I will shovel your walk and driveway this winter for $5 each event." Now let's say that the Smiths don't say "no" but they don't say "yes" either. Then the first winter snow comes. It is a medium storm dropping five inches. Mary goes out and shovels the Smith's walk and driveway. As in any instance of snow shoveling, there is some considerable noise as the metal shovel scrapes against the concrete. The Smiths open their blinds and watch Mary work. Mary looks up and waves at them. When Mary is finished, she knocks on the Smith's door. They thank Mary for her work. When Mary requests payment, they demur. "We never agreed to that, Mary," they said. But they never disagreed either. ■

What do you think? Was there an implicit contract? What are the grounds of there being an implicit contract? The standard account suggests acting in such a way that at least one of the parties believes there to be a contract and that the other party (knowing this) does not dissuade the party of the first part from her belief, then an implicit contract exists. This standard is accentuated when there is consideration (money) at stake.

In some ways, the concepts of implicit contracts are easier to conceptualize between individuals (a moral problem), than they are between individuals and a social group (a social/political problem). Both of these perspectives are at stake in contractarianism. Let us address these in reverse order.

SOCIAL CONTRACTS

The **social contract** tradition in the West gained new ascendancy in the seventeenth and eighteenth centuries. Key proponents such as Hobbes and Locke frame the question within various fundamental assumptions. Hobbes frames the argument this way.[3]

Argument 10–2: Hobbes' Theory of Social Contract

Leviathan, Chapter 13
   1. People may differ in strength or in cunning—Assertion
   2. [Nature acts to equalize the net sum of natural gifts]—Assertion
   3. In net sum, people are basically equal—1, 2
   4. There is greater net equality in prudence than in strength—Assertion

5. [Prudence contemplates (based upon experience) about means and ends]—Assertion
6. [Equality in the possession of a faculty implies equality of hope to attain the functional results of utilizing that faculty]—Assertion
7. Based upon prudence there arises an equality of hope at securing ends—4–6
8. [The desirable goods (ends) in the world are limited]—Fact
9. [When more people want more of a good than the quantity of that goods allows, then some will be left out (competition)]—Fact
10. [When people lose a good to others who are equal to them, there is a sense of unfairness]—Fact
11. [Having a sense of unfairness toward another breeds enmity (diffidence)]—Assertion
12. Man's equality breeds enmity—3, 7–11
13. The only way to avoid being a victim of unfairness is to use force and bypass the system—Assertion
14. [In general man would rather gain the good via force than lose the good unfairly and become diffident]—Assertion
15. Competition and diffidence lead to the use of force (war)—11–14
16. [Glory is about gaining more goods than one needs in order to achieve the good opinion of others]—Assertion
17. Striving for glory will involve one in competition and diffidence—Assertion
18. [Striving for glory will bring about war]—15–17
19. The only way to check man's natural inclination toward war is to threaten him with a pain greater than the prize he seeks (namely, death and punishment)—Assertion
20. Only a sovereign government can create a system to meet out punishment—Assertion
21. Only a sovereign government can save man from war—15, 18–20
22. The *right of nature* (*ius naturalis*) for each man is to use his own power as he sees fit—Assertion/ Chapter 14
23. Liberty is the absence of external hindrance—Assertion
24. The *law of nature* (*lex naturalis*) is that man is forbidden to act self-destructively—Assertion
25. [That which forbids is logically contradictory to that which extends license]—Fact
26. The *right* and *law* of nature work against each other and the medium is liberty—22–25
27. [War is self-destructive to man]—Fact
28. The law of nature forbids war—24, 27
29. The first law of nature is peace—28
30. To attain peace one must give up the liberty of doing what he pleases (right of nature)—Fact

31. The second law of nature is to give up absolute liberty—29–30

32. To fail to abide by the second law of nature is to open oneself to harm—Assertion

33. Man must assent to the second law of nature—24, 29, 31, 32

34. [The second law of nature implies interpersonal reciprocity]—Assertion

35. Interpersonal reciprocity involves mutual transference of the absolute rights of nature to absolute liberty—Fact

36. To mutually transfer a right is to be involved in a social contract—Fact

37. [There must be some institution in place for social contracts to be valid]—Fact

38. Social institutions should arise to authorize the social contract that will bring about peace—21, 26, 29, 33–37

Several points should be made about Hobbes' argument. First, he constructs a neutral space that he calls the "state of nature." Perhaps because of European attitudes concerning the conquest of other lands in which the Europeans depicted themselves as *in society* while others were merely *savages living in nature*, this sort of concept arose. Nevertheless, the thought experiment of there being a state of nature captivated philosophers from the early seventeenth century through (at least) the writings of Karl Marx in the nineteenth century—and perhaps even further to thinkers like Foucault in the twentieth century.[4] This constructional space called the *state of nature* is highly influential in contractarianism because it seeks scientifically to strip away the "nurture" from the nature-nurture construct so that we might see what humans are without perturbation: human nature.

Second, the goal is peace. Third, because of resultant equality (meaning I'm good at fighting and you're good at hunting and Juan's good at conniving—all end up the same) the economic competition results (unabated) in a war. The society arises for this. Also, in a subsequent argument, the sovereignty of that society sits with the monarch (who is given and kept in check by God). Social contracts exist for society to carry on peacefully. The result is a strong state.

Another approach comes from John Locke. Locke makes his argument this way.[5]

Argument 10–3: Locke's Theory of Social Contract

1. God made man to live in society—Assertion

2. The first society was the family—Assertion

3. [The family is the model for all other societies]—Assertion

4. In the family each person has different roles for the common good—Assertion

5. [All societies should be structured so that various people and groups perform different roles/functions for the common good]—1–4

6. Man is free while he is in nature—Assertion [Chapter 8]

7. Men only consent to give up their liberty in order to enhance their comfort and safety—Assertion

8. When men give up their freedom they do so to create a community—Assertion

9. Communities arise by the consent of the members to enhance comfort and safety—6–8

10. The liberty and power given up resides in the government—Fact

11. Once in a community the government is more powerful than the private citizen—10

12. [The spokesman for the community is the voice of the majority of citizens]—Assertion

13. Once in a community, a person must bend to the will of the majority—10–11

14. People leave the state of nature voluntarily for their comfort and protection which requires them to assume social roles and to bend their will to the voice of the majority—5, 9, 11

A key point here is that first people are cooperative. The state of nature is given up for enhancement—not because there is bloody awful war. Second, there is a depiction of the agent as very free and only giving up a limited amount of natural rights. The burden of proof is upon the state to convince the sovereign (in this case the people) to relinquish any given liberty for the sake of some stated benefit. The goal is the smallest state possible.

There were certainly others in this historical period (seventeenth and eighteenth centuries) who spoke about the social contract in this way—such as Rousseau, Hume, and Kant. However, for our purposes let us transition to two contemporary figures: John Rawls and David Gauthier. The former will represent contractarianism in the social sphere while the latter frames the question more individually.

RAWLS

Rawls begins his project by seeking back to the state of nature worldview of the seventeenth and eighteenth century theorists. Instead of envisioning forests with semi-savages running around, Rawls uses a different model. He employs modern game theory to set up Thought Experiment 10–1.[6]

THOUGHT EXPERIMENT 10–1: RAWLS'S ORIGINAL POSITION

Imagine a totally random group of people within some society. These individuals are considering what rules of justice should rule any given society into which they might be thrust. This choice situation is called the **original position.** Now also imagine that the people in this group are somehow stripped of any personally reflective understanding of who they are: male/female, young/old, rich/poor, holder of talents or what they are. They are also ignorant of the situations of the society into which they have been born: rich society in the twentieth century, middle society in the nineteenth century, or poor society in the eighteenth century. This situation of selective, rational understanding is called the *veil of ignorance.* Due to the veil of ignorance, the only thing left is human nature, as such. What sort of contract (under these circumstances) would be hammered out? ■

First of all, a reader of Rawls must accustom himself to the rules of the thought experiment: (a) the original position, and (b) the veil of ignorance. If these are agreed to, then Rawls contends that the following argument occurs.

Argument 10–4: Rawls's Argument for the Two Principles of Justice

1. The veil of ignorance ensures that the arbitrariness of the would not be present in the original position — Assertion (p. 141)
2. [When arbitrariness is gone, necessary principles of common human understanding result] — Assertion
3. The veil of ignorance allows common human understanding to prevail — 1, 2 (p. 142)
4. Rational self-interest means (aside from a unique understanding of his own good) maximizing his index of social goods — Fact (p. 143)
5. Envy, altruism, and other constraints on the parties are arbitrary — Assertion (pp. 149–50)
6. Rational self-interest must be a constraint upon the parties — 2, 4, 5
7. People will not exchange liberty for economic goods — Assertion (pp. 151–52)
8. Mini/max is the correct rational choice theory — Assertion (pp. 153–154)
9. Mini/max would adopt the equal liberty principle first — 3, 6–8 (p. 160)

10. Mini/max would hold for the highest floor for the least advantaged—Assertion (p. 176)
11. Mini/max would adopt the difference principle—3, 6, 10
12. Utilitarianism is the key alternative to the two principles of justice—Assertion
13. Utilitarianism does not treat people as ends—Assertion (pp. 180–182)
14. [Morality should recognize the dignity of all]—Assertion
15. Utility is not a tenable alternative—12–14

16. Through the veil of ignorance and the assumption of rational self-interest, the two principles of justice will be adopted—3, 6, 11, 15, 9 (p. 183)

There are several key turns to this argument. The first occurs at premise 4. It asserts rational self-interest. The reason for this is not because Rawls does not believe in the possibility of altruism, but because he is seeking a baseline description of humankind that is acceptable to economists (the ones who use game theory the most).

Second, premise 7 suggests a fundamental disposition toward liberty as inalienable. This may be controversial to some, but in the United States it is a part of our civic consciousness. Is it a part of the shared community worldview of all peoples? Does this matter for the claim to be true? This is an important query because Rawls's first principle of justice sets out liberty to all as a fundamental starting point that cannot be negotiated away: "Each person is to have an equal right to the most extensive basic liberty compatible with a similar liberty for others."[7]

Third, is the use of the mini/max choice model for the game theory occurring in the original position. The first member of the ordered pair, "mini," refers to risk. The second member of the ordered pair, "maxi," refers to the reward. Mini/max is asserted to be more rational than the other combinations: mini/mini; maxi/mini; and maxi/maxi. (More on this in the section on arguments against the theory.) Using the mini/max choice model in a situation of uncertainty, Rawls contends that any human would seek an acceptable social floor. This gives rise to Rawls's second principle of justice, the difference principle, that exhorts social institutions to first consider the effects of any policy changes upon the least advantaged as a first priority (after equal liberty, of course): social and economic inequalities are to be arranged so that they are both (a) reasonably expected to be to everyone's advantage, and (b) attached to positions and offices open to all.[8]

For example, the result of the second principle would be that if the country were to consider a revision of the tax code, the lot of the least advantage would be targeted first—and *not* as a trickle-down tax break that targets the wealthiest in society first.

The result of these two principles is meant to be an extensive governmental structure that offers a comprehensive safety net of social goods to all while stridently acting to defend political liberty throughout the society. Many philosophers in the Western tradition have found Rawls's theory of social contractarianism to be very attractive.

GAUTHIER

A second influential theory that is based upon contractarianism is that of David Gauthier. For Gauthier, the principal challenge to ethics is that of the moral skeptic.[9] If Hobbes is correct that, by nature, there are natural antagonisms between parties, then social harmony can only occur when one confronts challenges via a model of cooperative commerce. One famous characterization of such an approach can be seen via the **prisoner's dilemma** (Thought Experiment 10–2).

THOUGHT EXPERIMENT 10–2: THE PRISONER'S DILEMMA

Tanya and Cinque have been arrested for robbing the Hibernia Savings Bank and have been placed in separate isolation cells. Both care much more about their personal freedom than about the welfare of their accomplice. A clever prosecutor makes the following offer to each. "You may choose to confess or remain silent. If you confess and your accomplice remains silent I will drop all charges against you and use your testimony to ensure that your accomplice does serious time. Likewise, if your accomplice confesses while you remain silent, they will go free while you do the time. If you both confess I get two convictions, but I'll see to it that you both get early parole. If you both remain silent, I'll have to settle for token sentences on firearms possession charges. If you wish to confess, you must leave a note with the jailer before my return tomorrow morning."[10] ∎

What the prisoner's dilemma means to show is that if one is socially interested in her worldview perspective, then the best result is mutual silence. However, if one is individually oriented in worldview (such as is assumed by Rawls), then the best result is for you to confess (while the other remains silent). In versions of the dilemma where one party is able to cheat the other by making her think that she will be silent when really the agent has no intention of doing so, then this disconnect between social and selfish considerations is even starker. Thus, this thought experiment has been viewed by many as a watershed to separate the distinct worldview orientations of the social versus the egoistic.

However, if both parties are trying to cheat each other, then a bad outcome is likely to result. Gauthier wishes to enter this arena in which each party can put her mutual cards on the table in order to cooperate successfully. The same mini/max strategy is employed to minimize large-scale downside outcomes. However, Gauthier adds this twist that concessions calculated by mini/max be put into a context of the bargainer's ideal outcome. He calls this **mini/max relative concession**. This procedure is in everyone's interests. Just like Hobbes, it can be agreed that situations of extreme uncertainty work to no one's advantage.

The parties in Gauthier's system operate with full knowledge (no veil of ignorance). There is only the proviso that agents garner their advantages via positive personal production and not simply at the expense of another's loss. He calls this the "Lockean proviso" (after a similar stipulation by Locke). This constraint insures that agents are not engaged in what modern businesses sometimes call "cannibalism" (creating illusions of profit activity at the expense of an internal entity). Instead, positive activity is called upon that is in accord with the rule of mini/max relative concession. The upshot of this is a constraint upon traditional unbridled capitalistic economic theory. Agents should become constrained maximizers rather remain the sort of maximizers that they would be in a state of nature. This aspect of constraint separates Gauthier from other contractarians. Most of these who emphasize the individualistic standpoint turn toward libertarianism (see the next section).

In the end, Gauthier believes that parties employing these procedures will be liberal fair-minded people who individually contract with others according to a just process and who would collectively, voluntarily contribute to a Rawlsian-style supportive state.

THE ARGUMENT AGAINST THE THEORY

There will be two sorts of arguments against contractarianism: (a) from inside the theories of Rawls and Gauthier; and (b) from outside contractarianism.

FROM INSIDE THE THEORY

Rawls is really a neo-Kantian who emphasizes the second form of the categorical imperative dealing with nonexploitation of others (see Chapter 13). Most detractors of Rawls point to his justification thought experiment: the original position. There are several areas in which the original position may be disputed. The great advantage of the original position is as a fictive thought experiment. Thought experiments are engaging because they are so rich in empirical content that they bring the reader right into a similar worldview such as a short story or poem engages. The great disadvantage of thought experiments is that because they rely so much upon indirect discourse, they may falsify the underlying assumptions of the empirical world and the human condition. In some cases, this can lead to bizarre conclusions that really have no proper application at all.[11] Detractors of Rawls often cite first that there is no proper way to apply the veil of ignorance. Knowledge is not made up of discrete parts, but rather is a web of interconnectedness.[12] Any attempt to do otherwise is so far from how human knowledge actually operates as to yield false conclusions. Thus, if the veil of ignorance depicts an imaginary and false depiction of human intelligence, then any conclusions derived from such a premise are also suspect.

Along these same lines, one might quarrel with Rawls use of the mini/max choice strategy as the only one that is rational. Two other sorts of contenders might be mini/mini and maxi/maxi. If there are plausible reasons for choosing another choice matrix, then Rawls's original position justification system is flawed and the results are unproven.

The mini/mini advocates are essentially those who believe in the simple life. The most prominent of these in the United States are the Amish. The Amish (and other social groups such as the Mennonites advocating the simple life) do not take the maximization of outcome as valued end. Instead, they would prefer to mark off a modest terrain and seek its execution. This modest terrain is so achievable that large amounts of reserves can be set aside to guard against future losses. There is no real interest in maximizing total gain. Rather, the expectation level is well below expected output. Part of the good life is limiting desire to be within this realm. The Amish would contend that theirs is a legitimate choice strategy. It is not merely to be relegated to one's pursuit of the good (a consequence of Rawls's theory at the level of application). Instead, these individuals believe that this is a legitimate worldview standpoint that would not be extinguished by the veil of ignorance.

The maxi/maxi standpoint takes the view of the gambler. This sort of individual is willing to risk all for his pursuit of a dream. Is it really correct to say that gamblers are irrational? When one takes a big risk with knowledge of the upsides and downsides, is she irrational to such an extent that such an attitude should be discarded in the original position? Many of the most influential people in history were big gamblers. In science the progressive thinkers such as Galileo, Boyle, Pasteur,

Curie, Einstein, and others put themselves on the line for their conjectures. These conjectures might be accepted—probably not. If these conjectures were accepted, then there might be a high gain. But if they were not (especially in the seventeenth century when people were still being burned at the stake for heresy), there was *very* great risk.

In business the great entrepreneurs such as Carnegie, Vanderbilt, and Rockefeller gambled mightily that their concepts might prove to be profitable. The gain would be a fortune. The risk might be starvation (there was no social welfare network at the time).

In other fields as well—be it art or technology—the great rewards are always garnered by those who gamble (and gamble big!). If the gamblers are excluded from the original position, isn't it possible that something very valuable about human nature is being left out?

These are the principal arguments that have been delivered against Rawls from a methodological standpoint. Of course, others have attacked him based upon the social safety net that would result from adoption of his standpoint. Libertarians who think that everyone should be allowed to succeed or die trying would seek a smaller governmental structure than the one that Rawls's theory would suggest.

A related objection is also delivered at Gauthier. It stems from his Lockean proviso. Why should it matter if people make "new money" or just take a part of what is already there from someone else: cannibalization? Isn't this just what laissez-faire capitalism is all about? For example, Jan Narveson contends that a contractual relationship between unfettered parties should be able to proceed without regard to needless interference.[13] A contract between willing parties should be allowed to exist. The existence of the agreement, itself, is sufficient. If Nareson is correct, then the caveat of Gauthier for the Lockean proviso will not yield a similar protection to the disadvantaged (albeit indirectly under Gauthier's schema). For libertarians, such as Nareson, there is an awful responsibility to freedom. It allows one to soar and to crash land. For those who want to interpret "contracts" as being about laissez-faire capitalism, Gauthier slides in an unacceptable caveat.

These are the principal arguments against Rawls and Gauthier from inside the theory.

FROM OUTSIDE THE THEORY

The principal argument against contractarianism outside the theory concentrates upon the mechanics of creating a contract as it relates to the foundations of normative theory. *Why* do advocates believe that consent entails propriety? I am sure that something like the following argument must support this claim.

Argument 10–5: The Argument for Contractualism

1. The foundation of human action exists at the level of the individual—Assertion
2. Individual autonomy is to be valued above all else as the basis of ethics—Assertion
3. Each individual seeks to maximize what s/he believes to be an outcome that is best for her/his prudential interests—Assertion
4. The operational way to measure what one believes to be an outcome that is best for his/her prudential interests is when s/he exhibits behavior that demonstrates this—Assertion
5. The best and most reliable behavior that demonstrates the prudential interests of any agent is his/her freely entering into a contract—Assertion
6. The existence of a contract demonstrates what willing and free agents believe to be in their prudential interests—2–5
7. The foundation of human action rests upon contracts—1, 6
8. The foundation of human action ought to be the basis of all morality—Assertion
9. The foundation of all morality is demonstrated by individuals entering into contracts—6–8

Obviously, premises 2, 6, 7, and 8 underpin the claim of the contractualist that human agreement is sufficient to yield moral obligation. But what is the basis of this? The key premise is 2: individual autonomy is to be valued above all else as the basis of ethics. Now autonomy is important. It is our fundamental expression of who we are to the world. But what if "who we are" is severely skewed? For example, take an imaginary conversation between Adolph Hitler and Adolph Eichmann (architects of the "final solution" that resulted in the murder of six million Jews). "Say Hitler, I've got this plan to solve our problems: let's kill all the Jews." Says Hitler in reply, "Sounds good to me. Bring me a plan in the morning."[14]

The point in this example is to suggest that *agreement* is not sufficient to yield normative prescriptiveness. Agreement only indicates assent among like-minded people. But if the people are all corrupt, then the result will also be corrupt (as per the example).

Though autonomy is an essential ingredient in ethics, it is not sufficient. The sole agreement of agents creates only a situation in which two people think the same thing. But what if the same thing is evil? Agreement by evil parties yields only a stronger evil.

This is the principal argument of those opposed to ethical contractarianism from outside the theory.

KEY TERMS

- moral contractarianism
- social contract
- original position
- prisoner's dilemma
- mini/max relative concession

A CHALLENGING CASE STUDY

Directions: Write a two-and-a-half page essay (750 words) on the following case. Be sure to first set out what you believe the contractarian position to be. Second, evaluate whether you agree with this solution or not based upon personal worldview or community worldview tenets. Make your reasons very explicit. Be sure to make it clear whether you are referring to issues of autonomy or the nature of the contract in structuring your essay.

You are a married woman. You recently met a man at work named John. You think John is very hot. John thinks you are hot. The problem is that you are married. John is also married, but his spouse doesn't seem to care about what he does. John is making the move on you. You have the opportunity (due to a regular after-work function that you must both attend for your job). You really want to respond positively to John's advances, so you do. Both you and John have contractually agreed on having this affair (though not in so many words). You both enjoy each other. Is this right? What would contractarianism say? Who are the various parties involved? Are there several contracts involved? How does one adjudicate this?

NOTES

1. It should be said that Socrates was offered an alternative penalty. The intent was that he would offer a real choice to begin negotiations (since he wouldn't accept exile). Instead, Socrates made a faux offer of free meals and a stipend—no punishment, but a reward. This angered his despotic accusers.

2. Plato, "Crito" in *Platonis Opera,* vol. 1, ed. John Burnet (Oxford: Clarendon Press, 1900). All translations are mine.

3. Thomas Hobbes, *Leviathan,* eds. Richard E. Flathman and David Johnston (New York: W. W. Norton & Company, 1997).

4. Some of the key tenets in social construction are discussed by Helen E.

Longino, *The Fate of Knowledge* (Princeton, NJ: Princeton University Press, 2002).

5. John Locke, *An Essay Concerning the True Original, Extent and End of Civil Government; Chapter VII Of Political or Civil Society & VIII Of the Beginning of Political Society in Social Contract,* ed. Sir Ernest Barker (Oxford: Oxford University Press, 1947).

6. John Rawls, *A Theory of Justice* (Cambridge, MA: Harvard University Press, 1971), 118–194.

7. Rawls, 60–61.

8. Rawls, 60–61.

9. David Gauthier, *Morals By Agreement* (Oxford: Oxford University Press,

1986) and Gauthier, *Moral Dealing: Contract, Ethics, and Reason* (Ithaca: Cornell University Press, 1990).

10. The prisoner's dilemma was developed by Merrill Flood and Melvin Dresher for the Rand Corporation in 1950. There are many variations on the prisoner's dilemma. The above depiction is taken from Steven Kuhn, compare Steven Kuhn and Serge Moresi, "Pure and Utilitarian Prisoner's Dilemmas," *Economics and Philosophy* 11 (1995): 123–133.

11. I call this extreme sort of case, "the thought experiment fallacy." For a discussion of this see my book, *The Good,*

The True, and The Beautiful (London: Continuum, 2008).

12. An example of an advocate of the interconnectedness conjecture is Willard Van Quine and J. S. Ullian, *The Web of Belief*, 2nd ed. (New York: Random House, 1970).

13. Jan Narveson, *The Libertarian Idea* (Philadelphia: Temple University Press, 1988).

14. The rather casual tone of this dialogue is not meant to be disrespectful to the victims of Nazi atrocity.

Chapter

11

It's All About Your Character:
Virtue Ethics

- ❖ Snapshot
- ❖ The Problem This Theory Addresses
- ❖ The Argument for the Theory
- ❖ The Argument Against the Theory
- ❖ Key Terms
- ❖ A Challenging Case Study

SNAPSHOT

Another answer to the basic questions of being good concerns character. I have talked to people around the world for thirty years about what it means to be good, and probably the most popular answer was character. In the history of western philosophy this has been characterized as "virtue ethics." Now *virtue* in the classical Greek (its origin in this tradition) refers to "excellence." Thus the Greeks thought that to be an effective person in the world one must adopt various habits and characteristics that others would deem as praiseworthy. This is the origin of this theory.

Virtue ethics is also sometimes called agent-based or character ethics. It takes the viewpoint that in living your life you should try to cultivate excellence in all that you do and all that others do. These excellences or virtues are both moral and nonmoral. Through conscious training, for example, an athlete can achieve excellence in a sport (nonmoral example). In the same way a person can achieve moral excellence, as well. The way these habits are developed and the sort of community that nurtures them are all under the umbrella of virtue ethics.

THE PROBLEM THIS THEORY ADDRESSES

Do we judge a person to be good (or not) based upon some single pivotal action? Or do we take a longer look at a person's character over time? This is the fundamental question that character ethics addresses. In the nonmoral realm this is analogous to the U.S. Baseball Hall of Fame that looks at a whole career. A Roger Maris or Mark McGuire might not necessarily be admitted based upon one fantastic season. On the flip side, one is cut a little slack if one happens on some occasion to have had an "off year." The Baseball Hall of Fame is based upon a whole career. Likewise, in every day life, virtue ethics takes the long look at one's character and is somewhat forgiving of an occasional slipup that is not in consonance with that person's historical character.

The roots of the theory go back more than twenty-three hundred years. Although it is impossible to determine just when a theory based upon character began, we can assume that it predates history. A study of the Greek and Roman classics shows a developed theory of evaluating conduct based upon the excellence of an individual's character.[1] From our modern vantage point we see various public, competitive virtues given sanction by Homer, Hesiod, and the Tragedians. Once we get to Plato, however, the emphasis is far more introspective. "All courage is not created equal" *could* have been a subtitle for the *Laches*. Plato encouraged a "rethinking" of the virtues expressed by the dramatic poets. In the *Gorgias* Plato decries the traditional sense of good and bad (*agathos* and *kakos*) as only referring to personal gain or loss. Such pivotal conclusions as, "It is better to suffer injustice than to do it" serve to create another sense of good that is *other* directed as well as the traditional self-directed imperatives.

Aristotle extends this discussion in the systematic manner that characterizes his philosophy. In the *Nichomachean Ethics* and in the *Eudemian Ethics* he creates a model often called the **Aristotelian mean** between two extremes. Aristotle creates a model that I will describe shortly based upon achieving a mean between two extremes. Virtues are categorized in the context of what constitutes a "good person."

Aquinas took Aristotle's model and adapted it to a Christian perspective, adding a group of theological virtues to complement the moral virtues enunciated by Aristotle.

To some extent virtue ethics took a back seat in the beginning of the twentieth century, as various other moral theories seemed to fit the meta-ethical emphasis of the times.

In 1958 Elizabeth Anscombe's essay, "Modern Moral Philosophy" provided a harsh attack on post-Kantian rationalism and the way ethics was carried out in our universities. This was because ethics had strayed from the sources of normativity and ethical obligation. Anscombe would have us engage in a normative moral psychology that would determine what it would mean to be a flourishing person. The virtues would be the paths toward this flourishing.

Twenty years or so later Alasdair MacIntyre again renewed interest in virtue ethics in his book *After Virtue.* More recently there have been a number of articles on particular virtues and agent-oriented theories (as opposed to act-oriented theories). Some of these studies have created new forms of virtue ethics, like that of Michael Slote.

THE ARGUMENT FOR THE THEORY

CLASSICAL ACCOUNTS OF VIRTUE ETHICS

ARISTOTLE AND THE TELOS OF HUMANS

"Every art and every methodological investigation and every action seems to aim at some good, for this reason the good is rightly said to be that to which all things aim."[2] This famous sentence begins Aristotle's *Nichomachean Ethics.* If we think about this sentence for a moment we can get a sense of what Aristotle is talking about here. There are at least two ways to read this sentence:

Argument 11–1: Aristotle's Account of Action and Goodness

1. All deliberative/methodological actions are about something—Fact
2. [Any action which is about something is purposive]—Fact
3. All deliberative/methodological actions are purposive—1, 2
4. [Purposive actions are about their purpose]—Fact
5. [A purpose is an end]—Fact
6. Purposive actions and deliberative/methodological actions are about an end—3–5
7. ["To aim" is to exhibit a purpose]—Fact
8. "To aim" is about an end—6, 7
9. ["To aim" characterizes all deliberative/methodological actions]—Assertion
10. All deliberative/methodological actions are about an end—8, 9

11. All ends are good—Assertion

12. ["Good" means either: a. "Satisfaction of" (a functional concept), or b. "Approval of" (a normative concept)]—Assertion

13. ["Good" in this context means "Approval of"]—Assertion

14. All deliberative/methodological actions are about normative goodness—10–13

The most controversial premise is premise 13. "Good" here could either be a functional or a normative concept. Thus, the two ways to read Aristotle's sentence are as (1) a factual statement about the function of a human being and any purpose or aim;[3] or as (2) a normative statement about what humans ought to aspire. Traditionally, Aristotle is taken as assuming the normative—but by what reason? One of the problems is language. The Classical Greek word for "virtue" is *arête*—or excellence. This word, for Homer and many of the pre-Socratics, has a distinctly competitive and self-directed meaning: "I win if I can get what I want—even if that means taking from you what you have or want" (remember Paris and Helen!). "Excellence" in this context is functional egoism. Plato confronted this paradigm directly. He made frontal attacks against this position in *Republic I.* He sets out five refutations against Thrasymachus (a proponent of the position), who asserted, "Justice is the rule of the strongest." Again, Plato counters the position through the characters of Callicles and Gorgias in the *Gorgias* by supporting conclusions, which would be counterintuitive to the egoist (such as "it is better to suffer injustice than to do it"). In fact, Plato resorts to the *Iliad* and *Odyssey* to make his point about an equivocation in the terms, *agathos/kalos* and *kakos/aischron.*[4] The former pair is often translated as "good" and "noble" (while the latter pair is often translated as "bad" and "despicable"). Notice that the first member of this ordered pair displays the ambiguity mentioned in Aristotle's first sentence of the *Nicomachean Ethics.* "Good" can mean "good for me," namely, "lots of things and lots of sensualities." However, "noble" has a normative commending function built into the term that is more inclusive than mere self-interest. Since it is normative, we must commend it over ignoble "goods" which may benefit us but are not to be commended on the "nobility" scale.

Plato tries to have his narrator, Socrates, create a synonymy between "good" as functional and "good" as normative (with the latter being accepted as the primary meaning of the word and the former being subject to "shamefulness").[5] Thus a "good" which is beneficial to the agent but offends the *kalon/aischron* standard is shameful. No one wants to be shameful; therefore, only the sense of good that is noble is to be accepted in cases in which there is a conflict.

This is what a person of character would do.

Back to Aristotle. If we assume that Aristotle, as Plato's student, would be somewhat influenced by the work of his teacher, then it is plausible that the sense of "excellence" meaning "approve of" (as a normative concept) is the one intended. This still leaves open the question of whether Aristotle may properly argue for this position.

What is clear about the opening sentence of the *Nicomachean Ethics* is that "good" is defined in terms of an end. Morality is seen not as something to be done simply because it is right, per se, but because it contributes to the most choiceworthy of lives. This good is set in terms of the definition of humans as a species, "rational animal." Aristotle begins the *Metaphysics* by saying, "All humans, by nature, desire to know" (980b 20). This knowledge is of three sorts: theoretical, practical or productive. Ethics and politics are examples of practical reason *(phronesis)*. Ethics is about character and is often linked with politics as representing practical knowledge.[6]

Common opinion[7] dictates that what is most choiceworthy in life is *eudaimonia*. This word is tricky to translate. Often it has been translated as "pleasure" though this creates confusion with *hedone* (a more apt term for the English word, "pleasure"). *Eudaimonia* is different from pleasure because it suggests a permanent sense of serenity. The word, as used by Aristotle, also requires activity. For this reason a better translation would be "well-being" or "contentedness." This obviously gives a different twist to things. If the end of life were active pleasure, then we might act in one way. However, if the end of life were contentedness, then we might act differently. The contended person is more sanguine than the rash pleasure seeker. She is looking for some "compromise" between overly extreme expressions.

THOUGHT EXPERIMENT 11-1: WHAT MAKES A PERSON EXCELLENT

You are a college senior. You have a choice of taking a job at a private secondary school (that does not require teacher certification) for $47,000 a year (upside 80,000 at twenty years) or taking a job at your dad's brokerage firm for $65,000 a year (upside $1,000,000 a year in five years). You love teaching. You hate business people like your father. But the pay is nice. What do you do? ∎

You need to assess the various senses of "excellence." Which among the excellences in the thought experiment captivate you more? Is it money (thus making your job some sort of mask that you put on for another purpose) or is it intrinsic job satisfaction (thus making your job a part of your own quest for wholeness). This is not an easy choice.

THE ARISTOTELIAN VIRTUES

One way to understand the "compromise" between the extremes of various avenues to the good life is to consider some examples in striving for excellence. Consider the following chart:

Aristotelian Virtues[8]

Defect of Deficiency	Median = Virtue	Defect of Excess
Cowardice	Courage	Foolhardiness
[Asceticism]	Self-control	Overindulgence
Stinginess	Magnanimity	Spendthrift
No emotion	Proper emotion	Too argumentative
Obsequiousness	Friendliness	Flatterer
Silent malice	Righteous indignance	Obsession with vengeance

As the chart illustrates, Aristotle advocates that excellence is not an "overachieving" *(huparchein)*.[9] Rather, it is a considered balance among possible alternatives. This does not mean that whenever one is confronted with two extremes that one should always choose the middle course. This is false. There is no proper median between "torturer" and "murderer." We know this because "good" is not merely a functional term. If it were, then we could create a balance between anything and that would be "good."

Instead, we have a situation in that "appropriate" might well take the place of "median." In some situations it may be appropriate to be very angry and/or violent. Take the example of witnessing a person being robbed/beaten/raped. The appropriate response of a person of virtue would be to be outraged and for her/him to react with decisive measures.

For Aristotle, the question of something being "appropriate" may beg the question. How does one consider what is or what is not appropriate? The answer comes back to what people consider. Their common opinions rule the day. But what if the common opinion is skewed? This may be a potential problem.

Arête, then, is about achieving excellence within a particular functional task *(ergon)*. Possessing the functional skills to the appropriate degree confers excellence (virtue). If one, in turn, possesses a requisite number of excellent traits, then one is judged as a "good" person *(agathos)*.[10] This process can be represented as follows:

On Becoming *Agathos* and *Eudaimon*

> **Step One:** Master the functional requirements within a given type of task/behavior.
>
> **Step Two:** Possess habitual mastery of the functional requirements to an appropriate degree.
>
> **Step Three:** Steps 1 and 2 ⇒ excellence in that task/behavior.
>
> **Step Four:** Possess habitual excellence in a number of key tasks/behaviors.
>
> **Step Five:** Possess habitual excellence in those tasks/behaviors that the common opinion judges to be the most choiceworthy.
>
> **Step Six:** Steps 4 and 5 ⇒ *agathos* (good)
>
> **Step Seven:** Possessing *agathos* (good) ⇒ *eudaimon* (happy/contented)

This process illustrates why people wish to be excellent. Excellence is a necessary precondition to becoming *agathos* and *eudaimon.* Since everyone wishes to be *agathos* and *eudaimon,* it is necessary that people wish to be excellent. Being excellent is a *means* to achieving the ultimate contentment of life, *eudaimonia.* Only *eudaimonia is* prized for its own sake—everything else is merely a means to becoming ultimately content.[11]

Another dimension in the process are **habits of character**. This is an important component to Aristotle's theory.[12] It is not enough to do a single "great action." Those who are known for one single action are not excellent. Likewise those who can no longer perform excellently are not longer *eudaimon.* To say something is a habit means that: (1) One possesses mastery of the functional requirements of a task/behavior to an appropriate degree, in such a way that it has become imbedded upon one's character, (2) The imprinting upon the character takes time (years), (3) One is still demonstrating her excellence in the task/behavior.

Several consequences follow from this account. First, acquiring a habit takes time. The process of imbedding an acquired behavioral response is long term. Thus, young people cannot be excellent. They can be "on the way to becoming excellent," but they cannot *be* excellent. In an "action oriented/youth oriented" society (such as twentieth-century Occidental culture), this is rather jarring.[13] We worship youth and quick decisive action. For Aristotle it was different.

Second, one must continue to demonstrate her excellence. If one were no longer capable of performing the key task/behavior, then she would no longer be excellent. Take, for example a U.S. Supreme Court judge. She must have established herself over time to be considered excellent, but if she loses her ability to habitually do all the tasks of an excellent judge, then she will lose her excellence and the *eudaimonia* that being an excellent judge confers.

Obviously, one does not lose her excellence "all at once." Just as it takes time to *become* excellent, so it takes time to lose it. The implication of this is that we should judge the good person on her habitual behavior over a given period and not upon a single action (good or bad).

It is assumed that good personal character will exhibit good acts. This is because action is the result of deliberation, and deliberation about action (practical wisdom or *phronesis*) is encompassing of the whole person, that is, all your excellence traits and defects.

The whole person is part of the mechanism of practical wisdom such that if the mechanism is excellent the output of the mechanism will be sound (for the most part).[14] Thus, on balance, excellent traits in human character will generally produce excellent actions.

The problem for any human is to take stock of those virtues that he believes to be most choiceworthy and to work toward integrating them into his character. In this way a person "actualizes" himself.

ACTUALIZATION

"**Actualization**" means achieving the *telos* of personhood. As we said this is acting according to right reason.[15] The sort of reason which concerns itself with action is practical reason, *phronesis.* The achievement of the end confers *eudaimonia,* contentedness.

One can picture this journey as a move from potentiality to actuality as pictured in Figure 11.1.

Initially (as children, state 0) we are not wise in practical affairs. At that time we are at the left side of the chart. Though no one is *pure potentiality,* we all start somewhere on the left. Over time we acquire facility in more key tasks/behaviors until we are said to reach a requisite amount to count as an adult person (actuality-1, x on the chart).[16] It is at this point that the individual may set his sights upon self-improvement (in the direction of actuality-2, + on the chart). Actuality-2 is perhaps a limit that we may never achieve, however; it stands to give us direction in becoming "better" and thereby more contented in life.

Those who backslide because of bad or stupid choices, may regress away from actuality-1 and earn the epithet "bestial" or "brutish" as a result.

FIGURE 11.1   The Continuum of Actuality

0	x	+
potentiality	actuality-1	actuality-2

Thus, Aristotle's theory of ethics is tied into an a conception of human self-fulfillment in which self-respect and well-being are the result of creating a character that is excellent in those tasks/behaviors which common opinion judges to be choiceworthy along with personal realizations of objects of contemplation and study which, though outside of ethics per se, still can contribute to *eudaimonia* and the good life.

There are other compelling versions of virtue ethics, as well. The most influential of these is that of Thomas Aquinas who adds God's supreme goodness into the mix. We can thus amend Aristotle's argument as follows:

Argument 11–2: Aristotle's Argument as Amended by Aquinas

1. All deliberative/methodological actions are about something—Fact
2. Any action which is about something is purposive—Fact
3. All deliberative/methodological actions are purposive—1, 2
4. Purposive actions are about their purpose—Fact
5. A purpose is an end: either actuality-2 or a means to actuality-2—Fact
6. Purposive actions and deliberative/methodological actions are about either actuality-2 or a means to actuality-2—3–5
7. "To aim" is to exhibit a purpose—Fact
8. "To aim" is about either actuality-2 or a means to actuality-2—6, 7
9. "To aim" characterizes all deliberative/methodological actions—Assertion
10. All deliberative/methodological actions are about either actuality-2 or a means to actuality-2—8, 9
11. Actuality-2 is God—Assertion[17]
12. God is the epitome of normative good—Assertion
13. All deliberative/methodological actions aim at being closer to God—10–13

The import of this identification upon Aristotle's theory is enormous. If one accepts that actuality-2 is God,[18] then every act action and methodological inquiry is, in fact, about achieving the highest good, which is God. Distantly, the functional-normative problem vanishes. God is normatively good. Therefore, all right thinking about action is directed toward God.

This leads Thomas Aquinas to create a distinction between *types* of virtues (according to his Christian orientation).[19] There are the "philosophical virtues"[20] which are condensed by Aquinas as prudence, justice, temperance, and courage.[21] The philosophical virtues are supplemented by the "theological virtues": faith, hope, and charity.[22]

The second critical move that Aquinas makes concerns the question of a moral dilemma. Unlike a difficult moral decision (in which the decision can be known, but is difficult to employ), a moral dilemma means that if agent x does nothing wrong, then it might be possible that she is put into a situation in which she must commit an immoral action: 1. You must choose A or B. 2. Both A and B are immoral. Therefore, 3. You are doomed to act immorally. Any ethical system that aspires to being able to generate absolute moral commands, must account in some way for its own consistency. For clarity let us define moral consistency in Thought Experiment 11–2.

THOUGHT EXPERIMENT 11–2: MORAL INCONSISTENCY

A moral system is inconsistent only if it allows the possibility that, without any wrongdoing on her part, a person may find herself in a situation in which she can only escape doing one wrong by doing another.[23] ∎

St. Gregory was one of the first church fathers to write on moral consistency. His writings affected St. Thomas (and later writers) on this issue. St. Gregory cites three possible cases of moral inconsistency:[24] (1) secrecy, (2) obedience after having made an improper promise, (3) obtaining a cure of a disease incorrectly by a curate through simony. The curate must either abandon the needs of his parish or employ a wrongful authority.[25]

Or take these famous examples in Thought Experiment 11–3.

THOUGHT EXPERIMENT 11–3: MORAL PERPLEXITY

ALPHA:

Al has made a promise to Murder Incorporated to kill Professor B, who has given a low grade to one of the chief's favorite children. Al suddenly has a change of heart. But he has already made a promise. It seems Al can only escape one wrong by doing another.

BETA:

Jill must choose between telling the truth to the villainous man who wants to kill

Jackie, a materially innocent human agent. If Jill tells the truth about Jackie's whereabouts, Jackie will be murdered. It seems Jill can only escape one wrong by doing another. ■

These types of examples are said to illustrate **moral perplexity**. As a result of this perplexity any ethical system may be doomed to inconsistency. Aristotle's, Aquinas's, or any other system found to be inconsistent must be discarded as fatally flawed.

Aquinas begins his analysis of perplexity with an important distinction made:[26] moral perplexity can either arise *simpliciter* or *secundum quid*. Perplexity *simpliciter* is properly what Thought Experiment 11–2 describes. Perplexity *secundum quid* causes no difficulty to a moral system because it is a perplexity that follows from some illegitimate action previously committed. There is no logical inconsistency. This is roughly analogous to the maxim of logic that states that anything follows from a falsehood.

Thus the examples of St. Gregory and of case alpha are cleared up. In the first and second cases of St. Gregory, as well as in alpha, the previous wrong action was an antecedent promise that should not have been made. These promises have consequences that place the agents into their quandaries. St. Gregory's third example involves a curate wrongfully selling indulgences. As with the other cases, this improper, previous action has created subsequent dilemmas for the agent. Thus we have cases of perplexity *secundum quid*.

Case beta requires that we elucidate a further sense of *secundum quid*. Not only does the agent's previous wrongdoing skew the normal assessment of outcome, but it is also possible that other agents, by their actions, materially alter the situation. In this case the natural order does not obtain, but rather an unnatural order: the result of someone in a position of power creating an unnatural context. Any perplexity that results follows from the unnatural context. It would be roughly analogous in logic to someone randomly creating an unusual restriction on some operator, and then generating peculiar or inconsistent results. In beta we have a case of truth telling. Telling the truth means "Freely describing a state of affairs with the intent of properly informing an audience." This definition has three parts. The action is: (1) freely made, (2) factually true, and (3) intended to correctly inform an audience.

Obviously, in beta the first condition is violated. The villainous man creates an unnatural state of affairs. He is threatening the life of Jackie so that Jill is not in a position to act freely. She is being coerced on behalf of Jackie. The conditions for a promise thus do not exist and Jill may say anything she wants to protect Jackie. The perplexity is not *simpliciter* but *secundum quid*. The moral system is not endangered.

Most purported examples of perplexity are really cases like beta, in which we really have perplexity *secundum quid* following from an unnatural context.

Only cases of perplexity *simpliciter* would cause a moral system to be inconsistent. Since the cases just examined are really cases of perplexity *secundum quid,* they do not tell against Aristotle's or Aquinas's system (or any other similar, natural law system).

But this does *not positively* prove anything. Examining a few confirming cases does not convey confirmation (in the way that a single negative case *might* convey falsification).[27] This exercise in confirmation shares these structural problems with almost any theoretical system (as the history of post–World War II philosophy of science has shown). A further discussion of this issue will be continued in the chapter on deontology as the problem of perplexity is viewed from the context of deductive systems.

A final component of virtue ethics concerns the nature of community. Since the accepted standards of what constitutes a virtue is community based, it is essential to note that virtue ethics is an other-regarding theory of ethics. Thus, the community fixes the *meaning* of virtue or character that others within that community come to accept as being the criteria for being a good person. The individual cannot acquire or lose this appellation all at once. A good action is one that a person of character and integrity would commit. What does that mean? Find those that everyone admires and find out what they do. Take notes and do likewise.

THE ARGUMENT AGAINST THE THEORY

THE PROBLEM OF JUSTIFICATION

Critics will point to the fact that Aristotle and other advocates of virtue ethics do not engage in the kind of justificatory gymnastics that have been the focus of much of post-Kantian ethics. Why are the principles of virtue ethics accepted? This has been an increasingly important question—especially in this century among philosophers.

Virtue ethics relies upon common opinion. But this, in turn, is really intuitionism—at least level one. Therefore, the objections raised against intuitionism would be apropos here.

Further, along the same lines, is the objection that the specific virtues are too broad. Because of this they are not action guiding. The exact specification of what counts as courage, self-control, wisdom, and justice are basically worthless for guiding action.

Certainly, most people have *some* idea what excellence in these traits means, but the "devil is in the details." The way we specify these virtues can make all the difference. Unfortunately this theory does not specify *how* we are to make the fine distinctions that are crucial to any operating theory.

REPLY

It is precisely virtue ethics' strength (and, therefore, perhaps its weakness) that it does not focus so much on justification in the narrow sense of how some particular proposition should be defended. Rather virtue ethics appeals to the level of "lived experience." Who would deny that "courage," "self-control," "justice," and "practical wisdom" are virtues? *All* societies agree on this. If there are differences in the fine points of just what counts for these, then so be it. On balance all people agree with the essentials of the virtues because they objectively describe the human condition.

If we consider worldview and the personal worldview imperative in the context of justification here, then we might emphasize those factors that allow us, empirically, to integrate virtue ethics into our lives. These might include our survey of the common opinion and how it resonates into the life we intend to create. Virtue ethics can do very well here if our worldview is consonant with others with whom we live. In this case our own sense of right and wrong is harmonious with what others believe to be the case.

However, if we are a minority within a society, then it is very possible that our sensibilities will not be adequately represented or respected in the larger society. In this case, the personal worldview imperative would dictate to us to reject the mainstream culture and adopt some sort of countercultural idiom.

THE PROBLEM OF ACTION DIRECTIVES

Some would contend that virtue ethics does not give specific determination on what action should be performed. Virtue ethics emphasizes the development of *character,* but character is only remotely related to action. The proximate relationship might be the description of the action involved along with some covering rule(s) that are action guiding and which might prescribe a particular course. If the central problem in ethics is to answer questions such as: "How should I act in this particular situation?" or "Is an action of this description *right* or *wrong*?" then virtue ethics is lacking since it does not speak directly to these questions. To focus upon character instead of action is to remove ethics away from its proper focus and to fail in its basic mission.

REPLY

The central problem in ethics is *not* about whether some particular action is right or wrong, but rather how good people should act, in general. The question must be phrased in such generality, or else it will not be suffi-cient to cover societies everywhere. Since actions flow from character, it is unfair to say that virtue ethics ignores action. That it doesn't address action directly speaks to the fact that the most important element to liv-ing a good life is the character of the agents—and not simply the expres-sion of what the agents do. Begin with the agent and the rest will follow.

THE PROBLEM OF THE FUNCTIONAL AND THE NORMATIVE SENSES OF "GOOD"

This objection has already been discussed. However, the solutions pro-vided earlier may not be acceptable. If people do *not* understand courage as a normative virtue but merely as a cultural construct (sub-ject to much abuse, e.g., excessive militarism), then the advocates of virtue ethics are in trouble. If what we admire are not culturally and his-torically invariant, but rather speak to the spirit of various ages—and geographies, then virtue ethics cannot generate a normative good.

Further, Aquinas's solution is not sufficient for an atheist—or even for a theist who holds a different understanding of God, for example, Manichean Zoroastrians who hold that God is both good and evil.

REPLY

Here is an instance of immediate grasping. Certainly we could do a survey of all peoples and question them about the traits of character that they admire or value. This would be an exercise in empirical social science. But such a survey would only beg the question of whether the valued traits were valued *because* they were functionally prudent or because they simply "good." This latter sense is an immediate grasping. As such there is no available argument to those who don't similarly grasp that truth.

THE PROBLEM OF SELF AND OTHER REGARDING

The main thrust of the objection is that virtue ethics by its very description is about an individual regarding himself such that he develops a series of excellent traits of character—many of which (possibly all?) are excellent traits which the world regards functionally and rewards in its own way.

If morality *does* require that the agent be balanced, then how can virtue ethics accomplish this outcome? Without such a guarantee, it is unclear how virtue ethics is any different from Nietzsche's "noble nature" or from any theory of ethical egoism.

REPLY

The content of many of the virtues are other regarding already. Take "magnanimity," "courage," "friendliness," and "righteous indignance" from the Aristotelian virtues. All of these terms have at least one other individual built into them. You cannot understand these words without other people. Further, the attitude they express *toward* those other people is very positive and symmetrically directed toward interacting equally with them.

THE PROBLEM OF LIBERALISM AND HUMAN RIGHTS

Liberalism as a theory asserts that individual autonomy is quite important and the political liberties that individuals enjoy ought to maximized to the highest degree compatible with other people's expression of their liberties, too. The U.S. Bill of Rights is one example of a political document that asserts principles of liberalism. The U.S. Declaration of Independence is another example of a document that employs an argument of liberalism to support its overall conclusions.

One tenet that is often brought forward to support a theory of liberalism is that of human rights. These theories (generally deontological, Chapter 13) have a complicated structure of their own. However, for now suffice it to say that the emphasis upon individual freedom and various rights to well-being are important. Some would say that virtue ethics does little to ensure their continued existence. In fact it could be argued that virtue ethics promotes a community orientation that works in the opposite direction of the expression and protection of individual liberties and rights.

REPLY

From above we know that community is indeed an end result of virtue ethics. But why must this imply the loss of individual liberties and rights? Remember, the community is the result of individual friendships among interdependent groups. If friendships are built upon the highest principles, they will not be exploitative. To the contrary, they will seek the other's actualization and happiness along with their own.

What better type of community to exist in? Does this seem like a community in which oppression and totalitarian governments will flourish?

THE PROBLEM OF DIVERSITY WITHIN SOCIETY

Any community that has at its center a common, shared value structure will be or become homogeneous. The community that is built up from individual, interdependent friendships will be one based upon common shared values. Virtue ethics encourages just such communities, therefore virtue ethics encourages homogeneous communities.

The problem with homogeneous communities is that (a) they do not nurture diversity, and (b) they discourage conflict in favor of unity and harmony.

Diversity is a per se good in biological evolution. Many feel the same way about its sociological value as well. Even if it is not a value, it is a fact. Since it is a fact, one must approach it in some way. If we are encouraging homogeneous states, it is probable that those who are different will be discriminated against. Such discrimination is a per se evil. Thus, virtue ethics leads to a per se evil.

Homogeneous communities also discourage conflict in favor of unity and harmony. Plato and Aristotle (perhaps because of the chaos of factionalism in Athens during the Peloponnesian War) favored harmony over discord.

In one way all of us would favor harmony over discord. However, if we are creating a state we must be sure to protect the minority's ability to protest and petition their government. If we do not, we create a totalitarian state. If virtue ethics creates a homogeneous community and a homogeneous community squelches discord and squelching discord creates a totalitarian state, then virtue ethics can lead to totalitarianism.

REPLY

The objector overstates the force of conformity within the community formed by virtue ethics. There will really be a certain amount of diversity because diversity is a fact. Totalitarianism will not result because that assumes an attitude of greed and taking more than one's due *(huperarchein)*. This would be an extreme on the table of virtues; therefore, it would not be in the character of the virtuous person.

The objection only has force if we forget that the rulers of the virtue-ethics-oriented state are, themselves, virtuous.

THE PROBLEM OF THE ANALOGY OF THE UNITY OF SOUL WITH THE PARTS OF THE POLIS

Both Plato and Aristotle employed an analogy between harmony of the soul's parts and harmony among the types of people in the state. This is obviously a contingent relation at best. As such the theory that results is likewise flawed.

REPLY

It is true that the relationship between aspects of the soul and between types of groups within the state is contingent. The sort of harmony that can result within the former as it actualizes toward *eudaimonia* may be different from the harmony among groups within the state. However, this is a trivial objection because this is not used in the derivation of virtue ethics but only in the exposition of possible favorable consequences. Even if we concede this point, it does not alter the principal reasons supporting virtue ethics. All it does is eliminate one advantage of the theory.

CONFLICTS BETWEEN THE VIRTUES

If the virtue ethics advocate discards the harmony theory, there are difficulties (which may exist even if harmony among the virtues is granted). This objection obtains when two different virtues dictate two different types of actions. For example, what happens when a parent sees his/her child about to make a mistake that will cause the child some harm? One virtue might dictate that the parent save the child from any harm and thus advocate action to save the child. Another virtue might dictate that a child must learn through making bad choices that have consequences. This virtue advocates inaction. The agent thus has imperatives both to act and not to act (p and non-p). This is a logical contradiction. Any theory that creates contradictions is inconsistent and we should reject logically inconsistent theories such as virtue ethics.

REPLY

This problem is similar to the one raised earlier on moral perplexity. In that discussion Aquinas contended that moral perplexity does not arise in cases of virtue ethics. In that instance he was examining a dilemma situation in which an agent is forced to do wrong, having committed no prior evil acts.

This case is different because the issue is not between two bad actions, but between two different "solutions" to the problem. The virtue ethics practitioner must again rely upon intuitionism. This time it is level-two intuitionism dealing with the application of particular maxims to specific cases. By employing intuitionism in both recognition and application, the practitioner can decide which maxim is the most appropriate for this particular situation. Many of my students find this a particularly attractive feature of utilitarianism. Because of its more nuanced approach there is more flexibility than the rigid "decision-based" theories of utilitarianism and deontology. For these students the complexity of life demands more. They also like the greater conceptual space that Aristotle allows because it presents a more rounded model of the human decision maker, with all her resources—including emotions.[28]

In the end each reader must decide for herself whether the advantages of this theory outweigh the disadvantages.

KEY TERMS

- virtue ethics
- Aristotelian mean
- habits of character
- actualization
- moral perplexity

A CHALLENGING CASE STUDY

Directions: Write a two-and-a-half page essay (750 words) on the following case. Be sure to first set out what you believe the virtue ethics position to be. Second, evaluate whether you agree with this solution or not based upon personal worldview or community worldview tenets. Make your reasons very explicit. Be sure to highlight which virtues you think are at stake and why one will trump the other.

Case: You are a sales manager in an insurance company. One of your employees, Sally Boyd, wrote a life insurance contract on a career office worker, Shin Lee. Shin was suffering from carpal tunnel syndrome so Sally signed the application for him in his name. This is contrary to company policy. If the underwriters had known of Shin's condition, they may have asked for further underwriting information in order to determine whether Shin was an acceptable risk. In fact, Shin had an associated condition (unknown to him at the time) that later required treatment and as a result, went badly. The treatment for this condition was such that Shin was hospitalized, and after his operation sepsis set in and killed him. The life insurance money would help his family (otherwise destitute), but there is the issue of possible fraud on the part of Sally. The company decided to pay the claim, but has issued a request for an investigation that now stares you in the face. Sally has worked for the company for twenty years and has never had a complaint before. But now her decision to sign an application for someone else so that it didn't arouse suspicion has perhaps cost the company $50,000 (the face value of the life policy). What do you do? Turn Sally over to the police (fraud *is* a crime)? Fire Sally? Admonish Sally so that it makes an impact on her salary? Give Sally a slap on the wrist? Ignore the whole thing? Base your response upon virtue ethics.

NOTES

1. Writers who have documented the nuances of this process are E. R. Dodds, *The Greeks and the Irrational* (Berkeley: University of California Press, 1951); A. W. H. Adkins, *Merit and Responsibility* (Oxford: Blackwells, 1959; repr. Chicago: Midway, 1974); G. M. Calhoun, *The Growth of Criminal Law in Ancient Greece* (Berkeley: University of California Press, 1927); M. P. Nilson, *Geschichte der griechishen Religion, Handbuch der Altertumswissehschaft* (Munich, 1941). The questions here involve the transition of virtues that are attributed to (a) militarism, and (b) aggressive commerce as opposed to the so-called classical virtues of Wisdom, Temperance and Courage. In other terms, the transition from the competitive to the cooperative virtues.

2. *Ethica Nicomachea*, 1094a 1–4. Translation is my own from Ross's Greek text.

3. The reason this point is important is that if we accepted "good" only in a functional sense, then we would have to call a bank robber "good" if she performed all the duties of a bank robber, i.e., stole lots of cash, created the most effective amount of mayhem and terror, etc., and never got caught. Other grizzly examples of the "good" mass murderer, or the "good" instigator of genocide, illustrate that this sense of good alone would be totally unacceptable for ethics.

4. The power of this use reference to Hector is that Homer is a classic case of the confusion between the competitive, egoistic virtues and the emerging

dignity affirming quiet virtues. See note 1.

5. The situation in which functional good could become shameful would be when one is successful at a particular task to a high degree (therefore functionally good) and because of the manner or the way this task was "executed" the task became shameful. An example would be Achilles who performed his task of killing Hector in an excellent fashion, however; because Achilles paraded his feat by dragging Hector around Troy, his functional excellence was polluted with "shamefulness."

6. Whether ethics is a separate science from politics is a disputed question for scholars of Aristotle. Let it suffice for this context to point to *Posterior Analytics* 89b 9; *Politics* 1261a 31 etc. in which *ethike* is referred to as the discussion of character. Thus, character is primary in analyzing how a person acts in achieving the good.

7. For Aristotle the *endoxa* or "common opinion" was the measure of whether something was considered to be "good." What do we make of such appeals to "common opinion"? Some (like Plato) might contend that common opinion was the verdict of the lowest common denominator (the hoi polloi—in modern terms, the "television crowd"). What do *they* know about what is good, true, or beautiful? Aristotle is somewhat ambivalent on this issue, but I believe that, on balance, he is more of a democrat and therefore believed that the *endoxa* was important—though *whose* opinion was to be polled was another issue. See also Chapter 12 on *Utilitarianism*.

8. This list is only a sample and is not complete. For Aristotle's discussion of the virtues see *Nicomachean Ethics* III.6–V.11.

9. Aristotle's doctrine is not without controversy. In his day, as well as in ours,

there were those who believe that to be extreme in one's pursuit of excellence is the best model of virtue. In 1964 Barry Goldwater said in his acceptance speech to the Republican National Convention that extremism in the defense of liberty is no vice, and that moderatism in the pursuit of justice is no virtue. This is a totally anti-Aristotelian sentiment. Aristotle thought that moderation and not extremism was the path to virtue.

10. The word *agathos* here is the word of highest commendation possible. It is whatever everyone (the common opinion) thinks the most desirable person is. Obviously, the functional versus normative issues raised earlier are present here, as well.

11. *Nicomachean Ethics* 1095a, 14–20.

12. *Nicomachean Ethics* 1103a, 17–25.

13. In the West today we like to judge people by some single act of "greatness" such as a great athletic achievement, or a great artistic achievement, or a great scientific achievement. We especially prize these singular acts when done in youth. Aristotle's paradigm is rather different. One focuses upon the character that has been formed over some considerable time rather than upon the single prominent action.

14. No absolute necessity exists here. Human action falls within the biological realm and all biological phenomena occur "for the most part." We are thus dealing with a probability rather than a certainty.

15. *Kata ton okthon logon, NE* 11386 2.

16. The operative terms in this case are: (1) *dunamis* (potentiality), (2) *energia* (actuality-1), (3) *entelechia* (actuality-2).

17. This is the principal change: identifying actuality-2 with God.

18. Obviously, there are two types of objectors here: (a) Those who think that this sort of identification is wrong because God cannot be identified with

the natural realm in this way because of his/her/its transcendence, or (b) Those who do no believe there is a god at all and therefore any such identification would be nonsense.

19. In the Christian religion faith, hope, and charity are considered to be virtues due to their advocacy in the writings of Paul of Tarsus (see Corinthians I: 13).

20. Those virtues revealed by the use of reason, alone. These must apply to all regardless of religious faith. The second group asserts domain over advocates of Christianity. See the preceding note.

21. *Summa Theologica* I–II, q. 60, a.3.

22. *Summa Theologica* I–II, q. 62, a.3.

23. This, of course, requires someone to prove the system inconsistent. As such X is a negative or indirect argument for consistency. Positive proofs are hard enough to come by even within closed logical systems, much less open systems of possible ethical situations. In this regard one must agree with Church and Turing's conjecture that within open systems there are no complete positive proofs for consistency. Compare to Alan Donagan's discussion, *The Theory of Morality* (Chicago:

University of Chicago Press, 1978), 145.

24. "Moral perplexity," "moral dilemma," and "moral inconsistency" shall be used synonymously in this context.

25. St. Gregory the Great, *Moralium Libri*, xxxii, 20, 36–38. J. Migne, *Patologia Latina* Vol 76 (Paris: Garnier, 1878), 658.

26. Thomas Aquinas, *Summa Theologica I-II*, 19, 6 and 3.

27. The literature here is hopelessly large. An example of a valiant attempt would be R. Carnap, *Logical Foundations of Probability* (Chicago: University of Chicago Press, 1950), sec. 1–6. For two famous paradoxes of confirmation see Carl Hempel, "Studies in the Logic of Confirmation," Parts I and II, *Mind* 54 (1945): 1–26, 97–121; and Nelson Goodman, *Fact, Fiction, and Forecast* (Cambridge, MA: Harvard University Press, 1955), ch 3–4. On falsification see Karl Popper, *The Logic of Scientific Discovery* (London: Hutchinson, 1959).

28. It should be noted that Aristotle is rather ambiguous on this score. Though his picture of the human character is clearly a rounded one, he can be suspicious of emotions.

CHAPTER

12

IT'S ABOUT THE TEAM: *UTILITARIANISM*

❖ Snapshot

❖ The Problem This Theory Addresses

❖ The Argument for the Theory

❖ A Critical Evaluation of the Theory

❖ Key Terms

❖ A Challenging Case Study

SNAPSHOT

A very strong candidate for answering the searching basic questions is the team player. A team player is one who puts the good of the team before her own good. If you are on a sports team, for example, and you notice that Latisha has been playing better than you have lately and the coach asks your opinion on who should start, then if you are a person with the team's good at heart, you'll say, "Latisha" (knowing full well that this will mean you will sit on the bench). This orientation toward the team first can be given the name **utilitarianism**.

Utilitarianism is a theory that suggests that an action is morally right when that action produces more total utility for the group than any other alternative. Sometimes this has been shortened to the slogan, "The greatest good for the greatest number." This emphasis upon calculating quantitatively the general population's projected consequential utility among competing alternatives, appeals to many of the same principles that underlie democracy and capitalism (which is why this

153

theory has always been very popular in the United States and other Western capitalistic democracies).

THE PROBLEM THIS THEORY ADDRESSES

For any moral theory to work there has to be general agreement among citizens that the prescriptions are right. What is more right than maximizing everyone's happiness? This is a cause to which there might be almost universal acceptance. How best can we bring about this happiness? This is it in a nutshell.

In our sports example, people join the school team because they like the sport. The school supports the team because it's a part of an overall education (a healthy mind in a healthy body). Thus, virtually everyone in the school agrees that the sports teams are good for the school. The interest in the good of the school is given. It is thus assumed that the good of the team is also the good of the school. Therefore, being a team player is *right* because it maximizes the *good* (the morale, status, and so forth).

If there were ever any questions about the team, the deciding criterion would be the good of the team (and by extension, the good of the school). This would be calculated quantitatively by estimating the consequential pleasure that would occur. So, for example, if the team wanted to change its mascot from a bear to a snail, many might demur. This is because they might contend that a bear is a dynamic animal that gets things done while a snail is a disgusting, slow creature that never accomplishes anything. If teams (and the schools that support them) mirror their mascot (to some degree), then down the road the snail mascot would undermine the community worldview and lead to unhappiness. Better to stay with the bear and claw your way to the top of the standings!

THE ARGUMENT FOR THE THEORY

THE PLEASURE AND PAIN PRINCIPLE

One of the proponents of modern utilitarianism was Jeremy Bentham. He wrote in the early nineteenth century in England. He begins his work *An Introduction to the Principles of Morals and Legislation,*

> Nature has placed mankind under the governance of two sovereign masters, *pain and pleasure.* It is for them alone to point out what we ought to do as well as to determine what

we shall do. On the one hand the standard of right and wrong, on the other the chain of causes and effects, are fastened to their throne. They govern us in all we do, in all we say, in all we think: every effort we can make to throw off our subjection, will serve but to demonstrate and confirm it. In words a man may pretend to abjure their empire: but in reality he will remain subject to it all the while.[1]

Bentham makes the argument about the **pleasure principle** that "pleasure" is a clearly identifiable end to which all humans strive. This is set in the context of modern "science" versus antiquated notions of philosophy (nonempirical notions of "right and wrong"). Natural science demonstrates from an examination of animal behavior that only pain and pleasure are efficacious in causing conduct of one sort or another. The fascination with this idea has endured to the present day. In experimental psychology various modes of conditioning employing "positive" and "negative" reinforcement have been the basis of psychological behaviorism. One of the most prominent of the experimental psychological behaviorists, B. F. Skinner, writes, "Almost all living things act to free themselves from harmful contacts . . . Man's struggle for freedom is not due to a will to be free, but to certain behavioral processes characteristic of the human organism, the chief effect of which is the avoidance of or escape from so-called 'aversive' features of the environment."[2]

Like Bentham, Skinner sees a conflict between science and the illusory philosophical literature that asserts freedom of choice between "right" and "wrong." What is real is pain and pleasure.

No one would doubt that pleasure and pain *do* influence and/or determine many (if not most) of our day-to-day decisions. One does not go into a restaurant and order something on the menu that he/she believes to be nauseating. One does not ask the barber to cut his hair in a way that seems repulsive. Certainly, pleasure and pain are the basis of these sorts of decisions. The question is whether *all* decisions are governed by the principles of pleasure and pain (see Chapter 4 on altruism)?

John Stuart Mill puts the argument similarly in his book *Utilitarianism:*

> The creed which accepts as the foundation of morals, Utility, or the Greatest Happiness Principle, holds that actions are right in proportion as they tend to promote happiness, wrong as they tend to produce the reverse of happiness. By happiness is intended pleasure, and the absence of pain; by unhappiness, pain and the privation of pleasure. To give a clear view of the moral standard set up by the theory, much more requires to be said; in particular, what things it includes in the ideas of pain and pleasure; and to what extent this is left an open question.[3]

Second, notice that we have a new term in Mill's argument, "happiness."[4] This is not accidental. "Happiness" can be equated with elevated states while "pleasure" has the unpleasant association with low stimulations of the body. (This was especially repugnant to many in Victorian England.)

For B. F. Skinner (as well as for many behaviorists) pleasure is taken as a simple and not as a complex. This means that we are directly aware of being in the state of pleasure or pain. "If someone were to ask me if I were in pleasure, pain, or neither, I should be able to answer without any reflection. This is because one experiences simples 'all at once.' "

But in Mill, "pleasure" is depicted as a complex. This means that one might require reflection about whether he were in pleasure, pain, or neither. This calls for an analysis of pleasure.

Both Mill and Bentham were concerned that people not misunderstand what they meant by pleasure. Toward this end, Mill distinguishes between types of pleasures. For Mill pleasures are high or low, intense or weak.

The Varieties of Pleasures

High/Low	*Strong/Weak*	
High	*High/Strong*	*High/Weak*
Low	*Low/Strong*	*Low/Weak*

Thus, there are four sorts of pleasures for Mill: high/strong, high/weak, low/strong, and low/weak.[5] This means that in addition to *quantity,* one must factor in the *quality* of the pleasure, too.[6] This is a controversial move, because it is not clear on what grounds quality of pleasure is to be valued. Certainly examples that Mill would have considered to be of a low/intense pleasure—such as wanton drug use or promiscuous sex—are not the sort of pleasures he wishes to advocate. Rather he would prefer people cultivate the more "refined" pleasures of reading, debate, and charity.

However, how can I justify—on only the principle of maximizing pleasure—that I would choose the latter over the former? It might be possible to make distinctions such as "long term" and "short term" or other categories (see Bentham's categories in note 6). But it is questionable whether this really helps any.

Is it irrational to engage in low/intense pleasures? What really makes them "low"? Doesn't this constitute another set of standards by which something is of a higher quality than something else? Because we all want to praise reading a fine book over wanton drug use, we categorize the former as being of higher quality. But how do we do this on the principle of pleasure alone?

Mill says that anyone who has access to both will habitually choose the higher over the lower, thus proving that the higher quality pleasure is more choiceworthy (pleasurable). But is this *always* the case? How do we explain away the cases in which this does not hold? Are they merely cases of abnormal people? And how do we know whether the majority chooses the higher quality—because it is more pleasurable? Might they choose for some other reason? Is Mill begging the question?

These are important issues for the utilitarian to face because the theory seeks to be generated by a single principle. This single principle, in turn, claims to explain a wide range of phenomena.

Mill and Bentham believe that if people reflect they will engage the sentiment of Lucretius who said:

How brief our time that we not see
That nature asks *nothing* save
That we cast aside pain from our bodies
That in our mind—DELIGHT
May be
Alone, unmixed and free.

The real needs of our bodies are few
Simply—"That which chases the pain."
For Nature asks not
That we abide in luxury . . .

Anyone can be happy
As he lounges with friends
On the soft grass
In the shade of a tall tree
Beside the stream . . .[7]

The utilitarian will point to this aspect of Epicureanism and decry those who claim that a pleasure-based theory must be full of those "low" pleasures about which the general public is always so concerned. A truly hedonistic theory will create harmony with nature rather than a wanton rejection of the same.

THE MOVE TO GENERAL HEDONISM

If Mill and Bentham were only concerned about each person's personal calculus of pleasure, then they would be egoistic hedonists (those seeking the maximization of personal pleasure). However, this is not the case. Though Epicurus and Lucretius are egoistic hedonists, the utilitarians have a different direction to their hedonism. This is **general hedonism** (the pleasure of the aggregate body of people). Sometimes the statement of this sort of hedonism is depicted as "the greatest pleasure/happiness for the greatest number." Sometimes the statement is also depicted as "the greatest *good* for the greatest number." This second formulation is only different from the first when "good" is understood as being something different from "pleasure."[8]

It still remains for us to illustrate why the utilitarians believe in general hedonism over egoistic hedonism. This is a controversial issue.

This controversy can be highlighted via Thought Experiment 12–1.

THOUGHT EXPERIMENT 12–1: THE SCHOOL PICNIC

(A) The principal of the school wants to decide whether it would be better to serve hot dogs or hamburgers at the school picnic. (B) The principal loves hamburgers and hates hot dogs. (C) The students of the school by a four-to-one margin prefer hot dogs. (D) Only one main course can be purchased—either hamburgers or hot dogs. What should be purchased? ∎

(A) and (D) define the problem. It is a question of determining the right entree for the school picnic. Which choice is right for the principal to make: hot dogs or hamburgers?

Bentham addressed this issue by saying that every person counted as one.[9] This interpretation would imply that the problem identified is a group problem. If this is so, then it would be illogical to forget to count the other people involved in one's pleasure calculations. If there are 100 students in the school and 80 prefer hot dogs, and if the pleasure weight for hot dogs is four versus one for hamburgers, then alternatives work out to:

a. **hot dogs**—majority $(80 \times 5 = 400)$ + minority $(20 \times 1 = 20)$ + principal $(1 \times 1 = 1)$ = aggregate happiness/pleasure **421**
b. **hamburgers**—majority $(80 \times 1 = 80)$ + minority $(20 \times 5 = 100)$ + principal $(1 \times 5 = 5)$ = aggregate happiness/pleasure **185**
c. comparing the numbers: hot dogs (421) > hamburgers (185), therefore:
d. hot dogs yield the higher aggregate pleasure and *a fortiori* are the choice for the school picnic.

If the situation in question involves a group and if everyone in the group counts only for one, then the sort of calculation in the picnic example would seem appropriate. However, there are two possible difficulties to this stance. First, how does Bentham or anyone else justify the proposition that all people count as one equally? Could it be the case that some people are just more important (like the principal of the school)? Does it lead to general happiness that all people are treated equally?

What if there was a road crew and everyone on the road crew were paid according to how much work was produced? Each was treated as one equally and they finished x amount of work. However, at the same time another road crew was working and in this second road crew one person was selected to be the boss of the crew and that person, therefore, was treated above the others. In this case everyone is not treated as one. Assume also that the second road crew was more efficient (as many management studies have shown) and finished 2x amount of work and consequently was paid more money.

The result is that in the group that treated everyone equally as "one," ended up being paid less money. (Let us also assume that the only thing that these workers care about is getting the most money possible.) In this situation would people say that being "treated as one" really brought about greater general pleasure?

Second, what is to compel the egoist to agree that she should accept an equal accounting when clearly her own interests are the most important of all?

One could respond that it is logically evident or that an examination of Roman law (as Bentham did) showed that this was the case. However, this relegates a very important proposition to a posited, logical necessity. This sounds like the domain of the philosophers who were eschewed at the outset. (Appealing to Roman law only pushes the question of justification back one more step.)[10]

Another approach to this problem would be to say that one cannot justify the adoption of being a team player without moral education and sensitivity. Mill took this approach to the problem. If a society educated its population properly, the people would see that his or her own personal interests were not as important in the general scheme of things as the good of the whole. This only occurs when sympathy occurs. "Sympathy" is the connecting of the subject's feelings with the feelings or sentiments of another. When one exhibits sympathy, then one is automatically connected to others. My sentiment becomes tied to others and as a result I see the plight of others as important. The perfect expression of such sympathy is when I see my sentiments and others' sentiments in the same way. Neither is more or less important.

Can such sympathy be produced by education? Can the right environment foster such sentimental sympathy? And can the sympathy be developed to the degree necessary for the subject to view his interests as no more important than those of others? These are important questions that the utilitarian must answer.

Clearly, no one would argue that such "other regarding" behavior is not admirable and well suited to a moral theory. However, the key question is whether the utilitarian can justify such a position on the scientific, utilitarian principles espoused by its advocates.

Even if we accept the proposition that Mill's program of education might increase the general sentimental sympathy among the general population, it is not clear that it does so necessarily and universally. Unless it does this, the justification for the move from *egoistic* hedonism to *general* hedonism is undermined. There is no way to predict whether 5 percent, 50 percent, or 90 percent of the population will accept the authority of the duties derived from their moral maxims.

Henry Sidgwick continues the analysis of this issue in his work *The Methods of Ethics*.[11] Sidgwick takes as his goal uniting ethical intuitionism ("common sense morality") and utilitarianism. Sidgwick believes in level-one intuitionism in ethics, but believes that its extension to level two was problematic. For this function, utilitarianism is employed.[12] In most respects Sidgwick believes this combination works powerfully together to create an account that is noncircular (since utilitarianism at level one has an independent justification).

However concerning the problem of overlapping interests between egoistic and general hedonism, Sidgwick is not so sanguine.

> I do not mean that if we gave up the hope of attaining a practical solution of this fundamental contradiction [between egoistic and general hedonism] . . . it would be reasonable for us to abandon morality altogether: but it would seem necessary to abandon the idea of rationalizing it completely. We should doubtless still, not only from self-interest, but also through sympathy and sentiments protective of social well-being, imparted by education and sustained by communication with other men, feel a desire for the general observance of rules conducive to general happiness. . . . But in the rarer cases of a recognized conflict between self-interest and duty, practical reason, being divided against itself, would cease to be a motive on either side; the conflict would have to be decided by the comparative preponderance of one or the other of two groups of nonrational impulses (Sidgwick, p. 508).

Sidgwick recognizes Mill's proposed solution, but believes that in the end there is no necessary and universal argument that would make the egoistic hedonist accept general hedonism—especially in cases in which a person's own interests are severely compromised by the general happiness/pleasure. The advocate of utilitarianism must find a way to address this question.

Another question to consider is whether we wish to calculate utility on an *aggregate basis* or on an *average basis* (median or mode). The difference between these two approaches can be seen by Thought Experiment 12–2.

THOUGHT EXPERIMENT 12–2: DISTRIBUTION OF MONEY IN UTILITY-LAND[13]

1. In Utility-land there are five citizens: A, B, C, D, and E.
2. In Utility-land there is a debate on how money should be allocated. The two candidates are called $Model_1$ and $Model_2$.
3. In $Model_1$ A makes $180 and B, C, D, and E make $5 each. The aggregate amount of money paid to the citizens is $200.
4. In $Model_2$ A makes $40 and B, C, D, and E make $30 each. The aggregate amount of money paid to the citizens is $160.
5. A claims that money should be allocated according to utilitarian principles, "the greatest good for the greatest number." This means that since $Model_1$ produces the **greatest aggregate utility** that it should be the basis for money allocation. $Model_1$ produces the greatest amount of good (money).
6. The other citizens claim that $Model_2$ is better because both the median and mode calculation of averages dictate that the greatest number is benefited most by $Model_2$. Though the aggregate is less, more people are benefited. This is the **average utility**. ∎

Which model is the proper way to calculate utility? In $Model_1$ the "greatest good" is emphasized while in $Model_2$, the "greatest number" is highlighted. This is a tricky question. If you had to choose between the two, which would you choose? Part of the difficulty in evaluating these two interpretations of utilitarian calculation, from the point of view of a citizen in either $Model_1$ or $Model_2$, is that if she were to decide which model is better, there is some sort of mechanism at work which requires the citizen to engage in probability calculations about whether she might end up, like A at the top of the heap. Perhaps a person would like to gamble and take her chances in a $Model_1$ rather than take the safer bet and stay in $Model_2$.[14] Obviously the manner of utilitarian calculation is very important in any practical implementation of the theory.

Given this depiction, there are many reasons why someone would want to be a utilitarian. The first is that it accords so precisely to the way the macro perspective operates in economics and politics. If you were the chief executive of a large corporation and you were faced with a crucial policy decision that had no moral dimensions, wouldn't you be inclined to view the situation in terms of maximizing the profit of the company and thereby benefiting the greatest number? It is a "no-brainer." Of course you would. Cost-benefit analysis in nonmoral matters *is* what business is about. And since a very large part of our everyday life depends upon the actions of businesspeople, we all depend upon them acting in just that way. If they didn't, and if we were a stockholder in the company, then we could instigate a shareholders' lawsuit against the officers and directors of the corporation. They would be committing malpractice.

Likewise in the government, we expect our democratically elected officials to vote in the interests of the largest constituency (all things being equal and assuming there is no inherent moral question at stake). For example, if there were 100 million dollars for a road project and one claimant for the money could show that it would benefit two thousand people and the other claimant could show that it would benefit two hundred thousand people, then cost-benefit would lean toward the latter claimant.

Thus, in the macro sphere, when there are no moral issues at stake, we all believe that utilitarianism is the way the decision should be made. This is so deeply ingrained that if one were to act otherwise, we would declare that she was not carrying out her duties properly. This prudential acceptance makes appealing the possibility that it applies in the moral realm as well.

THE ARGUMENT AGAINST THE THEORY

I will highlight two prominent criticisms of utilitarianism: (a) The rights of minorities; and (b) The connection between pleasure and good.

THE RIGHTS OF MINORITIES

> DR. STOCKMAN. . . . D'you think I'm going to let public opinion and the compact majority and all that rigmarole get the better of me? No, thank you! . . . [the] policies of expediency are turning all our standards of morality and justice upside down, so that life's just not going to be worth living.[15]

Like Dr. Stockman in Ibsen's play we can all face the tyranny of the majority. Sometimes it seems that the majority isn't merely *sometimes* wrong, but is *always* wrong and driven by the politics of expediency (what gives general pleasure).

This sort of objection, by definition, affects the minorities. Consider Case 12–1.

CASES

CASE 12–1   MURDER IN NORTHERN IRELAND

You are a constable of a small, remote rural town in Northern Ireland. The town is divided into the Catholics (20% minority) and the Protestants (80% majority). All the Catholics live in one section of town that sits on a peninsula jutting out into the river just east of the main section of town.

One morning a young Protestant girl is found raped and murdered next to the town green. By general consensus it is concluded that a Catholic must have committed the crime. The Protestants form a citizens' committee that makes the following demand upon the constable: "We believe you to be a Catholic sympathizer. Therefore, we do not think you will press fast enough for this killer to be brought to justice. We know a Catholic did the crime. We have therefore sealed off the Catholic section of town. No one can go in or out. If you do not hand over the criminal by sundown, we will torch the entire Catholic section of town killing all 1,000 people. Don't try to call for help. We have disabled all communication devices."

The constable worked hard all day in an effort to find out who "did it." It was of no use. He couldn't find out. It was now one hour before sundown. He didn't know what to do. His deputy said, "Why don't we just pick a random Catholic and tell them he did it? At least we'd be saving 999 lives."

"But then I'd be responsible for killing an innocent man," returned the constable.

"Better one innocent die and 999 be saved. After all, there's no way the two of us can stop the mob. You have to give them a scapegoat." ■

There are at least two issues in Case 12–1: (a) the right of the majority to determine what is justice; and (b) whether pleasures and pains are additive, making it more of crime to kill two than to kill one.

The first issue pits theories of moral absolutism against moral relativism. If what is right and wrong are solely determined by the happiness of the majority, then it would seem that the Protestants' claim for a Catholic scapegoat is justified. It clearly meets the mood of the majority and will yield more pleasure to them by any scale that you might use. Thus, it would seem that the majority *could* dictate that justice requires Catholic blood.[16]

Such a conclusion is highly repugnant to most reader's intuitions. How could any theory sanction the persecution of a minority? Certainly cases like this are all too frequent across time and space in human history. No country is absolved from committing acts of vicious discrimination. Surely, utilitarianism could not be allowing this.

One way around the difficulties of particular implementations of utilitarianism to specific acts is to create general rules that, themselves, are justified by utilitarian principles. In our Case 12–1 this might mean: (a) that all accused criminals are entitled to a fair trial judged by a jury of their peers; and (b) that the killing of an innocent party is illegitimate. These rules could be justified independently of any particular situation. It would be seen as a good for society over the long run. Once the rule is set down it must be obeyed.

Thus, the Protestants could not justifiably believe that their particular happiness on *this* occasion might justify killing a person who has not gone through the legal process.

Also, from the constable's point of view, the second rule would prohibit knowingly killing an innocent party.

At first glance, the addition of rules to utilitarianism (called **rule utilitarianism**) seems to be an improvement. The various counterintuitive cases can be solved by creating a rule to protect against such applications. However, just as in level-two intuitionism, there is the problem of recognition and application. Is this particular event before me an instance of rule A or of rule B (recall the earlier example of abortion as either being described as murder or the permissible exercise of personal autonomy).

Unless utilitarianism wishes to revert to intuitionism, it must do better than merely create broad, general rules through which particular acts are subsumed by the agency of a theory which delegates this power through immediate recognition or application. This suggests that we make the rules very specific. But this also causes problems. David Lyons has argued that if the rules are too specific, then they are no different from maxims derived directly by reference to the principle of utility (**act utilitarianism**).[17] A proper rule must balance a careful line between being too general and being not general at all (pure act utilitarianism).[18] J. J. C. Smart has advanced this notion by criticizing both the ideas of the extreme Act and Rule Utilitarianism.[19] In its stead Smart has advocated "rules of thumb." These are similar to the prima facie duties described in Chapter 8 on Intuitionism. Rules of thumb are between the hard rules of Rule Utilitarianism and the sui generis applications of Act Utilitarianism.

Lyons develops this in his book *Rights, Welfare, and Mill's Moral Theory*.[20] Lyons believes that rule utilitarianism is not an ad hoc response to problems involved in act utilitarianism, but rather in the spirit of the founders—especially Mill. By "rules" Lyons means something closer to Smart's "rules of thumb."

The point, in this context, is that modern democratic societies emphasize institutions and the rights they engender. These, by their very definition, are general statements that cover a range of substitution instances. Thus, some sort of intermediary level is needed between the generating principle and the results of that principle.

In some ways this may be an artifact of the demands of this sort of formal structure rather than a trait of utilitarianism, per se (see the discussion of Kant in Chapter 13). What Lyons wants to assert is that the truth or falsity of utilitarianism as a system of ethics depends not upon these quibbles over the status of the rules (i.e., rules of thumb) but upon the thrust of the general principle.

If one acts in accord with the general principle and its corollaries (rules of thumb), then one is moral. However one might ask, "what of motives?" Motives are not often addressed in utilitarianism. Rather, it is a theory more akin to consequences only. But this is not always the case. One can modify utilitarianism to account for motivations, as well.[21]

The second issue deals with the additive nature of human crime. Is it morally *more* wrong to kill one than to kill two (or 999 as in the example)? This is an issue that is embedded in the utilitarian system. Can we say that the loss of two or more lives is morally worse than the loss of one? The so-called trolley dilemma (Case 12–2) captures this.

CASES

CASE 12–2   THE TROLLEY DILEMMA

1. You are the engineer of a trolley.
2. The trolley has gotten almost out of control.
3. Your only choice left is to switch at Lincoln Junction between A-track and B-track.

4. You are approaching Lincoln Junction and on the RIGHT track is a school bus filled with 50 innocent young children whose bus got caught in the trolley tracks.

5. The LEFT track is occupied by a homeless person whose poor-fitting shoe has caught in the trolley tracks.

6. As the engineer, you have the choice of moving your lethal train to the right or to the left. This is your only choice. ■

The key question to ask in Case 12–2 is whether one has any moral justification for going to the right or to the left? This is an important question. Clearly most of us would kill one rather than fifty. The question is whether we have moral justification for doing so? Is human life additive? How can we assess such examples? Is it the case that there are no *moral* reasons for choosing one track over another (as a deontologist might argue), and that if one chooses to save the school bus, you do so for other nonmoral reasons?

In ordinary act-aggregate utilitarianism human life is additive because pleasure is additive. Rule utilitarianism or average-utility utilitarianism might not have to make the same claim, but the inclination is in that direction.

Theories that hold that each human life is priceless are bound to say that addition is impossible—for who can add together that which is priceless? This is an important divide between utilitarians, who base the rightness of an act on the calculations of consequences, and nonconsequentialists, who might set out a premise such as "the preciousness of human life trumps any calculation of group utility." In the end, you—the reader—must decide whether the basic strategy of consequentialism can work to protect the interests of minorities—or not.

THE CONNECTION BETWEEN PLEASURE AND GOOD

The last issue to be discussed is the relation between pleasure and good. In utilitarianism good is defined as that which maximizes pleasure. A detractor might say that there is really no connection between pleasure and good. They are two different concepts.

If we remember the Bentham selection at the beginning of the chapter, it emphasized the scientific nature of this claim.

1. Pleasure is a natural end in itself—Fact
2. [Nature is good and whatever follows from its laws is good]—Assertion
3. Pleasure is good—1, 2

Obviously, the key premise to be examined is 2. Why is nature, and what follows from its laws, good? Well, if one were a theist who believes in divine creation, then one might say that since nature is created by

God and that since God is good, and that since the artifact takes on the character of its artisan, then nature is good. This was the direction of some early utilitarians like William Paley.[22]

However, Bentham does not take this tack. He links more directly with the emerging attitude that empiricism alone is the basis for knowledge. Since science is governed by empiricism, science provides a better foundation upon which to construct philosophical theories. If we discard theistic ties to nature, it is not altogether clear why pleasure is good. If nature, itself, is morally neutral, then laws derived from nature would be morally neutral as well. How does "good" emerge from "pleasure"? The utilitarian response must be rather like Sidgwick's, that this tie is immediately grasped. Utilitarianism may not be able to justify its own first principles, but that should not count against the theory. Many useful theories cannot justify their origins. What counts for the utilitarian is that once accepted, the principle of utility is a prescription that is easy to understand, apply, and fits the moral inclinations of many people.

KEY TERMS

- utilitarianism
- pleasure principle
- general hedonism
- aggregate utility
- average utility
- rule utilitarianism
- act utilitarianism

A CHALLENGING CASE STUDY

Directions: Write a two-and-a-half page essay (750 words) on the following case. Be sure to first set out what you believe the utilitarian position to be. Second, evaluate whether you agree with this solution or not based upon personal worldview or community worldview tenets. Make your reasons very explicit.

CASE:
You are living in the United States of America. The president has declared a national emergency. The president has declared that terrorism threatens our very way of life due to the 9/11/2001 event at the World Trade Center in New York City. The only way to really track terrorists in our country is to declare that the Bill of Rights privileges will now be granted only at the discretion of the president. Each and every right may be temporarily suspended at his discretion until the danger to our country has abated.[23] Is the president justified in making this executive order? Base your response only upon utilitarian reasoning (quantifying where possible).

NOTES

1. Jeremy Bentham, *An Introduction to The Principles of Morals and Legislation* (Oxford: Oxford University Press, 1789), 1.

2. B. F. Skinnner, *Beyond Freedom and Dignity* (New York: Alfred A. Knopf, 1971), 26, 48.

3. John Stuart Mill, *Utilitarianism* (London, 1863, repr. 1979 Hackett Publishers), chapter 2, 7.

4. Bentham uses the word "happiness" as a synonym for pleasure, too. Like Mill, Bentham will try to distinguish categories for ranking pleasures; see *Principles of Morals*, 31.

5. Mill, *Utilitarianism*, 8.

6. Bentham sought similar distinctions as he distinguished first the sources of pleasure being physical, political, moral, and religious (24–28), then the scale of measurement due to intensity, duration, certainty, propinquity, fecundity, purity, and extent (30). However, Bentham did not allow for a distinction in the quality of pleasure. He is quoted as saying that "the quality of pleasure being equal, pushpin is as good as poetry." This marks a distinction between Mill's depiction and Bentham's.

7. Titus Lucretius Carus, *De Rerum Natura*, ed. C. Bailey (Oxford: Clarendon Press, 1922); translation is mine.

8. G. E. Moore declares in *Principia Ethica* a utilitarianism of this other sort. "Our 'duty,' therefore, will cause more good to exist in the Universe than any possible alternative" (148). Our duty is to maximize the amount of good in the world. "Good" is a nonnatural property and cannot be identified with "pleasure," as the standard utilitarians would have it. For Moore, whatever "good" is, it is something that is grasped by intuition. We may term this sort of utilitarianism "agathistic utilitarianism" (see Chapter 8).

9. "Each to count for one, and none for more than one."

10. This is one of the perennial questions in legal positivism that was developing during the late eighteenth and early nineteenth centuries. In this instance the historical precedent was considered to be adequate without independent foundational justification; cf. John Austin, *The Province of Jurisprudence Determined,* ed. Robert Campbell, 5th edition. 2 vol. (London: John Murray, 1885).

11. Henry Sidgwick, *The Methods of Ethics,* 7th edition (London: Macmillan, 1907).

12. Sidgwick, *Methods,* IV.3.

13. The assumption on this model is that A is extremely productive and that given a model in which his/her productivity is highly compensated and very little social redistribution is taking place, that A would drive him/herself so as to achieve the high monetary rewards. In Model$_2$ one can assume a taxation policy or some other redistribution device which does not reward A as highly so that greater equity is paid for with lower efficiency.

14. An economic discussion of the principle of "maximizing" vs "maximinizing" is found in William Fellner, *Probability and Profit* (Homewood, IL: R. D. Irwin, Inc., 1965), 140–42. The philosophical implications of a similar choice situation are set out by John Rawls, *Theory of Justice* (Cambridge, MA.: Belknap Press of Harvard University Press, 1971), sections 25–28.

15. Henrik Ibsen, *An Enemy of the People* trans. James McFarlane (Oxford: Oxford University Press, 1983), act 5.

16. Of course one might contend that to protect a minority would, in the long run, better promote the greater good. But it is difficult to see how one would justify this on purely utilitarian principles (as so far presented). If one were to try such a tack, s/he is open to the charge that s/he is begging the question by introducing an unjustified moral criterion. Of course if intuitionism is added to utilitarianism, then such a difficulty might be met.

17. David Lyons, *Forms and Limits of Utilitarianism* (Oxford: Clarendon Press, 1965).

18. In this context pure act utilitarianism means that each individual act is measured by the general utilitarian maxim. However, it is not clear that Mill, Bentham, or Sidgwick actually advocated what we have called act utilitarianism.

19. J. J. C. Smart, "Extreme and Restricted Utilitarianism" *Philosophical Quarterly* 6 (1956): 344–54; cf. J. J. C. Smart and Bernard Williams, *Utilitarianism: For and Against* (Cambridge: Cambridge University Press, 1973).

20. David Lyons, *Rights, Welfare, and Mill's Moral Theory* (Oxford: Oxford University Press, 1994), pp. 77–78, 139–142.

21. See Derek Parfit, *Reasons and Persons* (Oxford: Oxford University Press, 1984); cf. Michael Slote, *Common-Sense Morality and Consequentialism* (London, 1985).

22. William Paley, *The Principles of Moral and Political Philosophy* (London, 1785). Paley believed that pleasure and happiness were part of God's natural law and that they were therefore good. Thus maximizing general happiness is also good.

23. The Bill of Rights says—Amendment I: Congress shall make no law respecting an establishment of religion, or prohibiting the free exercise thereof; or abridging the freedom of speech, or of the press; or the right of the people peaceably to assemble, and to petition the government for a redress of grievances. Amendment II: A well regulated militia, being necessary to the security of a free state, the right of the people to keep and bear arms, shall not be infringed. Amendment III: No soldier shall, in time of peace be quartered in any house, without the consent of the owner, nor in time of war, but in a manner to be prescribed by law. Amendment IV: The right of the people to be secure in their persons, houses, papers, and effects, against unreasonable searches and seizures, shall not be violated, and no warrants shall issue, but upon probable cause, supported by oath or affirmation, and particularly describing the place to be searched, and the persons or things to be seized. Amendment V: No person shall be held to answer for a capital, or otherwise infamous crime, unless on a presentment or indictment of a grand jury, except in cases arising in the land or naval forces, or in the militia, when in actual service in time of war or public danger; nor shall any person be subject for the same offense to be twice put in jeopardy of life or limb; nor shall be compelled in any criminal case to be a witness against himself, nor be deprived of life, liberty, or property, without due process of law; nor shall private property be taken for public use, without just compensation. Amendment VI: In all criminal prosecutions, the accused shall enjoy the right to a speedy and public trial, by an impartial jury of the state and district wherein the crime shall have been committed, which district shall have been previously ascertained by law, and to be informed of the nature and cause of the accusation; to be confronted with the witnesses against him; to have compulsory process for obtaining witnesses in his favor, and to have the assistance of counsel for his defense. Amendment VII: In suits at common law, where the value in controversy shall exceed twenty dollars, the right of trial by jury shall be preserved, and no fact tried by a jury, shall be otherwise reexamined in any court of the United States, than according to the rules of the common law. Amendment VIII: Excessive bail

shall not be required, nor excessive fines imposed, nor cruel and unusual punishments inflicted. Amendment IX: The enumeration in the Constitution, of certain rights, shall not be construed to deny or disparage others retained by the people. Amendment X: The powers not delegated to the United States by the Constitution, nor prohibited by it to the states, are reserved to the states respectively, or to the people.

IT'S ABOUT DOING YOUR DUTY: *DEONTOLOGY*

- ❖ Snapshot
- ❖ The Problem This Theory Addresses
- ❖ The Argument for the Theory
- ❖ Arguments Against the Theory
- ❖ Key Terms
- ❖ A Challenging Case Study

SNAPSHOT

Deontology is a moral theory that emphasizes one's duty to do a particular action just because the action, itself, is inherently right and not through any other sorts of calculations—such as the consequences of the action. Because of this nonconsequentialist bent, deontology is often contrasted with utilitarianism that defines the right action in term of its ability to bring about the greatest aggregate utility. In contradistinction to utilitarianism, deontology will recommend an action based upon principle. "Principle" is justified through an understanding of the structure of action, the nature of reason, and the operation of the will. The result is a moral command to act that does not justify itself by calculating consequences.

THE PROBLEM THIS THEORY ADDRESSES

Moral theories operate in the realm between commending and commanding. Commending comes from the Latin, *commendare* and denotes representing something as worthy such that it is recommended to do. For many, this is too weak. Ethics goes beyond commending. It is about commanding. The word "deontology" comes from two Greek words, deion + logos. *Deion* comes from the particle *dei* which means "must." *Logos* (in this context) means "the account of." Thus, the whole meaning refers to "the account of the 'musts.'" In this instance, "musts" refer to human action: what "must" we do, that is, what is our duty? "Duty" is all about commanding. Commanding is a much stronger goal than commending. Those who seek this stronger structure are attracted to deontology.

But what is the foundation of these commands? Two contenders are: (a) human conventions, such as laws or customs; and (b) natural moral duties. No one would deny that there have always been duties of type (a)—even before Solon "the lawgiver." In order to have any civil government or working society, there have to be laws and customs. These laws and customs prescribe a duty. All citizens, if they want to remain in the society (and avoid punishment), *must* obey the law. Likewise all citizens, if they wish to be accepted in the communities in which they seek to live, must accept a set of social standards. Such duties are called "conventional" because they owe their origins solely to a set of conventions.

The more interesting question (from the ethical point of view) is when this question was recognized to have taken on the sense of type (b). These sorts of duties would owe their origin to some overarching natural order that would transcend any particular civil or social attempt at the depiction of the same. This question is somewhat vexed and will be discussed later in this chapter, but the answer to it is very important to how we react to duty-based theories.

In the "modern era" (post-1600), it is clear that writers such as Locke, Hobbes, and Rousseau concerned themselves with aspects of natural rights and duties in a contractarian tradition (see Chapter 10), while others such as Kant wanted to assert the existence of categorical duties whose origins resided in reason, itself.

The sorts of duties that Kant is thinking about fall into two categories: *prohibitions* (things you shouldn't do—often called negative duties), and *obligations* (things you are required to do). Whatever is not a prohibition or an obligation becomes a *permission* (things you may do if you want to—generally determined by personal assessments about individual happiness). A permission is not a duty. It is a class of action that can be determined individually based upon one's personal worldview. For Kant, most actions in life are permissions. Morality is a special subclass of action that calls for special behavior that is not self-interested (see Chapter 4). Whatever is not commanded by ethics as either a prohibition or an obligation is free game for the agent to do whatever he or she wants to do.

THE ARGUMENT FOR THE THEORY

As indicated above, there is no one single "deontological" theory. There are many practitioners. If one were forced to choose a prominent "standard bearer," it would probably be Kant, but it would be a mistake to identify "deontology" solely with Kantian ethics. Instead, let us begin our examination of the reasons deontologists profess their theory with the question posed above: "When does recognition of moral duty begin?"

To give even the barest answer to such a difficult question, let us begin with several key distinctions. First, there is an intricate relationship between duties and rights.[1] These **right claims** relationships can be explained by the following sentence:

i. "X has a right against Y to Z in virtue of P."

X is a person(s) and Y is a person(s) and Z is a good (such as the liberty to vote, or to have adequate health care, or to maintain ownership of the automobile that is titled under your name, or to be able to purchase a new consumer product) and P is a legitimating moral institution (in the sense of type (b) above).

This rights claim implies a correlative duty:

ii. "Y has a duty to provide X with Z in virtue of P."

Let's consider Thought Experiment 13–1 and see how I and II might be used to formulate a solution.

THOUGHT EXPERIMENT 13–1

Charles Rudd is an African American living in the Southern United States in the 1950s. His particular state has a poll tax in order to vote and also a literacy test. In the literacy test the applicant must demonstrate competence with complicated legal concepts often reserved for law schools. The reasons for these two requirements are that the citizens of that state want to be sure that (in the spirit of the U.S. Constitution) those voting are financially sound and that they are capable of complicated contemplation about the issues (making them informed voters). Are these two requirements reasonable? ∎

Thought Experiment 13–1 requires that we consider just what is intended in the legitimating institution. It is true that the Constitution of the United States as originally written did restrict voting to landowning males. However, if one believes that the U.S. Constitution is an evolving document that can be amended and interpreted by the Supreme Court, then the sense is to open things up via the 13th Amendment—outlawing slavery; the 14th Amendment assuring equal protection of rights to all under the law; the 15th Amendment that directly addresses the rights of African Americans as being upheld; and the 19th Amendment that extends the right to vote to women. Clearly, the intent of these amendments (as interpreted by the Supreme Court) is to confer the privilege of voting to all citizens regardless of race or gender. If we understand the Constitution in this way, then we can assert that the import of I and II above is to say: "John or Kinshasa Doe has a right to vote against the citizens of the United States in virtue of the Constitution of the United States and the moral principles upon which it stands." Now assume that Kinshasa Doe is an African American in a southern state in 1950s where there were poll taxes and literacy tests that were only given to African Americans with the effect of denying these individuals their opportunity to vote.

The correlative duty statement would read: "The citizens of the United States have a duty to provide John or Kinshasa Doe his/her voting privileges in virtue of the Constitution of the United States and the moral principles upon which it stands."

The Voting Rights Act of 1965 might be considered as a moral response to this question. A law was passed that created safeguards against spurious devices (such as poll taxes and various "citizenship/civics" tests which served to deny universal suffrage).

Some examples are not so evident—such as the right to adequate health care. Can we say, "John or Kinshasa Doe has the right to adequate health care against the citizens of the United States of America in virtue of a natural moral principles"? I have written in the past on this subject[2] suggesting that the answer is "yes," but it has been obvious that in the United States (at the writing of this edition) this is a controversial position.

However, it is clear that the two examples given above are of a different type than those that describe less essential goods such as an automobile or a cellular phone. Can we say in the same way (as we did with voting rights) that: "John Doe has a right to an automobile against the citizens of the United States in virtue of a natural moral principle"? or "John Doe has a right to a cellular telephone against the citizens of the United States in virtue of a natural moral right?" Certainly not. The type of good involved is different. (The *way* it is different and how competing goods can be ranked would be the heart of a theory describing duties—see the table of embeddedness, Chapter 1.)

At least we have established that rights, duties and types of goods are related, and that reasons for favoring some over others (when those reasons follow from *natural*, as opposed to merely *conventional* reasons) are the basis of a deontological theory.

A second issue is the question of *recognition* of rights/duties. Some authors such as H. L. A. Hart and J. L. L. Austin have emphasized an examination of legal statutes and the general literature of the period as a way of addressing this issue.[3] They contend that without actual words for "right" or "duty" which are employed in the literature or legal statutes, that there is no operational concept of "right" or "duty."[4] If there is no "operational" right or duty, then the concept does not exist and it is not a legitimate category by which to judge societal/individual conduct.

Such arguments have also been made about Chinese culture in recent times.[5] The claim is that since there has never been a recognized tradition of human rights observance in China, then the individuals in China have no moral claim to such. This is based upon the proposition that only publicly recognized rights are valid. This sort of claim asserts that the legitimatising institution for human rights is a descriptive public agreement. Such a claim might fit very well within the contractarian approach or within the emotive/ethical intuitionist linguistic approach that sees ethics as a project of description. This sort of argument contends (quasi-operationally) that: (a) if the literature and law statutes of the time (such as we have it) in some well-recognized society would support a duties/rights analysis, then such an attribution is appropriate, and (b) if the actions of the people would support a duties/rights analysis, then such an attribution is appropriate.[6] But beyond such sociological or linguistic analysis there are no natural rights that belong to people, *as such.*

Obviously, *duties* have existed both in principle and in practice since the beginning of civilization. *Socially*, neighborhoods and communities exert a "must" upon their members. *Politically,* the despot or government does the same. "If you want to stay alive (or out of jail), submit or be crushed."

This sort of duty is certainly different from a moral duty whose sanction may only be one's conscience. The two *may* overlap, but they *may not.* The concept of a "right" is other oriented. It creates some conception of a community of agents who want to assert their individual claims for desire fulfillment. In this instance, the agent is forced to view action from the point of view of others' competing claims.

"Moral" status does not attach itself to a purported right merely because a legislature has put it forward, nor because some society says this is the way "proper" individuals behave.

Because such a conception is different from an anthropological methodology, "rights language" will be "moral" only if the right exists in some other realm than mere convention. Thus, a "natural" right is one that may be attributed to every agent in virtue of his/her being an agent. This right need not be "claimed" to be activated, nor must the agent be aware that s/he has it. Agents possess this right simply by being people existing in the society.

KANT

Immanuel Kant is depicted by many as the quintessential deontologist. His work in ethics is very influential because he looked for the "science of right and wrong in human action" in a different place, namely through an understanding of the structure of action, the nature of reason, and the operation of the will. The way Kant understood the ethical enterprise was for an individual to contemplate about acting in the world and what reason requires us to do in order to obtain/create a good will.

This procedure seeks to discover clear actions demanded by morality (both negatively—that is, what to be avoided, such as murder—and positively—that is, what is required by all to perform, such as the duty to assist another.

The language of these positive and negative duties is set in the form of an imperative or command. We will examine the form of these imperatives shortly.

Kant set out his ethical theory in several key works that include *The Groundwork of the Metaphysics of Morals; The Metaphysics of Morals; The Critique of Practical Reason,* and *The Lectures on Ethics.* Each of these works gives a slightly different slant on the moral enterprise. Various contemporary commentators on Kant favor one book over the others and there is some dispute on how Kant is to be understood.[7] Some contemporary commentators disagree because Kantian scholarship is undergoing a thorough re-evaluation.[8] However, most of the points examined here will not be affected by these debates.

THE SORTS OF IMPERATIVES

As I mentioned above, Kant viewed the prohibitions and obligations of actions in the form of imperatives or commands. Kant believed that all questions of morality could be decided by referring to the proper form of the **categorical imperative** (his supreme principle of morality). Before exploring this further we need to obtain an understanding of the various sorts of imperatives.

According to Kant there are two sorts of imperatives: hypothetical and categorical.[9] A hypothetical imperative means that the consequent depends upon the antecedent. The categorical imperative is a command that depends upon nothing else aside from the rational grounds for the command, itself. Since deontology is wholly dependent upon principle alone,[10] it is the categorical imperative that is most important in understanding the basis of how we should act in any particular situation.

Let us therefore examine the forms of the two sorts of imperatives.

THE FORM OF A CONDITIONAL OR HYPOTHETICAL IMPERATIVE

A hypothetical imperative can be expressed in the following form: "If p then q." Q (the consequent) is viewed *conditionally*. Now there may be other antecedents that might cause q,[11] but in this case we look to p as a prior event that is requisite to determine q. Whenever p occurs, then q will also occur.

The nature of the possibility here is whether the hypothetical is *problematic* or *assetoric*. In the former case, its modal nature is largely contingent—while in the latter, it is less so. Most hypothetical imperatives revolve around the best strategy to achieve some "bottom line"—often money or some other good that is supposed to lead to happiness. Cost-benefit analysis is an instance of employing hypothetical imperatives. Most business schools teach this sort of analysis as a way of "maximizing the 'bottom line.'"

The other sort of imperative is *categorical.* In a categorical imperative nothing detracts from the exhortation to act. This is because it does not depend upon a logically prior condition. An example of a categorical imperative might be: "Get up!"

This sentence is in the imperative mode, that is, it is a command. The linguistic form of the command seems to depend upon nothing other than itself, but this misses the dynamics of any actual situation. If someone were to tell me, "Get up!" I would reply, "Why?" A truly categorical imperative must contain within it the ground for compliance.

THE WAY THE CATEGORICAL IMPERATIVE WORKS

The existence of a categorical command, in itself, is not sufficient to insure its adherence. We need to know more—that is, the groundwork or rationale of the command. For example, if someone were to say to me: "There is a deadly cobra under your chair," and "Get up," then I would get up (given that I have no hidden "death wish").

In some ways this sort of categorical imperative is not completely categorical at all.[12] It assumes various predispositions such as: (1) "I wish to be a rational person"; (2) "I wish to follow what rationally determined duty dictates"; (3) "I agree that some particular maxim 'x' is an instance of a more general principle, 'y,' and so on."

These are not exhaustive, but they point to the fact that categorical commands of any sort are also dependent upon some logically prior context. We do not simply act upon a command (such as "kill him!" where the "him" refers, for example, to some oppressed minority such as an African American, Jew, or Moslem). To act upon a command, we require a background (such as "this person before me is about to murder me unless I kill him").

For Kant, the general features of this background seek to be the foundation of reason itself: the principle of noncontradiction. The principle of noncontradiction $\{-(p \text{ and } -p)\}$ is fundamental to all human thought. If one found that a particular maxim of action—such as "Mary should lie to Max about his tax refund"—fit a more general type of action, namely, "x should lie to y," and that said action involved one in a logical inconsistency (i.e., a logical contradiction), then said type of action is irrational.

If morality is said to accord with logic, then to be illogical is to be immoral.

But why is morality said to be in accord with logic? This is because morality (the science of the right and wrong of human action) is a function of human action.[13] Action is a function of human reason (given an account of human freedom based upon reason), so that morality is a function of human reason. Reason is governed by logic which was to be demonstrated, to be irrational is to be inhuman.

I would personally assert that there are other aspects of being human, as well. For example, the ability to love or care for another person is a significant part of our humanity. This sort of love is not mere emotion, but an amalgam of emotion and reason. These react dialectically to inform upon a command of action.[14]

Now, none of us wish to be inhuman, for it would declare a preference to become a lower biological species (assuming a linear expression of the biosphere). Therefore, we must all accept the dictates of reason on the pain of being expelled from the species: Homo sapiens. This is what Kant means when he says that to be irrational is to "degrade" oneself.

This will best be shown by an example. But before presenting this example we need to present one more operation: the universalization of a maxim of moral action. For Kant, a universal moral law should aspire to the generality of a Newtonian law of physics (such as $F = ma$, force equals mass times acceleration). Such laws cover all possible instances regardless of time or space. They are always true everywhere there are rational beings. The structure in physics is to subsume particular events under the appropriate law and then mechanically to determine the consequences. This process recognizes three components: the particular event, a characterization of a generic event, x, and a law that governs events of type x. One begins with the particular event. Then, in the process of trying to identify what this event *is*, one characterizes the event of belonging to some generic description. Once a description is made (such as its being of type x), then one can plug type x into the appropriate covering law and generate a conclusion.

Kant aspires to a similar process in the realm of morality. Moral maxims are normative statements that tell us what to do in a given particular situation. "John should pay his bills" is an example of a moral maxim. Moral maxims give us advice on how to act in life. The process of universalization begins with moral maxims. Since the moral maxim is particular in nature (dealing with an actual person contemplating some action in the world), and since moral laws only cover over generic forms, one is required to determine what *type* of action is involved.

Now Kant believed that in this process of universalizing the maxim one could ascertain the logical character of such a maxim (as being logically coherent or not). Let's proceed now to Thought Experiment 13–2.

THOUGHT EXPERIMENT 13–2: CHEATING ON YOUR TAXES

Maxim under consideration—Mary should lie to the IRS about Max's taxable income.

Maxim universalized: [*All particular maxims should be generalized to depict the generic type of action involved.] The maxim universalized is: "X will lie to Y about Z" (where X and Y are people and Z is some state of affairs).

Analysis of universalized maxim upon a general sample space: If there were a society of liars, would this society be rationally coherent?

One way to describe this process (there is no single agreed upon way) is to begin with the definition of a lie: "A freely says B to his audience, C, knowing that B is false and with a sincere intent to deceive C."[15] Under these conditions, is it logically coherent to contemplate a society of liars? And if not, then what does this entail? Is there a permission, prohibition, or a duty involved with the generating maxim? ∎

Here are some thoughts on Thought Experiment 13–2. All conditions must be met in order for a particular speech act to be a lie—the two major ones being (1) A freely says something false; and (2) A sincerely intends to deceive C. If either is missing, then there is no lie.

In the case of a society of liars, one of two situations would occur.

Situation One: A habitually says that which is false (because A is a member of the society of liars trying to satisfy the first criterion). If A has said B to C, then A cannot legitimately expect that C will believe B to be true. This is because A habitually says that which is false. So if A tells C, "It is raining outside," C will think it is sunny since A habitually says that which is false. Therefore A cannot sincerely intend to deceive C (because C will always take whatever A says and believe just the opposite—and with good justification).

Situation Two: What if A focuses upon the second condition, that is, "sincerely intending to deceive." In this case, A will say that it is sunny outside when it really *is* sunny. C will think that the opposite of what A says is true and so believes it to be raining. A has thus deceived C.

But still we do not have a lie, because though the second condition is met (a sincere attempt to deceive), the first condition is not met, namely, A has said something which is untrue.

It would thus seem that a society of liars could not be constructed. The reason for this is that there is a logical incoherence in the concept of lying when it is generalized. The process of universalizing the maxim makes evident the logical incoherence, but the logical incoherence resides in any individual maxim, which advocates lying, as well.

Obviously, this assumes that the character of the individual maxim does not alter significantly when it is generalized. If it did, then the process of universalization would prove nothing about the individual maxim (more on this point in the evaluation section of this chapter).

There may be different ways to uncover the "inconsistencies" involved in particular maxims that have been universalized. The example I gave of lying above is merely one way to draw out an inconsistency. There are others. I would encourage the reader to try the process of universalization him/herself.

Four candidates that are suggested by Kant are: (1) John is contemplating suicide because he is depressed. What happens if his maxim were universalized as a law of nature? (2) Mary is contemplating making a promise she doesn't intend to keep in order to get out of some difficulties. Suppose she were to borrow money with no intention of paying it back—even though she said she would. What happens to her maxim if universalized? (3) Malcolm is a person who is filthy rich. He desires to chase women and take drugs rather than to increase his natural aptitude to teach others (in school he was a gifted tutor). Can Malcolm legitimately universalize his maxim of self-indulgence? What would such a society be like? (4) Marcia sees a family in her neighborhood whose major breadwinner suddenly becomes unemployed through no fault of her own. Should she just say, "What will be, will be" or "Let them eat cake!" or "This isn't my problem." What would happen if everyone turned her back on her fellow human being in distress?

The first two examples set out actions to be avoided: suicide and making a promise that one does not intend to keep. The duty not to perform these actions can be characterized as "perfect" because they follow directly from an application of the universalization of the categorical imperative (as per above).

The latter two examples can be characterized as "imperfect" because they follow from the categorical imperative only after considering some facts of human nature (such as all of us, ceteris paribus: seek our own happiness). If this addition is made, then one cannot fail to develop his/her natural capacities or to help another in distress (since one could not will to be ignored if s/he were in distress). The words "perfect" and "imperfect" do not signify gradations of strength or priority, but instead merely indicate their point of origin. An imperfect duty is just as strong in its action guiding force as a perfect duty.

These examples are difficult. They suggest that the foundation of compassion is in a disinterested, rational individual. This is different from others who may ground charity in sentiment or emotion.

THE SECOND FORM OF THE CATEGORICAL IMPERATIVE[16]

The second form of the categorical imperative is one that emphasizes **human dignity**. Kant asserted that among the goods that exist, some may be substituted for others.[17] For example, a car may be stolen from me and its loss can be compensated by some amount of money or by another like car. But there is no such compensation possible for intrinsic goods, namely, humans. This is because intrinsic goods are unique. They are priceless. As such, we assign them the designation, "dignity." People have dignity because they are not a commodity. They must be respected per se because they are unique and their uniqueness is grounded in the highest power we apprehend: REASON.

From this Kant derives the following imperative: "Act in such a way that you always treat humanity whether in your own person or in the person of any other never simply as a means, but always as an end."[18] Now it is important to be clear about the meaning of this second form of the categorical imperative. There are at least two key parts to this imperative: (a) the symmetry of one's attitude about oneself and other people, and (b) the invocation to recognize humans as ends. Let's address these in order.

First there is the symmetry of one's attitude about oneself and other people. This is a feature that is not explicitly stated in the first form(s) of the categorical imperative. I, as a human agent, am identical to all other human agents respecting my potential agency. Thus, the fact that I desire "x," does not mean that my claim for x is any greater than any other agent's claim for x. All count equally.

Second, humans are ends and this status (including their dignity and personal goals, values, and aspirations) must always be recognized. Since we live in an interdependent world, it is impossible not to depend upon others for the execution of various tasks—many of which are beneficial to us. This is using another as a "means" but not necessarily as a "means *only*." A few simple examples can describe the difference: I want to know the time of day. I can say to someone, "Hey, buddy, gimme the time," grabbing his wrist myself if he doesn't respond fast enough.

This is treating the other person as a means only. He is merely an instrument or tool for providing my wants. The alternative would be to say, "Excuse me, could you please tell me what time it is?" This way of responding to another recognizes that he is doing you a favor at his discretion.

THOUGHT EXPERIMENT 13–3: PEOPLE AS ENDS

You are a mid-level manager at a large corporation and you have a secretary. You have many tasks to present to him. How do you present these? If you treat him as if he were merely a robot that will pick up your laundry, make your coffee, and do your every bidding with a "yes ma'am, right away ma'am," then you are treating another as a means only. The alternative would be to take some interest in your secretary as a person and affirm his dignity by affording him respect and consulting him in areas in which he may have expertise. This latter behavior would allow his work to be as rewarding to him as is possible. ∎

According to Kant, the mid-level manager in Thought Experiment 13–3 should treat her secretary with dignity and respect. This is because the second form of the categorical imperative commands that we treat all people (ourselves and others) as ends and never as means only. To treat your secretary as if he were merely a robot would be to commit a category mistake. He is an independent person living in the world who cannot be exactly replaced by anyone. He is unique. His dignity arises from this uniqueness. To fail to recognize this uniqueness is to be illogical. One mistakes one sort of entity for another, that is, a human for a robot. The manager who does this demonstrates her ignorance. She is acting illogically. For Kant, the source of unethical behavior is always a logical mistake.

THOUGHT EXPERIMENT 13–4: PEOPLE AS MEANS

You own a factory that manufactures automobiles. You have a very efficient assembly line in which every worker executes one and only one task. You have time and motion experts that walk about the assembly line with stop watches in order to determine whether your production quotas will be met. You look down at your workers from your catwalk high above the production line and you dream up new slogans that are meant to impress upon your workers that they each comprise a cog in a well-oiled machine that produces cars. Yet you wonder why you have so much labor trouble and why every so often one of your workers throws a screwdriver into the interior of a passenger door that namelessly passes by her. What can Kant tell us about solving this labor problem? ■

In Thought Experiment 13–4, the boss is treating his employees as a means only. The alternative would be to involve the unions into the management process. Create teams that build cars together and assume responsibility and accountability for the cars they create. Encourage employees to master several tasks so that they are better able to feel a part of the entire production of the finished product. Such a strategy recognizes the dignity and creative element of the workers by engaging them as artisans or craftsmen and not merely cogs in a machine. The metaphor and its expression moves from viewing people as parts of a machine to a guild of skilled people whose personal pride is involved in each vehicle they produce.

Thought Experiments 13–3 and 13–4 are one dimensional, but they suggest an attitude in which people are unique and valuable and should be respected throughout any transaction—business or otherwise. The "kingdom of ends" is a community of compassionate and sympathetic people who are committed to one another's growth: individually and collectively.

CATEGORICAL IMPERATIVES ONE AND TWO

Together, the two forms of the categorical imperative work together to provide: (1) a formal justification of action which highlights perfect and imperfect duties, and (2) a materially concrete depiction of the way such a society would behave towards themselves and towards each other.

The categorical imperative (in each of its two forms) provides a candidate for the ground of all moral duty.

THOUGHT EXPERIMENT 13–5

Think about your own life. Have you had any important decisions of late? Your major? Your boyfriend/girlfriend? You thoughts about a career? Issues at home? List a few of these important decisions on a sheet of paper. Then examine each to see whether there is a prohibition, obligation, or permission involved. Once you have made this classification, then set them out into Kant's framework for solving the issue.

Are you happy with these prescriptions? Is "happy" the right way to ask the question? What do you ultimately think that you should do—and *why*? ■

One's response to Thought Experiment 13–5 moves you into internalizing the machinery of Kant's ethical theory. He may be right. He may be wrong. But before you can evaluate him, you must learn how to manipulate his theoretical system.

ARGUMENTS AGAINST THE THEORY

The principal criticism of deontology is that "duty" is too thin a concept upon which to base a moral theory. One is inclined to ask, "Duty to do what? And why?" The answer to the first question is dependent upon the answer to the second. And the justification to the second can be very abstract and divorced from the realm of human action (i.e., day-to-day life).

This can become a problem if the process of abstraction "changes things." Wittgenstein thought a test of whether philosophies were working properly was whether it was merely a tool to explore truth, that is, it "left things alone." Well, in this case of abstraction, "leaving things alone" is precisely what is at issue. Do we leave things alone when we abstract, or do we alter the *explanandum* (the phenomena which we seek to explain)?

One might say that the answer to this would lie in whether the essential character of the *explanandum* alters in a significant way when it is abstracted. This is not an easy problem. It is the exact complement of the same issue of "reduction" in philosophy of science. In this case, the question is whether one "changes" the *explanandum* by reducing it to a lower level (e.g., in philosophy of biology moving from the phenotype to genotype to explain the dynamics of evolution). Some say that things change, while others demur.

In order to evaluate this question in the context of deontological ethics, one must determine whether the abstraction that Kant uses in the first form of the categorical imperative really changes things. If they do, and if "changing things" is really a good test, then there may be a lacuna between what the deontologists claim to have justified and the concrete lives of humans living in the world.

One problem that vexes modern Kantians and modern neo-Kantians is which Kant to support? The author of the first form of the categorical imperative in its two versions, or the author of the second form of the categorical imperative? They recreate a Kant in that image. Others have thought that the first form was the essence of Kant. Still further, there are others beginning with Bruce Aune and followed by Barbara Herman, Onora O'Neil, Christine Korsgaard, and Thomas Hill who seek a more integrated Kant by emphasizing Kant's other works on morality (such as *The Critique of Practical Reason, The Metaphysics of Morals,* and *The Lectures on Ethics,* among others). These authors seek to present a unified Kant and to assert that the *Groundwork of the Metaphysics of Morals* should not be overemphasized in evaluating Kant's moral theory.

There is some justification in these remarks. A balanced view of any author should rest on his/her views in his/her entire corpus. Still, the *Groundwork* has been the work of principal focus because of the unity and structure of its argument.

At any rate, some may criticize Kant for holding what seem to be various views on the foundations of morality. These critics would try to emphasize incoherence between the various positions.

Hegel leveled another criticism of Kant. What it amounted to was that the abstraction of Kant's forms of the categorical imperative ignored the concrete reality of the family, community, and the nation. In both *The Philosophy of Right* and *The Phenomenology of Spirit* Hegel criticizes Kant for failing to account for concrete reality.[19] This is similar to the general criticism discussed above, but its particular instantiation with Kant vis-à-vis Hegel is that Kant does not recognize the *sitten* (customs) in his title *Grundlegung zur Metaphysik der Sitten.* Where should the starting point be when exploring ethics? The abstract form of reason, as such, or the existing, concrete moral community?

For those who think the latter, Kant's whole enterprise is doomed from the start. By failing to account for the concrete reality, these detractors will say that Kant divorces himself from actual human experience. This means that he creates an empty set of rules "full of sound and fury and signifying nothing."

THOUGHT EXPERIMENT 13-6

You have lived in Plattsville all your life. It is a small town of 25,000 people in the middle of nowhere, USA. However, some notable people have come from Plattsville. For example, the inventor of the rotary dial on the telephone was born and raised here, as was an inventor who discovered several key patents essential for the hybrid automobile engine. There were some bad types, too. The founder of the Ku Klux Klan hailed from Plattsville. The town has two lynchings of innocent African Americans in its history. Also, a key accountant in the X-Ron scandal (that brought down a Fortune 100 company and ruined millions financially) hailed from here.

So what do you have to say? Do you agree with Hegel that with time, the culture of a town will overcome all and move forward to ethical rectitude? Or do you agree with Kant that we need firm principles that common folk can use to reform the system from without? Will the spirit of the culture be enough? Can we appeal to anything else? ■

Proponents of Hegel suggest that there is an evolutionary direction to human history. Things are getting better—especially in societies that have a tradition that accept concrete values that bounce dialectically against aspirational visions of the good (in the context of real, everyday demands).

Essentially this is a problem of method. What model should we choose? If it is one that relies upon the instincts of the social scientists, then Kant has made a grave error. If logic and mathematics are a better paradigm, then Kant is vindicated.

Of course, this overemphasizes the place of Kant's first form of the categorical imperative. If we accept the "integrated" vision, then one would have to modify this objection to one that objects to "rationality" as being the ground of ethical theory.

Such a critique is rather specific: it depends upon one's depiction of rationality and how one applies it. The reader should view writings of the "integrated" vision in order to ascertain whether they present an unreasonable vision of rationality.

The last problem to be considered here is whether a "**claims right**" must be actually "claimed" by the agent in question (instead of merely being properly attributable to him/her). If a claims right must be claimed to be operative,[20] then our inquiry must take in descriptive features concerning why some groups may or may not claim rights during various historical epochs. The question then takes on a political/sociological dimension. Such a direction would go against the universality and timelessness that many deontologists (including this author) seek to obtain.

If, on the other hand, the claims right need not be claimed in order to be properly attributed, then one can ascribe rights to various individuals and groups of individuals regardless of whether or not they actually made such a claim. For example, the United Nations Universal Declaration of Human Rights (1948) takes such a view. Basic human rights are possessed by all, even if those people live in a culture that has never recognized such rights and even if those people, themselves, have never explicitly demanded that those rights be recognized.

The difficulty with such a position is that it creates another realm in which said rights exist or else it asserts a form of essentialism that includes human rights in the package. Either of these alternatives presents problems to those who desire a sparser and less populated metaphysical realm.

A response would be to deny the efficacy of Hegel's criticism. Alan Donagan believes that Hegel's criticism would lead to a bipolar view of morality such as espoused by Michael Oakeshott in *Rationalism in Politics*.[21] Oakeshott adopts one sort of morality, which Donagan depicts as Hegel's *Sittlichkeit* (the domain of the accepted customs within an ethical community). This sort of morality proceeds as custom until it is in need of critical revision, at which time it reverts to a stance of traditional morality, *Moralität*.

But Donagan believes that unless one has a timeless, universal morality, one will never know when to make the switch. Indeed, when you really need it (such as the case of the martyr against the Nazis, Franz Jägerstätter) the *Sittlichkeit* within an ethical community comes up short. The *Sittlichkeit* becomes the empty vessel instead of *Moralität*.[22]

In the end of the day, the detractors of Kant characterize him as being rigid and driven by an unyielding logic. They say that this misses much of what it really means to be a person living in the world: emotion, spontaneity, and joie de vivre. It is up to you to make this determination for yourselves. There is certainly a hard line that is necessarily advocated by all who believe in a moral personal worldview. The question is whether Kant has got it right?

In the end each reader must decide whether the advantages of this theory outweigh the disadvantages.

KEY TERMS

- deontology
- categorical imperative
- human dignity
- claims right

A CHALLENGING CASE STUDY

Directions: Write a two-and-a-half page essay (750 words) on the following case. Be sure to first set out what you believe the deontological position to be. Second, evaluate whether you agree with this solution or not based upon personal worldview or community worldview tenets. Make your reasons very explicit. Be sure to highlight one of Kant's categorical imperatives regarding prohibitions, obligations, and permissions in formulating your answer.

You go to a small university. You are very much in love with your boyfriend, Micah. He is a strong, loyal, plodding type, and you think that you definitely want to marry him. You have been living with him for the past eighteen months. The problem is that you met Jemal. He is a sports star and you think he is really hot. One night after he scored 35 points to lead the university to an important win, you were in a coterie who surrounded Jemal. Micah was studying for his math exam. On that night you had sex with Jemal. You know that Micah is a very traditional person. He doesn't even look at other women because he is attached to you. After the game and the affair you return to Micah and have sex with him, but he becomes suspicious (because he says it's different). He asks you whether you have been with someone else. What do you say? Direct your responses to the rules of deontology.

NOTES

1. Wesley N. Hohfled, *Fundamental Legal Conceptions* (New Haven, CT: Yale University Press, 1919).
2. Michael Boylan, "The Universal Right to Healthcare" in *Ethical Issues in Business,* (New York: Harcourt Brace, 1995).
3. H. L. A. Hart, "Are There Any Natural Rights?" *Philosophical Review* 64 (1955): 176–177; John Austin, *Lectures on Jurisprudence,* 5th ed., ed. Robert Campbell (London: John Murray, 1883).
4. See the essays by Beth Singer and Virginia Held in *Gewirth: Critical Essays on Action, Rationality and Community,* ed. Michael Boylan (New York: Roman and Littlefield, 1999).
5. Ibid.
6. This is a question of some dispute. See Singer and Reiman's comments in Boylan, *Gewirth* 1999.
7. By and large I will follow H. J. Paton, *The Categorical Imperative* (London: Hutchinson, 1947). This is often depicted as a traditional reading of Kant.
8. Any historical figure in philosophy undergoes a "revision" regularly if she is considered worthy of the time. The reader is directed to the suggested readings at the end of this section for alternative understandings of Kant.
9. Kant, *Groundwork*, 40–44/414–417.
10. Save for some commentators such as David Cummiskey, *Kantian Consequentialism* (Oxford: Oxford Press, 1996): 47–50
11. One does not want to fall into the fallacy of "denying the antecedent," i.e., just because the antecedent is false, that the consequent must also be false. "F ⇒ T or F" in truth functional logic is true. Kant did not have these points in mind when he was writing *Groundwork*, but it does not matter. Kant's point is not "truth functional logic," but some sort of existential claim. If the antecedent does not occur in a *uniquely defining relationship*, then the

consequent will also fail to be. This is the difference between a general "truth functional" conditional and an "existential conditional" whose antecedent relates to the consequent as a uniquely determining relationship.

12. See David Cummiskey, *Kant's Conse-quentialism* (New York: Oxford University Press, 1996).

13. Though I depict morality as fundamentally based upon reason, this does not mean that there are not other important imputs, as well. These might include the overlays of emotion (such as sympathy and love), religion, professional, and aesthetic values.

14. For a further discussion of these issues see Chapter 7.

15. The addition of 'freely' to this commonly accepted definition is to eliminate cases of coercion such that Thomas's dictum of "*novus actus interveniens*" is not violated.

16. Strictly speaking there are three forms of the categorical imperative. The first occurs at 421/52 and says, "Act only on that maxim through which you can at the same time will that it should become a universal law." The second occurs at 421/52 and says, "Act *as if* the maxim of your action were *to become* a universal law of *nature*" (tr. Paton, italics are mine). The difference between the first two forms revolves around the perfect and the imperfect duties (i.e., perfect duties flow from the first form while imperfect duties are associated with the second). In the above examples, the first two are said to flow from the first and the second two from the second.

Then there is the third form (which I am calling the second form — above). In this case Kant has created a much more empirically rich principle which is built upon nonexploitation of others: "Act in such a way that you always treat humanity whether in your own person or in the person of any other, never simply as a means, but always at the same time as an end" (429/66–7).

17. Ibid, 435–437

18. Kant's *Groundwork*, 429.

19. G.W.F. Hegel, *Hegel's Philosophy of Right*, trans. T. M. Knox (Oxford: Clarendon Press, 1942), 90–91. Hegel, *Hegel's Phenomenology of Spirit*, trans. A.V. Miller (Oxford: Oxford University Press, 1977), 29–32 Cf. also to W.H. Walsh's discussion in *Hegelian Ethics* (N.Y.: St. Martin's Press, 1969), chaps 4–7.

20. Beth J. Singer makes just such a point in her book, *Operative Rights* (New York: SUNY Press, 1995).

21. Michael Oakeshott, *Rationalism in Politics and Other Essays* (London: Methuen, 1962), 65–70.

22. Cf. Donagan's discussion, 13–16.

PART

3

PUTTING IT ALL TOGETHER

CHAPTER

14

FORMULATING YOUR OWN ANSWERS

- ❖ Snapshot
- ❖ The Problem
- ❖ The Topography of Theory Evaluation
- ❖ How To Choose an Ethical Theory
- ❖ Key Terms
- ❖ A Comprehensive Integrative Exercise

SNAPSHOT

This chapter will examine the criteria that one ought to adopt when evaluating an ethical theory. It will be suggested that logical justification *alone* is not sufficient to choose a moral theory. What is needed in addition is the more robust vision of the agent's personal worldview. This creates a richer environment in which to consider which ethical theories and positions to embrace. Two worldview standpoints will be examined: the personal and the community.

THE PROBLEM

It has been widely held among philosophers, at least since Kant, that providing a firm, internally consistent foundation to an ethical theory offers a good and *sufficient* reason for believing in and personally adopting said theory. Other approaches considered in Part 1 of this book — such as the personal worldview imperative, feminist ethics, religious ethics, and others offer a more holistic vision. For ease in reference, let's agree to call this approach the mode of rational justification. Other modes of belief acceptance come from other values in one's worldview more broadly considered. These can also be described as **understanding the theory**.

The initial appeal of the rational mode of justifying a theory of morality, or of any other theory, is the paradigm of Euclid's or Hilbert's axiomatic geometry.[1] These authors seek to mechanize what, at first, seems to be an unruly discipline.[2] Indeed, the lure of such theories seems to be that: (a) one is presented with a system that contains only a few generating principles (fewer initial axioms one must defend lessens one's "burden of proof"); (b) the theorems which are proven from the axioms and the primitive rule(s) of inference, are true due to "heritability," that is, traits of the "progenitor" which are thought to transfer to the "offspring;" (c) the "closed nature" of the system dictates that indeed there are theorems within the system which cannot be proven (thus, on one level, ensuring its coherence)[3] and, therefore clear, robust boundaries are created around the theory. There is a sense of what is "inside" and "outside" the theory.[4]

This strategy demarcates the realm of the theory. If one were faced with competing theories in mathematics or logic one might appreciate such a clearly demarcated theory. It would resemble theories of science (in the modern sense) as presented to us in reconstruction by philosophers of science.[5]

This work is important. There is no getting around the fact that the phase of logical justification of an ethical theory is important. Axiomatic theories create a self-contained, "law-governed" universe that is finite and can be tested.[6] One aspect of our rational natures is supremely satisfied with the logical necessity derived from such an exercise. Thus, the **rational justification of a theory** of ethics is very appealing.

THE TOPOGRAPHY OF THEORY EVALUATION

The last section touted the role of rational justification. Certainly, much of the appeal of a theory based upon a supreme principle of morality is its affinity to closed logical systems and the formal necessity attributed to them. One might be led to the conclusion that if one provides a *justification* within the style of a closed, deductive system, that she has done enough. Once the reader logically accepts the argument as presented, and has exhausted her rebuttals, then she must accept and act upon the conclusions of such a system.

However, as suggested earlier, Part 1 of this book has shown that there may be more important aspects to our worldview than merely logic. These values are important for determining action and the rules that govern action. This is a complicated process that can be assessed in various ways. One manner of holistic examination might go according to Case 14–1.

CASES

Case 14–1   THE WAY WE CONFRONT NOVEL NORMATIVE THEORIES

I. OVERVIEW AND JUSTIFICATION

A. Stage One

1. CONSIDERING THE THEORY. When we consider an ethical theory fully, both *its justification* and *our understanding* of its application need to be considered (i.e., the kind of world that would be created if we accepted the theory). If the theory is sufficiently interesting in these ways, we create a favorable overview of the theory. This prompts more careful, formal analysis (justifying the theory).

2. JUSTIFYING THE THEORY. We logically justify the theory by testing the theory on its own terms for logical validity, soundness, and cogency. If the theory passes our test(s) we move to stage two.

II. DIALECTICAL UNDERSTANDING

A. Stage Two

1. REFLECTING ON OUR OWN WORLDVIEW. We entertain our own worldview with all its various components including our metaphysical, epistemological, ethical, and personal convictions and judgments.[7]

2. COMPARING OUR WORLDVIEW TO THE NEW THEORY. This involves an interaction between the two stages.

3. UNDERSTANDING THE THEORY. From this comparison one of three things will happen: (a) **coinciding and amplification:** The model and one's worldview will coincide and the model will enhance one's worldview by giving it additional structure; (b) **dissonance and rejection:** The model and one's world view will be far apart and we will reject the model (in this case we may return to *justifying the theory* for a time and then possibly onto stage three—although complete theory rejection is more likely); and (c) *worldview overlap and modification:* The model and one's worldview will not be identical, but there is at least some consonance so that one continues a more complicated examination that will identify anomalies in either the theory (in which case we may modify the theory or reject it) or our worldview (in which case we may modify our world view because of the theory—assuming we are seekers of truth). In most cases *worldview overlap and modification* will cause us to move to stage three.

B. Stage Three

1. DIALECTICAL INTERACTION. This stage is a rather long process of dialectical interaction between the agent's worldview and the theory itself. As in Hegelian dialectic, both poles cannot be viewed *simpliciter,* but only mediately through the other at the same time. As we progress through these dialectical moments, we observe a modification of the theory and worldview occurs so that when equilibrium is achieved, the result is a transformation in which both the novel theory and the old worldview are discarded. In their place is a new amalgam that owes its origins to the generating poles, but like any offspring, although it may display various resemblances, it is own entity.[8] ■

Let's examine two examples to better understand how this process works. Since *coinciding and amplification* is not problematic, there is no need for an example here. In *dissonance and rejection*, the best example is Zeno's paradoxes of motion.[9] Zeno offered strong deductive arguments arguing that all is static: there is no motion. To the ancient Greeks these are powerful arguments that, if accepted, would imply that our empirical sensations (that report to us that there is motion in the world) are false. If motion is false, and our senses are mistaken, then the sources of knowing and what is good would lie elsewhere.

Did the ancients simply accept Zeno's argument and agree that "what is" consists of a motionless and static One? The answer is largely, "no!" Why is this? The reason is that when confronted with a theory that describes or prescribes propositions that are different from our worldview, we act cautiously. The inclination in *dissonance and rejection* is to reject the new theory. The most obvious way to do this is to provide an internal refutation. But in the ancient world this was not so easy. Indeed, it was not until the development of transfinite numbers and the resultant application of transfinite sums (in the latter nineteenth and early twentieth centuries) that Zeno's paradoxes were refuted.[10] But even in the ancient world there were attempts at dealing with infinitesimals through the theory of exhaustion. As Ian Mueller points out, Euclid XII.2 suggests the groundwork for such a theory that was also used to "square the circle."[11]

The point is that though many thinkers could not come up with an adequate refutation of Zeno, they did not simply *accept* Zeno either. The reason for this is that Zeno's theory and the consequences it suggested did not square with their fuller worldview. This larger picture suggested that though one could not come up with an adequate argument to prove Zeno wrong, still one was not prepared to accept the theory, either.

Now some might argue that *dissonance and rejection* will lead to blind prejudice. A person hears a logically persuasive position and though he cannot come up with a rejoinder, will nonetheless reject the theory.

Descriptively I believe this to be true.[12] Much of the work over the last 35 years on so-called revolutions in the history of science documents that theory changes do not come easily.[13] In fact, Hilary Putnam has suggested that the more reasonable approach to a theory replacement situation is to "fix" the old theory rather than adopt a new one.[14] This is because without proven anomalies in the existing theory (in our case the subject's worldview), there is no reason to change. "If it ain't broken, don't fix it" is the old adage. *Dissonance and rejection* describes a situation in which one is inclined to remain in his existing worldview even when confronted with a logically sound argument.

Does this mean that the dynamics of *dissonance and rejection* are always arbitrary and prejudicial? I don't think so. There are some touchstones of value that are independent of the proposition at hand. These touchstones come from our other core values. For example, in the case of Zeno's paradox, one may have a core value in a realist epistemology that is offended by Zeno's contention that empirical data are somehow illusions.

Still another person may have a core value in religion. In this situation let us imagine a Jewish philosopher who believed that his God was not a trickster. Thus, it would be impossible (given that belief) for God to create an intricate set of illusions meant to test humankind's faith.

A third person might be a devoted artist whose mission in life is to imitate nature for the purpose of conveying truth. If nature, itself, were merely an elaborate ruse, then his entire stock of values would be wholly misplaced.

In each of these three cases, it is the core values of the adherent that serve as a check upon untenable theories and occasion the reaction of *dissonance and rejection.*

It is also possible that an irrationally based value comes into play that most would judge to be evil. For example, say a Nazi were to address some maxim concerning the universal rights of all humans, for example, "All humans have the right to their basic goods of agency against their society and the world community in virtue of Kant's categorical imperatives."

The Nazi says, "This is crap. I won't buy this. Jews and Gypsies are a scourge on our Fatherland; they must be eliminated!"

"But upon what do you base such an opinion?" asks the philosopher.

"It's what I've always believed. Ask anyone else; they believe it, too."

"But what is the alternate core value that is being violated by the principle of universal human rights?"

"Are you kidding? It's that these Jews and Gypsies are a scourge on our Fatherland. Haven't you been listening?"

"But *where* does that value come from?"

"I don't know. From my parents, friends—the *Sittlichkeit*, don't you know? Where else?"

What position does this put us in?

Well, it is not the absolutely content position of those who only appeal to the logical justification mode. No, that complete comfort has been set aside. But it is not a relativist position either. This is because one can evaluate the principles upon which these side values are based and let them stand on their own stead. If they are complete, coherent, and good, then so be it. But in the above example, they are not. When one presses on *why* these groups are a scourge, she is left vacant. There *is* no consistent reason aside from anecdotal fabrications (e.g., the Jews are stealing all the money from our country or the Gypsies are kidnapping children and drinking their blood). It seems to me that, for the most part, such pretenders to legitimate *dissonance and rejection* are, in fact, easily depicted illogical shams.

When there is some connection between the presented theory and the worldview of the person considering the novel theory of good, then the interplay of *worldview overlap and modification* and stage three dialectical interaction become possible. A good example of this can be found in the Reverend Dr. Martin Luther King, Jr. The proposition that Dr. King was trying to get white America to accept was that African Americans were living under oppressive Jim Crow laws in the South and vicious de facto apartheid in the North. His enormous task was to alter the shared community worldview and thereby create theory acceptance of racial equality.

This was not an easy task.

What Dr. King did was to bridge the two worldview of black and white America. On the side of black America, King (like his father before him) ministered daily to the victims of racial oppression. On the white side King was a Christian minister (the principal religion of white America) and a PhD in divinity from Boston University (white America respects those educated in its own institutions). In this way Dr. King had enough commonalities with white America that when white people turned on the evening news and saw peaceful African American protesters signing Christian hymns while being beaten by police, knocked down by fire hoses, and attacked by fierce police dogs the television watchers were confronted with cognitive dissonance. On the one hand, they honored the police and the white power structure that ruled the nation—because that's the way it always had been. On the other hand, they sang hymns in church each Sunday about a peaceful God who loves all people. Who did they want to identify with: peaceful black folk or over zealous policemen bent on cruelty? Their own personal world-views dictated the former. Their own personal worldviews said that Dr. King's logical argument for racial equality was valid. But it took the stage three dialectical process occasioned by *worldview overlap and modification* for any real progress to be made in the *actual* acceptance of King's ideas. And though the struggle for racial equality isn't over by a long way, most people who lived through that era would agree that Dr. King, over time, won over a majority of white America. The process of theory acceptance depended upon more than a strong logical argument for its justification. It also required the dialectical interactions brought about by worldview overlap and modification.

It is the contention of this book that the above process of overlap and modification constitutes the way we actually accept novel norma-tive theories. Certainly, there is a stage of deductive and inductive argu-mentation. But then there is the inevitable sorting of those predisposed to be in favor of the novel theory (coinciding and amplification) and those predisposed to be against (dissonance and rejection).[15] When either of these alternatives results, then the existing worldview and not the argument at hand decides whether the agent will accept the theory put before him or not. In the vast majority of cases this is the end of the story. But there is also that glimmer of hope that the purveyor of the new theory can find enough common ground in order to initiate the sort of dialectical worldview interactions that Dr. King was able to initiate.[16]

Case 14–1 is offered to readers as a device to both explain the process of worldview shift (both personal and community) as well as an explanatory tool to justify such shifts in a more holistic way than mere logical justification (see the next section).

HOW TO CHOOSE AN ETHICAL THEORY

The basic strategy recommended in this book for choosing an ethical theory is to first consult your personal and shared community world-views against the relevant imperatives so that one might begin from a recognized and chosen position. In the case of this book that will mean coming to terms with the basic questions highlighted in Part 1. These questions are challenging, but do not represent *all* the questions one must ask himself. Each reader will have additional personal issues that were highlighted in the exercises at the end of Chapter 2 on personal and community worldview. All of this material must be viewed together so that one's standpoint is self-consciously accepted.

The second phase is to undergo the process recommended in Case 14–1. The best way to do this is to break the process down into its component steps. For example, in step one a person should consider just how the theory works and what difference it would make in your life and in your community if the theory in question were to be adopted. How does such a theory square with your own worldview and that of your community? What other values are at issue in this overview? How deeply embedded are these issues? Do any of them appear to be show stoppers?

If you are still comfortable in continuing, then re-examine the logical justification that was given to support the theory. How do you evaluate the justification? Are the premises true and the inferences sound? If so, proceed to step two. You may want to refer to your work on the exercises at the end of the chapters in Part 2 to help you go through this stage of evaluation.

In step two, you need to imagine accepting the theory for yourself and for your community. How would things be different? What are the most controversial aspects of the theory? How do they match up against your personal and community worldviews? The result of this will either be *coinciding and amplification, dissonance and rejection,* or **overlap and modification.** If either of the first two outcomes occurs, you're done. Either you already believe in the theory in some form, or its controversial features are so contrary to pivotal worldview tenets that you have to reject it at this point.

If you elicit overlap and modification, then you are ready to undergo stage three. Stage three is less regimented than the other two stages. There is not single formula for matching your new potential worldview or worldview tenet against your existing one. The two are brought together in various ways: justification, predicted results, and compatibility with other worldview tenets. The point is that you have to understand why a change is being suggested and whether, all things considered, you believe the change to be for the better. It is not an easy project, but it will lend an authenticity to your beliefs.

Now that we've reviewed the process, it's time to test drive it.

KEY TERMS

- rational justification of a moral theory
- dissonance and rejection
- coinciding and amplification
- overlap and modification

A COMPREHENSIVE INTEGRATIVE EXERCISE

The following two-part exercise is meant to assist the reader to bring the whole text together in a personal way for each person.

EXERCISE ONE

Using the work from the personal worldview exercise in Chapter 2 and some of the other exercises from favorite chapters in Part 1, isolate two or three challenges to your personal worldview as it is now just as you read the words on this page. (A "challenge" here will be defined as an intriguing possible change or alteration to your personal worldview.) Write down those challenges and the chapters that discuss them.

Next, run each challenge through the process described in Case 14–1 and generate an outcome (describing your worldview interactions that lead you to your conclusion): *dissonance and rejection* or *overlap and modification.* If it is the latter, continue through the dialectical interactions of stage three. After this is complete, give an account of why you have modified your worldview in these respects or not.

EXERCISE TWO

Using the work from the community worldview exercise in Chapter 2 and some of the other exercises from favorite chapters in Part 2, isolate two contenders to being your preferred ethical theory according to your work in exercise one and your

shared community worldview as it now is as you read the words on this page. (A "contender" here will be defined as an intriguing possible change or alteration to your personal/community worldview.) Write down those contenders and the chapters that discuss them.

Finally, run each contender through the process described in Case 14–1 and generate a preferred theory (describing your worldview interactions that lead you to your conclusion): *coinciding and amplification, dissonance and rejection,* or *overlap and modification.* If it is the latter continue through the dialectical interactions of stage three. After this is complete, give an account of why you have modified your worldview in these respects or not.

Your final product from this exercise will be your own assessment of the various controversial tenets of personal and community worldview that have been presented in this book. The outcome is an ethical theory and standpoint of life that you can legitimately call your own. Congratulations!

NOTES

1. Euclid, *Die Elemente*, trans. C. Thaer (repr. Darmstadt: Wissenschaftliche Buchges, 1969); D. Hilbert, *Grundlagen der Geometrie,* 10th ed., with revisions and additions by P. Bernays (Stuttgart: Teubner 1968).

2. The point being made here is a general one. Obviously, there are other disputes such as the difference between mechanizing elementary geometry versus mathematical reasoning with mechanical theorem proving. For a discussion of these finer points see H. Poincaré, "Review of D. Hilbert," *Grundlagen der Geometrie, Bulletin des*

Sciences Mathématiques, 2nd series, 26 (1902): 249–272.

3. Kurt Gödel spells out these implications in "Über formal unentscheidbare Sätze der Principia Mathematica und verwandter System I," *Monatschefte für Mathematik und Physik* 38 (1931): 173–198; trans. J. van Heijenoort, *From Frege to Gödel, Sourcebook on Mathematical Logic* (Cambridge, MA: Harvard University Press, 1967).

4. The literature on boundary conditions is rather more in philosophy of science. For some of the central issues see: Rudolf Carnap, "The Logical

Foundations of the Unity of Science" in *International Encyclopedia of Unified Science: Volume I,* ed. O. Neurath, R. Carnap, and C. Morris (Chicago: University of Chicago Press, 1938–55), 42–62; and Paul Oppenheim and Hilary Putnam, "Unity of Science as a Working Hypothesis," *Minnesota Studies in the Philosophy of Science,* vol. II, ed. H. Feigl, M. Scriven, and G. Maxwell (Minneapolis: University of Minnesota Press, 1958), 3–36. These two essays set the logical empiricist position from which most of the "reactions" have been from biology. See especially: Alan Garfinkel, *Forms of Explanation* (New Haven: Yale University Press, 1981), 49–74; and J. Sterelny and Philip Kitcher, "The Return of the Gene," *Journal of Philosophy* 85, no. 7 (July, 1988): 339–361. In philosophy of biology (as in the logical empiricist account) boundary conditions are important. However, in biology the contention is that there is causation from "top" to "bottom" and vice versa, as opposed to the logical empiricists who claim only "bottom" to "top" causation.

5. In fact, it is my contention that the literature in philosophy of science is very useful to this question from the point of view of the axiomatic approach—given that the logical empiricists were greatly influenced by the mechanized-application models which aspired to the design of Euclid or Hilbert as a perfect end.

6. Onora O'Neill would contend that Kant's Single Principle Theory offers not only the supreme principle of morality, but of reason, itself—see "Reason and Politics in the Kantian Enterprise" in *Constructions of Reason: Explorations of Kant's Practical Philosophy* (Cambridge: Cambridge University Press, 1989).

This is typical of the attraction of Single Principle Theory advocates—though O'Neill would also contend that the first form of the categorical imperative, by itself, does not properly describe Kant.

7. For personal convictions I am primarily thinking about aesthetic and/or religious beliefs and judgments we may hold. These may, of course, follow from our metaphysical, epistemological, and ethical positions.

8. This entity may exhibit more traits of one or the other progenitor. Just because the offspring is born of dialectic does not mean there is equal mixing.

9. The four paradoxes of motion can be found in Aristotle: (a) The Stadium, *Phys.* Z9, 233a 21–24; *Topics* 160b 7–11; (b) The Achilles, *Phys.* Z9 239b 14–16; (c) The Flying Arrow, *Phys.* Z9 239b 30–31; (d) The Moving Rows, *Phys.* Z9 239b 33.

10. See especially G. E. L. Owen, "Zeno and the Mathematicians," *Proceedings of the Aristotelian Society,* 58 (1957–58): 199–222; J.F. Thomson, "Tasks and Super-Tasks," *Analysis* 15 (1954): 1–13; Gregory Vlastos, "A Note on Zeno's Arrow," *Phronesis* 11 (1966): 3–18; Gregory Vlastos, "Zero's Race Course," *Journal of the History of Philosophy* 4 (1966): 95–108; James Watling, "The Sum of an Infinite Series," *Analysis* 13 (1953): 39–42.

11. Ian Mueller, *Philosophy of Mathematics and Deductive Structure in Euclid 's "Elements,"* (Cambridge, MA: M.I.T. Press, 1981), 234; compare T. L. Heath, "Greek Geometry with Special Reference to Infinitesimals," *The Mathematical Gazette* 11 (1922–1923): 248–259; Simplicius, *Commentary on Aristotle's Physics,* ed. H. Diets, 2 vol. (Berlin: G. Reimeri 1882, 1895). Simplicius gives an account of Antiphon's reasoning on page 54.

12. It is my opinion that prejudice is *unfortunately* a very real fact of Homo sapiens' behavior. This does not mean that I condone it in any way. It *does* mean that it is not surprising that there is so much prejudice that exists all over the world. From the United States, to the Congo, to Cambodia, the history of the world reflects this prejudice. What we must therefore do, as moral thinkers, is to think of ways to alleviate this natural inclination. The only hope for change is in the mode of overlap and modification.

13. The classic example of course is Thomas S. Kuhn, *The Structure of Scientific Revolutions* 2nd ed (Chicago, Illinois: University of Chicago Press, 1970).

14. Hilary Putnam, "The 'Corroboration' of Theories" from The Library of Living Philosophers, vol xiv, *The Philosophy of Karl Popper,* ed. Paul A. Schilpp (LaSalle, Illinois: Open Court, 1974), 221–240. Putnam is arguing against Popper's thesis in *The Logic of Scientific Discovery* by discussing the actual behavior of scientists when Uranus's orbit was found to be incorrect (before the discovery of Neptune). This behavior was directed at modifying existing theories rather than discarding them. Thus the goal of "all or nothing" does not describe the way scientists act.

15. There is also, of course, those who properly use dissonance and rejection as in the earlier example involving Zeno's paradoxes.

16. This is also the model of Plato's depiction of Socrates as well as most other philosophers who have chosen the dialogue form to express their philosophy.

GLOSSARY

All terms in the glossary come from the key terms listed at the end of each chapter.

ABSOLUTE GOOD   From the realistic perspective, this refers to the actual existence of goodness in the natural and/or supernatural realm; from the antirealistic position there is no absolute good. (It is all defined functionally or via linguistic convention.)

ACTUALIZATION, PERSONAL   In virtue ethics, creating an integrated character with the middle way of moderation in accord with reason.

ACT UTILITARIANISM   The interpretation of utilitarianism that says that each moral situation should be subjected to the utilitarian formula "the greatest good for the greatest number."

AGGREGATE UTILITY   The view that general hedonism is measured through an aggregate counting of happiness/pleasure as measured via money or some other externalist currency. The highest aggregate counts as satisfying the formula "the greatest good for the greatest number." This may conflict with average utility.

ALTRUISM   Acting from the motivation of principle or duty rather than from the motivation of any personal advantage.

ANTIREALISM, MORAL   See moral realism and antirealism.

APPLIED ETHICS   Deals with applying normative theories to actual moral situations.

ARISTOTELIAN MEAN   The doctrine that the way to be good is the middle way between extremes: for example courage is midway between cowardice and foolhardiness. The person seeking this lifestyle will aim to be moderate in all that she does. Moderation is excellence (virtue).

AVERAGE UTILITY   The view that general hedonism is measured through the average (mean, median, or modal) happiness of representative people in the society. The highest average counts as satisfying the formula "the greatest good for the greatest number." This may conflict with aggregate utility.

BLIND PREJUDICE PROBLEM   Asserts culturally based preferences that are not functionally tied to the phenomena they are describing.

CARE AND JUSTICE   Care is generally characterized as emphasizing *relationships* and *emotive connection* (sympathy). It is contrasted with "justice," which focuses upon abstract principles of equality and fairness.

CATEGORICAL IMPERATIVE   The categorical imperative is the supreme principle of morality for Immanuel Kant's deontology. There are two versions of the imperative that generate ethical prohibitions and obligations. The categorical imperative constitutes a command of moral absolutism coming from moral realism.

CHARACTER   See habits of character.

COHERENCE/INCOHERENCE   With respect to the personal worldview imperative coherence/incoherence comes in two varieties. Deductive incoherence is an instance of direct contradictory behaviors. Inductive incoherence is an instance of contradictory life policies that lead to a sure loss contract.

COINCIDING AND AMPLIFICATION   This is one of three reactions that agents exhibit when they move into stage two of process of evaluating normative theories. This reaction is one that says the new approach is basically the same or reinforces one's own personal or community worldview.

COMMON BODY OF KNOWLEDGE A set of factual and normative principles about which there is general agreement among a community or between communities of people. This includes (but is not limited to) agreement on what constitutes objective facts and how to measure them. It also includes (but is not limited to) what counts as acceptable values that will be recognized as valid in the realms of ethics, aesthetics, and religion.

COMPREHENSIVENESS With respect to the personal worldview imperative, is the same as completeness. It means that whenever one is presented with a novel situation in life, she has an answer that comes from her personal worldview. The two forms of the goodwill: Kantian and Augustinian (rational and emotive) ensure that this will be the case.

CONTRACTARIANS See ethical contractarianism.

CULTURAL RELATIVISM, LEGITIMATE See legitimate cultural relativism.

DESERT—The theory that legitimizes one's claim to social goods. Feminist ethics often supports a definition that looks at actual accomplishments minus preferment.

DEONTOLOGY The moral theory that suggests that an agent's duty is based upon principle. The theory bases its duties on the nature of human reason or on the nature of human action. It asserts the existence of moral facts and so is a moral realist theory.

DISSONANCE AND REJECTION This is one of three reactions that agents exhibit when they move into stage two of process of evaluating normative theories. Under this reaction the agent summarily rejects the novel normative suggestion.

DIVINE COMMAND THEORY The theory that says we ought to be moral because God commanded us to do so.

ETHICAL EGOISM Presents an agent with the liberty and mandate to strive to optimize her general *flourishing* that is heavily weighted toward long-term calculation.

ETHICAL INTUITIONISM An immediate grasping of normative truths based either on: (a) social norms or (b) direct contact with truth, itself. There are two levels of ethical intuitionism: level-one describes intuitionism about principles; level-two describes intuitionism about the propriety of applying some principle to this particular case. See, also, intuitionism.

ETHICAL NONCOGNITIVISM The belief that there are no moral facts (antirealist) so that one must turn to social norms and their expressions in language and customs to determine what moral terms mean and the extent of their action-guiding force.

ETHICS The science of the right and wrong in human action. (Some writers in Part 2 define ethics as what is socially taken to be the right and wrong in human action.)

FREE RIDER An individual who takes the benefits of the community but tries not to reciprocate either through voluntary acts of goodwill or through illegal schemes to break the law.

FREGE-GEACH PROBLEM Peter Geach attacked ethical noncognitivism by noting that when combining statements (that are asserted to have no truth content) into linguistic contexts, they yield results that, in fact, do appear to have truth content. In this context Geach builds upon the philosopher Gottlieb Frege's distinction between assertion and predication, in other words, between illocutionary force and propositional content, respectively. This seems to confute the mission of the noncognitivists who want to maintain that there is no truth functional content in moral discourse.

GENERAL HEDONISM The notion that the pleasure principle (that supports egoistic hedonism) can be expanded to the group so that agents are interested in supporting actions that promise more general happiness than other proposed alternatives.

GOODWILL With respect to the personal worldview imperative, good will comes in two forms: Kantian and Augustinian (rational and emotive).

HABITS OF CHARACTER In virtue ethics, it is assumed that the habits we possess are under our control. The project of ethics is for each person to habituate himself toward the acquisition of propensities toward the moderate way.

HEINZ DILEMMA In the Heinz dilemma there is a man called Heinz who considers whether or not to steal a drug that he cannot afford to buy in order to save the life of his wife. The feminist critique of Kohlberg's understanding of this dilemma underscores the need for ethics to reflect the role of care.

HOBBES ON HUMAN NATURE Hobbes believes that humans, by nature, are self-interested and competitive. Using these inclinations they will act to satisfy their own designs within the constraints of contrary power structures.

HUMAN ACTION The goal of each person to pursue his or her own goals. Human action is purposive and requires certain goods in order to make this teleological design possible. See, also, table of embeddedness.

HUMAN DIGNITY For Kant human dignity signifies that humans cannot be intersubstituted. Everything that can be substituted without difference constitutes a functional tool that has a price. That which cannot be substituted has no price — instead it possesses pricelessness: human dignity. Human dignity is closely associated with the second form of Kant's categorical imperative.

ILLOCUTIONARY See locutionary.

INTUITIONISM The immediate grasping of truth. See also ethical intuitionism.

KRATERISM The theory that says that "to each according to his ability to snatch it for himself." The acquisition and ability to hold onto power, money, or any other good is the criterion of making something right. See, also, might makes right.

LEGITIMATE CULTURAL RELATIVISM Different practices between cultures are permitted at will (either between countries or within a single country in a well-defined social group) that does not violate either the personal worldview imperative or the shared community worldview imperative.

LOCKE ON HUMAN NATURE Locke believes that humans are cooperative by nature. This should be the default interpretative mechanism. Those who are not cooperative should be dealt with via fair societal mechanisms.

LOCUTIONARY, ILLOCUTIONARY, PERCULOCUTIONARY Describe the communication flow of the speaker making the sorts of statements that are empirically factual (locutionary), or point to a feature of linguistic/social analysis (illocutionary), or finally that the speech act is instrumental to persuasion or other effects (perlocutionary).

METAETHICS Metaethics is a series of investigations that intend to offer critical support to the process of creating a moral theory and the operation of its implementation. (In Part 2 of this book some noncognitivists describe metaethics as talking about normative ethics in a linguistic context.) See, also, metalanguage.

METALANGUAGE Refers to statements about other statements. In these referential propositions, it is important to distinguish the locutionary, illocutionary, and perlocutionary force of the newly created context.

MIGHT MAKES RIGHT The theory that the ability to use power to one's advantage means that the consequent realm is morally right. See, also, kraterism.

MINI/MAX RELATIVE CONCESSION The strategy of Gauthier to solve the prisoner's dilemma by putting into the bargainer's ideal outcome. That result is in everyone's interest.

MORAL ABSOLUTISM Moral Absolutism defines ethics as the science of right and wrong in human action. It asserts that there is a single correct ethical standard that applies across different socio-geographical-historical contexts. Moral absolutism is often the consequence of adopting the moral realism position.

MORAL CONTRACTARIANISM Declares that the ground of moral obligation lies in fact that agents (individually or collectively) have agreed to accept the obligation. Normative force follows from that agreement. They are generally moral antirealists unless the grounds for the contract are, themselves, moral facts.

MORAL PERPLEXITY The situation in which an agent (through no fault of her own) finds herself in the situation in which she cannot act without doing evil. This is said to count against an ethical theory based upon the criteria of deductive coherence.

MORAL REALISM AND ANTI-REALISM Moral realism contends that there are empirically factual criteria that support universal moral claims. The moral antirealists deny that there are any factual criteria that support universal moral claims. What one is left with are various analyses into language and cultures to determine what these particular societies believe to be right and wrong within the context of their traditions.

MORAL RELATIVISM Moral relativism defines ethics as the perceived or recognized right and wrong in human action. It allows for different ethical standards to legitimately arise in different socio-geographical-historical contexts. Moral relativism is often the consequence of adopting the moral anti-realism position.

MOST PLAUSIBLE HYPOTHESIS MAXIM In those situations in which the rationality incompleteness conjecture holds, one may employ the selective faith maxim to accept the most plausible hypothesis based upon all relevant information given to the agent (relevance here is defined via the personal worldview imperative and operates according to "the way we confront novel, normative theories").

NORMATIVE ETHICS Creates a system by which a large number of similar cases can be dealt with under the constraints of acting under some well-defined prescription.

ORIGINAL POSITION A thought experiment set out by John Rawls to integrate rational choice via game theory into what social/political principles anyone would choose for structuring society under conditions of uncertainty.

OTHER, THE STANDPOINT OF Those who are oppressed are often unintentionally marginalized just because they are different from the ruling group.

OVERLAP AND MODIFICATION This is one of three reactions that agents exhibit when they move into stage two of process of evaluating normative theories. In this reaction the agent finds support in some of her personal or community worldview to consider changes, be they minor or major.

PERLOCUTIONARY See locutionary.

PERPLEXITY See moral perplexity.

PERSONAL ACTUALIZATION See actualization, personal.

PERSONAL AUTONOMY Personal autonomy is about the power of individuals to successfully complete what they aim to do. The individual is the rule maker in this process. The right to personal autonomy in the realm of liberty is a second-level basic good. Personal autonomy is sometimes brought forward as an argument for moral relativism. The limit to personal autonomy is the shared community worldview imperative.

PERSONAL WORLDVIEW IMPERATIVE All people must develop a single comprehensive and internally coherent worldview that is good and that we strive to act out in our daily lives.

PLEASURE PRINCIPLE The assertion that pleasure is the highest and ultimate motivation of human behavior (scientific fact). If a theory of ethics seeks to be realistically grounded, then it needs to find its foundation here (as per Bentham, Mill, and Sidgwick).

PRISONER'S DILEMMA A fictional account of two prisoners being held in separate cells. The inquisitor wants to get a confession or some sort of statement that can be useful. The dynamics of the dilemma are whether prisoner A should confess while prisoner B remains silent, or vice versa, or whether they should both be silent or whether they both should confess. It is meant to illustrate a problem between cooperation and self-interested calculations.

PRUDENTIAL ADVANTAGE Means the advantage of one's own personal interests based upon the principle of happiness (or perceived happiness).

PSYCHOLOGICAL EGOISM We only voluntarily do that which we think will satisfy our own perceived interests.

RATIONALITY INCOMPLETENESS CONJECTURE Rationality seeks demonstrably to prove all propositions. However, in cases in which there is no empirical, non-question begging, test for verifying a principle, the best reason can do is to offer various plausible alternatives. The resolution can only come about through appeal to the personal worldview imperative and its application in the way we confront novel normative theories. See, also, the most plausible hypothesis maxim.

RATIONAL JUSTIFICATION OF A MORAL THEORY The rational justification of a moral theory sets as its domain of discourse rational deductive systems of expression. Those that pass the test are justified. Those that do not are not.

RIGHT CLAIMS Deontologists situate rights claims as legitimating the possession of some morally justified good against the social order who, in turn, possess a correlative duty to provide the morally justified good to the claimant. The grounding of deontological right claims is either through an analysis of reason or of human action.

RULE UTILITARIANISM The interpretation of utilitarianism that says that each moral situation should be guided first by prima facie rules (that themselves are justified by utilitarianism). Thus, the agent assesses a situation on act-utilitarian principles but within a framework of prima facie rules that can override apparent act-utilitarian outcomes.

SELFISH GENE STRATEGY Each agent acts according to biological determinism in order to maximize the chance that his genes will follow through to the next filial generation. All other actions can be interpreted through this general evolutionary strategy. The result is some sort of biological determinism.

SHARED COMMUNITY WORLDVIEW IMPERATIVE Each agent must contribute to a common body of knowledge that supports the creation of a shared community worldview (that is itself complete, coherent, and good) through which social institutions and their resulting policies might flourish within the constraints of the essential core commonly held values (ethics, aesthetics, and religion).

SOCIAL CONTRACT THEORY Originated in the seventeenth century principally in the writings of Hobbes and Locke, social contract theory posited a unrestrained state of nature that is abandoned for the state in favor of certain benefits such as the rule of law.

TABLE OF EMBEDDEDNESS The table of embeddedness is an hierarchical listing of the goods to which humans can claim in order to fulfill autonomous human action. There are two general divisions: basic and secondary goods. Basic goods have two subsequent levels while secondary goods have three. It is assumed that claim rights to more fundamental goods, such as food and water, trump claims to less fundamental goods, such as luxury vacations. The table of embeddedness gives a blueprint for morally justified social/political philosophy.

THEISTIC ETHICS (TWO THEORIES) Philosophical ethics will be grounded without reference to God; a second theory that embraces a theistic understanding of the good is also acknowledged.

UNDERSTANDING AN ETHICAL THEORY A person understands an ethical theory when she can visualize it within the context of her personal and community worldview, including an empirically rich vision of possible application.

UTILITARIANISM The theory that suggests that an action is morally right when that action produces more total utility for the group as a consequence than any other alternative does. See, also, act utilitarianism and rule utilitarianism.

UTILITARIANISM, ACT OR RULE See act utilitarianism; rule utilitarianism

UTILITY, AVERAGE OR AGGREGATE See average utility; aggregate utility

UTOPIAN VERSUS ASPIRATIONAL Utopian visions of the world focus on the best of all possible situations that could occur, regardless of facts about human nature and the state of history concerning the communities in the nation and the world. Aspirational accounts look at what is possible. They will frame moral oughts in terms of what is possible.

VIRTUE ETHICS Virtue ethics is also called agent-based ethics. Its position is that we become good when we cultivate excellence (virtue) by pursuing the moderate course between excess and defect. Since the origin of the virtues is in question, some practitioners of virtue ethics are moral realists while others are not.